Loyalties in Conflict
A Canadian Borderland in War and Rebellion, 1812–1840

Despite their strategic location on the American border, the townships of Lower Canada have been largely ignored in studies of the War of 1812 and the Rebellions of 1837–8. Originally settled by Loyalists from New York, and followed by much larger numbers of land seekers from New England, this was a potentially volatile borderland during British–American conflicts. J.I. Little's *Loyalties in Conflict* examines how the allegiance to British authority of the American-origin population within the borders of Lower Canada was tested by the War of 1812 and the Rebellions of 1837–8.

Little argues that while loyalties were highly localized, American border raids during the war caused a defensive reaction north of the 45th parallel. The resulting sense of distinction from neighbouring Vermont, with its radical religious and political culture, did not prevent a strong regional reform movement from emerging in the Eastern Townships during the 1820s and 1830s. This movement undermines the argument of Quebec's nationalist historians that the political contest in Lower Canada was essentially a French–English one; however, the dual threat of French-Canadian and American nationalism did ensure the border townships' loyalty to the government during the rebellions. The following years would witness the development of an increasingly conservative and distinctly Canadian cultural identity in the region.

Loyalties in Conflict is a rigorous study of the conflicting forces that shaped a Canadian region in a pivotal period in North American history.

(The Canadian Social History Series)

J.I. LITTLE is a professor in the Department of History at Simon Fraser University.

Loyalties in Conflict

A Canadian Borderland in War and Rebellion, 1812–1840

J.I. Little

UNIVERSITY OF TORONTO PRESS
Toronto Buffalo London

ISBN 978-0-8020-9773-6 (cloth)
ISBN 978-0-8020-9525-1 (paper)

∞

Printed on acid-free paper

Library and Archives Canada Cataloguing in Publication

Little, J.I. (John Irvine), 1947–
Loyalties in conflict : a Canadian borderland war and rebellion,
1812–1840 / J.I. Little.

(Canadian social history series)
Includes bibliographical references and index.
ISBN 978-0-8020-9773-6 (bound)
ISBN 978-0-8020-9525-1 (pbk.)

1. Canada – History – War of 1812. 2. Canada – History – Rebellion,
1837–1838. 3. Americans – Québec (Province) – Eastern Townships –
History – 19th century. 4. Americans – Québec (Province) – Eastern
Townships – Social conditions – 19th century. 5. Americans – Québec
(Province) – Eastern Townships – Politics and government – 19th century.
6. Eastern Townships (Québec) – History – 19th century.
I. Title. II. Series.

FC442.L56 2008   971.03'4   C2008-904276-X

University of Toronto Press acknowledges the financial assistance to its publishing program of the Canada Council for the Arts and the Ontario Arts
Council.

University of Toronto Press acknowledges the financial support for its publishing activities of the Government of Canada through the Book Publishing
Industry Development Program (BPIDP).

This book has been published with the help of a grant from the Canadian
Federation for the Humanities and Social Sciences, through the Aid to Schol-
arly Publications Programme, using funds provided by the Social Sciences
and Humanities Research Council of Canada.

Contents

Preface / vii

Introduction / 3

The War of 1812 / 11
The Militia Prior to the War / 12
An 'exposed and defenceless situation': The Outbreak of
War / 18
'Delay, backwardness, and want of zeal': The Conscription
Crisis / 24
'Making the fur fly': Resisting American Invasion / 37
'Like herds of buffalo': The Smuggling and Counterfeiting
Frontier / 43
'Improper communication': Policing Cross-Border Migration / 49
Conclusion / 54

The Rebellions of 1837–8 / 57
Postwar Developments / 57
The Political Culture / 64
'Incurably cursed with Radicalism': Prelude to Rebellion / 67
'I shall die defending my home and family': Rebellion / 77
'These dreadful frontiers': Post-Rebellion Conflict / 96
Conclusion / 100

Afterword / 107

Appendix A: Volunteer Corps in the Eastern Townships as of
29 December 1837 / 111

Appendix B: List of Prisoners Confined in the Common
Gaol at Sherbrooke Charged with Political Offences,
21 December 1838 / 113

Notes / 113
Bibliography / 161
Index / 175

Illustrations follow page 54

Preface

While Ontario and three of the Atlantic provinces are separated from the United States by bodies of water, the same is not true of Quebec. Yet that province's historians have only begun to grapple with the issue of *Américanité*, and the long-settled borderland alongside the forty-fifth parallel has been largely ignored. It lay beyond the colonization zone during the French regime, and, as English-speaking Protestants, the early settlers did not contribute to what Jocelyn Létourneau refers to as the province's 'great collective narrative of *la survivance*.'[1] Furthermore, the subsequent demographic victory of the French Canadians in the region fails to conform to the defensive nature of that narrative, and it is certainly not predisposed to celebrate the accommodations characteristic of cultural contact zones. The history of the region known as the Eastern Townships would clearly be better known had there been less accommodation and more conflict, for even the two major crises of the early nineteenth century – the War of 1812 and the Rebellions of 1837–8 – saw no major battles in the region. If Canada deserves the title the 'peaceable kingdom,' however, and if the two largest 'threats' to our survival as a country have long been the external influence of the United States and the internal aspirations of the Québécois, the story of how the people of the Eastern Townships responded to those two crises should be of more than local interest.

During the French regime the land east of the Richelieu and west of the Chaudière served as the hunting territory for Abenaki warriors, whose raids into New England slowed the northward expansion of the British colonial frontier. The first settlers to arrive in this northern Appalachian region were New York Loyalists during the American War of Independence, but they were quickly outnumbered by

land-seekers from New England. Less than two decades later, the War
of 1812 would represent this population's first test of allegiance to
British authority. While one might have expected most of these Yankee settlers to have been sympathetic to the American cause, Vermonters themselves initially showed little enthusiasm for the war.
Loyalties were localized and the people on both sides of the border
resisted playing more than a defensive role. But local loyalties also
meant that, just as the British invasion of Vermont in 1814 stimulated
sharp resistance in that state, so American raids north of the forty-
fifth parallel caused a defensive reaction in the Eastern Townships.
As Peter Sahlins (echoing Benedict Anderson) has noted, 'imagining
oneself a member of a community or a nation meant perceiving a significant difference between oneself and the other across the boundary.'[2] That difference would become more real as the war-caused
break in New England preaching circuits, followed by the arrival of
British missionaries, gradually resulted in the development of a more
conservative religious culture north of the border, a process that I
examined in *Borderland Religion*.[3]

This volume complements that study insofar as it focuses on the
evolution of the region's political culture, culminating with the
Rebellions of 1837–8, when the dual threats posed by French-Canadian and American nationalism accelerated the shift towards a pro-
British political allegiance. The Eastern Townships may have been,
until recent years, an exception to the rule of a French-speaking Quebec and English-speaking rest-of-Canada, but the region represents a
microcosm of a country largely shaped by the interaction of American and British influences, as well as French-language and English-
language ones. The forces that led to the development of a distinctive
English-Canadian identity in this cultural borderland were not so different from those at work in other parts of early nineteenth-century
British North America. This study, then, is not simply another example of the 'limited identities' approach to Canada's history that has
been criticized by its more nationalist historians.[4] It does argue that
local loyalties remained a powerful force in the pre-industrial Eastern
Townships, but it also examines the development of a civic culture, a
regional outlook, and a growing identity as British subjects and Canadians. This is not an intellectual history, however, but a socio-politi-
cal one, for the emphasis is less on how a regional elite articulated
that identity than on how the population as a whole manifested it
through their responses to the crises posed by war and rebellion.

Many people contributed to the completion of this volume, but I
would like to thank Patricia Kennedy of the National Archives in par-

ticular. Her generous and very knowledgeable assistance has been indispensable for nearly all my research projects during the past three and a half decades. I am also very grateful to the two anonymous assessors for their constructive recommendations, to John Scott for sharing his remarkable knowledge of the local family histories, and to James Leahy for the expert copy-editing. The unfailingly supportive Len Husband proved, once again, to be all one could ask for in an editor, and I also wish to thank Greg Kealey for taking this project on board. The always professional staff of the University of Toronto Press made the production process a smooth and expeditious one.

Books such as this would not be possible without public funding, and I am very pleased to acknowledge the research grant provided by the Social Sciences and Humanities Research Council, as well as the publication subsidy from the Canadian Federation for the Humanities and Social Sciences. I am also grateful to Simon Fraser University for providing the administrative leave that made the writing possible. To acknowledge the essential role in gathering and preserving historical records played by the region's local historical societies, I wish to dedicate this book to Marion Phelps, who has provided over half a century of volunteer service to the rich archival collection of the Brome County Historical Society. It is particularly fitting that she and the BCHS be recognized as they both celebrate their hundredth anniversary in 2008.[5] Finally, my deepest thanks, as always, goes to Andrea for her love and support.

Loyalties in Conflict

Introduction

The picturesque region south of the St Lawrence River and north of the American border, known as the Eastern Townships or les Cantons de l'Est (more recently, l'Estrie), has had a long history as a contact zone between Canada's French-speaking and English-speaking communities. Even before that history began this territory was a rather permeable buffer zone between the warring French and British empires. Then, after being opened to settlement, it became a borderland between competing British and American influences. In short, the Eastern Townships was like much of the rest of English-speaking Canada insofar as it represented a middle ground in which a hybrid collective identity emerged from the interaction between conflicting political and cultural forces.

During the French regime, western Abenaki hunters had this wilderness region mostly to themselves. The northward expansion of the British colonial frontier had caused them to abandon all their traditional villages except for the one on the western edge of their territory at Missisquoi Bay on northern Lake Champlain. Most of the western Abenakis retreated to the Jesuit missions at the mouths of the St Francis and Bécancour rivers that drained the northern Appalachian range into the St Lawrence. Beginning in 1690 the warriors from these two villages served as the shock troops of the French war effort by raiding the frontier New England settlements that were occupying what had once been their homeland.[1] After the French defeat in the Seven Years' War, the British continued the ban on settler encroachment on the Abenaki hunting grounds but refused to recognize that the Natives had any legal entitlement to this territory.

3

The Abenakis' position was further weakened by the War of Independence, when they were torn between alliance to Britain or to the rebelling colonies. When the Treaty of Paris extended the boundary between New York and Quebec eastward to define Vermont's northern border, the Missisquoi Abenakis found that not only had their traditional hunting and fishing territory been divided but their village lay south of the forty-fifth parallel, leaving them to the mercy of hostile American settlers.[2] Lacking official recognition of their land rights, the Missisquoi Abenakis soon scattered in small bands or migrated to the St Francis village of Odanak. The expansion of the settlement frontier would gradually force the St Francis and Chaudière Abenakis to shift their hunting grounds north of the St Lawrence.[3] In contrast to most North American borderland regions, then, the history of the indigenous population in what would become the Eastern Townships largely ended soon after the imposition of the international boundary.

The governor of Quebec, General Frederick Haldimand, did attempt to delay settlement of the Missisquoi Bay area by insisting that the Loyalists who had arrived there during the war move once again to the St Lawrence valley west of Montreal. Haldimand claimed that he wanted to prevent border conflicts, but he was probably more concerned about smuggling and the development of close ties along the border that would weaken the colony's defences – hence, his stated preference for French-Canadian settlers. But a sizable minority of the Loyalists refused to leave the fertile area even after Haldimand cut off their provisions and threatened to burn their houses. In 1785, only two years after the war had ended, a petition of 380 names was submitted for land titles in the area.

Meanwhile, prominent Loyalists were able to remain on the Vermont side of the border as long as its government was flirting with allegiance to Britain, but that independent republic's entry into the American Union in 1791 intensified pressure to open the region north of the boundary to colonization. As Alan Taylor has noted, recruiting Americans was a dangerous gamble, but colonial authorities were convinced that the American states were filled with suppressed Loyalists, anxious to escape republicanism by returning to the empire.[4] British officials may also have viewed American settlement as a means of diluting French-Canadian influence in the elective Legislative Assembly, which was granted by the constitution that separated Upper and Lower Canada in 1791.

That constitution declared that the seigneurial system was not to be extended, but, in an attempt to ensure that a landed aristocracy would dilute the republican American influence, each newly surveyed township of approximately sixteen square kilometres was to be granted to a leader and his associates. While the standard grant was supposed to be only 80 hectares, the prevailing assumption was that each associate would receive the supposedly exceptional amount of 480 hectares, then sign over 400 hectares to the leader as compensation for the time and money invested in obtaining the land title and developing the economic infrastructure. But this system, which had originated in New England, was more capitalist than feudal because the leader was financed by outside investors and protracted delays in securing land titles caused their number to multiply, making the venture increasingly speculative in nature.[5]

These delays were caused by British officials in the colony who remained concerned about American expansion, especially as fears of French invasion gave rise to a garrison mentality in Quebec City.[6] In his recent study of the borderland between New York and Upper Canada, Taylor defines the land-granting process as one in which the state 'derived revenue and power by surveying property lines and selling sovereign title to enclosed parcels,' and 'the recipients returned allegiance to the government that issued their land titles.'[7] But the process was not quite so clear-cut in the Eastern Townships. Because Quebec officials were eager to discourage American settlement and acquire much of the land for themselves, they insisted that an oath of loyalty be administered to every settler before he became eligible for a grant, then delayed the appointment of the oaths commissioners for two years. Settlers who had little choice but to begin improving their land claims in the meantime because they had sold their properties in the United States subsequently found that those claims were transferred to Quebec officials and their merchant allies.

The most persistent American township leaders finally did acquire land titles in 1802, by which time most of them had amassed debts that prevented them from developing or even holding onto much of their land grants. The Loyalist township leaders may not have become a landed aristocracy, but the government did, as we shall see, bolster their social leadership role with appointments as militia officers and justices of the peace. In the meantime, the arable tax-free land in the border townships had attracted 8,300 New England settlers by 1803, a number that would reach approximately 18,500 in 1812. Not only could very few claim to be Loyalists, but many were squatters with no expressed loyalty to the state.[8] As in Upper Canada, where the population was 70,000 in 1815, the immigration from south of the border was driven not by an antipathy to republicanism but by the fact that the War of Independence had left the new country with a large debt. The result was the large-scale alienation of public lands in the United States to speculators as well as a heavy tax burden, while in the remaining colonies Britain assumed the cost of government and taxes were only nominal.[9]

As for the British and Irish immigrants who disembarked at Quebec following the Napoleonic Wars, the vast majority made their way to Upper Canada or the United States, and most of the relatively small number who did settle in the Eastern Townships remained in the more economically marginal outlying areas. The French Canadians who would eventually dominate the region numerically only began to arrive in the later 1830s.[10] For all intents and purposes, then, the southern heartland of the Eastern Townships was the northern frontier of New England settlement.

While Canadian historians have tended to stress metropolitan links and influences on the settlement frontier,[11] the governing officials and influential merchants who became absentee proprietors in the Eastern Townships did little more than hinder the region's development, and they were resented accordingly. Economic links with the principal external markets of Montreal and Quebec were tenuous because there were no obstacle-free river arteries to the St Lawrence, and the absentee proprietors only posed an obstacle to road construction. The political connections to the colonial capital were also weak for many years because the Eastern Townships did not have its own electoral constituencies until 1829. Other state ties were equally limited for there were no local courts prior to 1823. While justices of the peace were authorized to fulfil low-level legislative and administrative functions such as the regulation of markets, they remained few and far between, and there was only one police constable for the entire district, appointed in 1824.[12] The militia was the one institution that represented a formalized link between most of the local population and external authority, but it was of little significance outside wartime, and we shall see that the men of the Eastern Townships tended to march to their own drummer during the War of 1812.

Formal institutions that would promote internal cohesiveness were also somewhat lacking because the New England missionary societies neglected the region, especially after the War of 1812, and it took a number of years for the British-based Wesleyan Methodist and Anglican churches to gain a firm foothold. The largest religious category in the census of 1831, at 37 per cent, was the one that declared no denominational affiliation whatsoever.[13] But churches rapidly gained in influence thereafter, as attested by the rise of a number of temperance societies, and local notables exercised some influence through Masonic lodges, though these went into decline in the 1830s. The town meeting system that had fostered a strong sense of civic consciousness in New England was forbidden in Lower Canada, but local residents did take matters into their own hands by building schools and, when the need arose, organizing vigilante societies. For example, Hatley's society 'for the suppression of Felonies, Vices and Misdemeanors' assessed the property of subscribing members and paid 'pursuers' to apprehend offenders.[14] The threat posed by the conflicts examined in this study also called for a united local response. It is safe to assume, however, that the Eastern Townships was rather slow to evolve from the egalitarian, self-sufficient, and family-centred society described by Frederick Jackson Turner's western frontier thesis.[15]

But even though American historians of religion view northern New England's frontier conditions as an important factor in the radical revivalist and political protest tradition that developed there during the late eighteenth and early nineteenth centuries,[16] that tradition failed to take deep root in the neighbouring Canadian townships. Despite the experience of an even stronger social atomization process, there were three important distinguishing features on the northern side of the boundary. Firstly, settlers in a British colony could obviously not rely upon the revolutionary tradition of sacrifice made during the American Revolution to justify their political demands. (Sacrifice for the Loyalist cause, which relatively few had supported in any case, clearly had more conservative connotations.) Secondly, as already noted, the town meeting system that provided the organizational framework for those demands in New England was prohibited in Lower Canada; and, thirdly, this meant that Canadian settlers were not subject to the taxes that led to major protests south of the border.[17] Added to those differences was the impact made by British-funded missionaries even before state-controlled schools would begin to have a major influence in the 1840s.[18] Finally, the two armed conflicts examined in the following pages would, themselves, play a role in transforming the cultural identity of an American-origin people living adjacent to the New England border into a distinctively 'Canadian' one insofar as it represented a synthesis of American and British values.

The main advantage of the borderlands approach is that it shifts the focus from the central state to the local communities as active agents in history, but borderland historians are generally most interested in the common features of the contiguous societies, as well as in how state-imposed boundaries were defied or ignored by the people they divided. Lauren McKinsey and Victor Konrad of the Northeastern Borderlands Project go so far as to state that borderlanders have 'more in common with each other than with members of their respective dominant cultures.'[19] In contrast to old-world countries, however, the boundary between Lower Canada and Vermont was established before all but the earliest settlers arrived, and they were attracted in part by the freedom offered from taxes and religious conformity. Furthermore, because the border did not divide an already established population, once the indigenous inhabitants had been pushed aside, the cross-border political networks that characterize First Nations borderlands as well as those in other continents did not exist here.[20] Although the people of the border townships and northern Vermont and New Hampshire shared similar origins and geographical propinquity, a more interesting question than what they had in common is: when and how did this borderland become a bordered land?[21]

In taking this approach, Adelman and Aron focus largely on the power exercised by the state, but simply pointing to state imposition of the border by 'fences, gates, and other signs and systems of control' would not take us very far in understanding the Eastern Townships because the Canadian–American border did little to impede regular communications or contact.[22] Indeed, the state's influence was somewhat limited in what Michiel Baud and Willem Van Schendel would refer to as an unruly borderland because there was for many years a lively traffic in counterfeit American bank bills manufactured in the Eastern Townships and exchanged for stolen American livestock.[23] And, as we shall see, the fact that the sale of American livestock to Britain or its colonies was prohibited by Jefferson's embargo only increased the northward flow, as did the outbreak of war in 1812.

The armed conflicts studied in this volume obviously brought the state into play, but it lacked the coercive power to enforce loyalty during the war, and it had little need to do so during the Rebellions. It was only the American side of the forty-fifth parallel that threatened to become a rebellious borderland during the War of 1812, and the enthusiasm of the American border communities to 'liberate' the Canadas in 1838 through the Hunters' Lodge movement was not reciprocated in the Eastern Townships. As Peter Sahlins points out in his study of the Spanish and French Catalonians, borders are not simply products of central states but of local social relations as well.[24] Benjamin Johnson also notes that borderlanders were never unaware of the border, often using it for their own purposes.[25] To take one local example, the inhabitants of the border townships may have opposed the state's imposition of the boundary by forcefully resisting the local customs officers' attempts to collect duties on regular cross-border exchanges, but they did tolerate the presence of those same officers because they also resented the competition posed by imports of American livestock.[26]

As with all the young settlements of British North America during the early nineteenth century, loyalty was largely restricted to a community that – as Jane Errington has noted for Upper Canada – 'was confined to those in his or her family and to the few settlers he or she met occasionally at the mill, at work parties, or at social occasions.'[27] During the War of 1812 most settlers of the Eastern Townships rejected allegiance to their country of birth, while also remaining deaf to the colonial authorities' orders to send recruits who would fight outside the region. But by activating the militia and forcing the settlers to take sides, the war did foster a nascent sense of regional identity, one that was loosely associated with the fact that they were residents of a British colony even though regional grievances gave birth to a lively political protest movement in the 1820s.[28] That movement was cut short in the mid-1830s by the prospect of French-Canadian rebellion. The outbreak of armed conflict saw the formation of volunteer units in the Eastern Townships eager to join the British forces, though their only active role would be to repel invaders from the United States. Reform sentiment certainly did not die with the Rebellions, but the American revolutionary tradition had failed to take root in the region.

Baud and Van Schendel caution that historians who ground their research on one side of an artificial line in social space run the risk of confirming the nationalist claims that borders represent.[29] As if to illustrate that observation, Elizabeth Jameson and Jeremy Mouat argue that by dividing 'U.S. cultural and economic savagery from Canadian civilization' the forty-ninth parallel (which, they fail to point out, only begins in Manitoba) continues to play a role in Canadian history similar to that of Turner's frontier in American history.[30] This study does not ignore developments to the immediate south of the border, but they are not a major theme because there is little to suggest that the cultural values and identity of the American borderland population were significantly influenced by its proximity to a British colony.

These observations notwithstanding, I am not adopting a nationalist stance in arguing that a more conservative cultural identity devel-

oped north of the forty-fifth parallel. Indeed, my thesis is that localism, not nationalism, was the dominant force in the early nineteenth
century, albeit a localism that was gradually complemented (perhaps
even weakened, but not replaced) by broader regional, provincial,
and imperial identities. In that sense, this study conforms to Nancy
Christie's recent appeal that pre-Confederation history be read as an
extension of British cultural, institutional, and social frameworks,
though I would add that historians should not neglect ongoing American influences nor the persistence of local traditions and loyalties
well into the industrial era.[31] Almost by definition, then, my findings
will be unique to the Eastern Townships in many respects, but local
loyalties were a defining feature of what Randy Widdis, echoing
Northrop Frye and Cole Harris, refers to as an 'archipelago of soli-
tudes.'[32] And the fact remains that the experience of British political
domination, American military threat, and French-Canadian unrest –
all themes explored in this study – helped to define how the 'imagined' community known as English Canada came into existence.[33]

The War of 1812

The causes and general progress of the War of 1812 are too well known to require more than a brief outline here. Native unrest in the Ohio country was blamed on British interference, and the Americans also resented the British naval blockade of continental Europe. Jefferson's retaliatory Embargo Act of 1807 and its successors failed to change British policy, and the impressment of British-born sailors from American ships was considered a severe provocation, leading to the declaration of war in June 1812. As for the war's progress, British seizure of the American posts at Michilimackinac and Detroit restricted the early fighting to Upper Canada, where it remained focused until the autumn of 1813, when a half-hearted American attempt was made to take Montreal. The two-pronged American attack was turned back at Châteauguay and Crysler's Farm, and, with the defeat of Napoleon the following year, the British took the war to Lake Champlain. Their defeat at Plattsburg Bay in September 1814 helped set the stage for the Treaty of Ghent, which effectively restored the antebellum status quo the following December.

Even though the thinly settled country north of Vermont and New Hampshire served as a smuggling frontier across which New England livestock were moved to feed the British army,[1] and Lake Champlain became a two-way invasion route during the later stages of the war, the Eastern Townships escaped with relatively little armed conflict. The war's many historians, preoccupied largely with military events, have therefore found no reason to give the region more than a passing mention.[2] But the history of war concerns more than military conflict; it is also social and cultural history, exploring the role played by, and the impact felt by, the civilian population. S.F. Wise has claimed

11

that, while most American histories of the War of 1812 'have as their central matter the grand evolution of the country and its people,' the Canadian studies 'remain local in outlook.'[3] But he and other historians have argued, nevertheless, that the war fostered a conservative nationalist elite and ideology in Upper Canada, strongly influencing the developing English-Canadian identity.[4]

If the presence of the British army helped to ensure a certain degree of loyalty in Upper Canada during the war, what about the Eastern Townships, where there was no military garrison to provide a market for local farmers, shopkeepers, artisans, and tavern owners or to signify that this was British territory?[5] Still more importantly, the Loyalist ratio of the Eastern Townships population was much smaller than in the neighbouring colony, and the border was not a major body of water but a largely unguarded line passing through hilly wilderness areas as well as between adjoining villages where Americans and Canadians were close neighbours. As we have seen, the Eastern Townships had only been officially opened to settlement twenty years earlier, and the great majority of the inhabitants were New Englanders (or their offspring) who had little contact with the rest of British North America,[6] yet they were called upon by the government to serve in the militia and fight their American kin and neighbours, if necessary. Understanding the somewhat complex way in which they responded provides insight into the self-preservation impulses of a rural population caught up in an international conflict with which it had no reason to identify. But it also helps us to understand the longer-term impact of such a conflict on the development of a sense of community, both local and national, on one side of an international borderline dividing what had once been a common people.

The Militia Prior to the War

Abolished after the Conquest, the Canadian militia was restored in 1777, two years after the French-Canadian habitants had refused to take up arms against the American invaders. All able-bodied males aged sixteen to fifty were now obliged to serve in local units known collectively as the Sedentary Militia. It was meant to protect the home front, but members between the ages of eighteen and thirty could be conscripted by ballot to defend the border regions in active battalions known as the Select Embodied Militia.[7] In 1805 three battalions of the Royal Eastern Militia Regiment were established under the command of Colonel Sir John Johnson, the leading Loyalist in the colony. The First Battalion was located west of the Richelieu, and therefore outside the Eastern Townships, but the Second – with fourteen township companies – covered the area between Missisquoi Bay and Lake Memphremagog, and the Third consisted of the sixteen township companies to the east of Lake Memphremagog.[8] Rapid settlement made the two Eastern Townships battalions unwieldy by 1808 when the Fourth Battalion (in the Loyalist-settled St Armand–Dunham area) was carved out of the Second, and the companies in the Fifth Battalion (located in the densely settled townships of Stanstead, Barnston, and Hatley) were extracted from the Third.[9] The number of men in each company varied greatly, according to local population density, for in 1813 the eleven companies listed for the Third Battalion ranged in size from twenty-two to sixty-four ablebodied men, aged sixteen to fifty, with an average age of thirty-six years. Not all these men by any means were fit for duty, and the returns from one of the Hatley companies reveal that nine of the thirty-two non-officers were infirm. Only eleven of the fit were unmarried men and therefore suitable for extended duty outside the region.[10]

As in the seigneuries, the local organization of the militia reinforced the landed elite, for the aging senior officers were township leaders.[11] Lieutenants-Colonel Henry Ruiter of the Second Battalion, Philip Luke of the Fourth, and Patrick Conroy of the Fifth were also all prominent Loyalists who had served as oaths commissioners at Missisquoi Bay, while Henry Cull of the Third Battalion had arrived in the colony from England. When Conroy died at the outbreak of the war, however, he was succeeded by the surveyor Jesse Pennoyer, whose three years of service on the rebel side during the War of Independence did not prevent him from being appointed as an oaths commissioner as well being recognized as the leader of Compton Township. Pennoyer was promoted from captain to major in 1813 and remained the only battalion commander in the colony below the rank of lieutenant-colonel.[12]

Despite their sizable land holdings, these men were not wealthy, and their unpaid positions represented a considerable personal burden during the war. The former Quebec merchant Henry Cull had acquired 1,680 hectares in Hatley Township by 1805 and had purchased many militia grants in Windsor Township. Befitting the status of a landed gentleman, his library of some 500 volumes was said to include 'the best of the British classics, ancient and modern history and valuable miscellaneous works.' But Cull's farm at the outlet of Lake Massawippi (today's North Hatley) was more scenic than productive, and he asked for a salary in January 1814,[13] later complaining that his expenses were much greater than the £15 per annum provided by the government. He explained that a militia officer in the densely settled French-speaking parishes could simply

> appoint the day & number of men wanted & nothing more is requisite than for him to get into his Caleche or Cariole – meet his Batt^n & the business is ended – here it is totally different – after wading through miserable roads to the place of the rendez-vous perhaps not one half of the Officers or Privates will attend, & the same Tour is to be performed five or six times, & the Command^g officer here has not a good comfortable Habitant-house to go to where he is kindly & hospitably received, but must go to some place of Public entertainment, & glad to pay very dear for indifferent accommodations, and is regarded every where as one coming to deprive the Country of its young men, rather than that of assisting in the glorious cause of defending the Country from Pillage & Invasion.[14]

The Fifth Battalion's Jesse Pennoyer had the advantage after 1812 of a salary of £200 a year for five years, plus £100 annually for expenses, in order to promote the production of hemp in the region.[15] But this did not save him from being constantly hounded by creditors. Explaining his failure to appear in Montreal to pay off a debt in June 1813, Pennoyer wrote that command of his battalion required all his attention; he could not even afford 'to keep a hired man to assist me in carrying on my farm,' making it necessary to cut his own hay.[16] By November Pennoyer had sold the only oxen he owned, but this did not prevent the bailiff from seizing many articles which Pennoyer claimed would fetch only a fraction of their value when sold at auction.[17]

Meanwhile, the embargo against British trade imposed by Jefferson in 1807 had brought a flurry of militia activity. Colonel Commandant Johnson announced a tour of inspection in the Eastern Townships, requesting that those townships too remote for him to visit send their captains and other officers to meet him. They were to bring lists of all the men in their townships over the age of sixteen, identifying one-fifth of each company, generally bachelors 'and those less usefull [sic] to their families,' for the possibility of active service in case of war.[18] On 28 September Lieutenant-Colonel Cull announced that 'the militia of this District conducted themselves with the greatest Loyalty and the best order that their undisciplined state could possibly promise.' Cull admitted that 'some few stragglers who had been influenced by the American News papers' had gone as far as Stanstead on their way to the United States, but added that the inspecting officer's address 'had the happy effect of sending those of the above description to their places of residence and of confirming all in a determined resolution to conform to the Laws.' To make the militia laws better known in the region, Cull requested books of exercise and recommended that arms be furnished 'under certain restrictions.' The Stanstead militia also requested the formation of a 'Troop of Horse,' which was granted on the grounds that the border township was more densely settled than the others.[19]

The following February, Cull reported to Johnson's adjutant, Captain Jacob Glen, that he believed most of his men were ready for duty, adding that 'as they are mostly young men it must be expected some of 'em are charging about from place to place but I believe very few have left the Country in *consequence* of the *command*.' Cull stressed the importance of uniforms, pistols, holsters, and cutlasses in encouraging their participation, adding that the cavalrymen in particular were willing to make a small financial sacrifice to equip themselves.[20] A year later, in 1808, Cull reminded Colonel Johnson that 'men are growing Rich in this fertile Country – and as militiamen are anxious for a Uniform, and only wait the honour of your Commands to say the Colour you approve mostly of, and I believe the greatest part of them will furnish themselves immediately on receiving a Pattern.' He added that the Vermont unit to the immediate south 'have a handsome uniform particularly Hatt & Feather – your third Battalion are desirous of *appearing*, as well as *acting* better than their neighbors.' Cull also felt that if the government could not supply arms, the men would submit to a law requiring them to pay for them provided they were made available at a reasonable price.[21] But the government was very hesitant to arm the Townships militia, as we shall see, and uniforms for the Sedentary Militia appear to have been out of the question. Even the cavalry was neglected, for as late as June 1812 only thirty of Stanstead's sixty-one cavalrymen were in uniform, 'with Swords Pistols Holster etc compleat – the rest are tolerably well mounted but without the necessary requisites.'[22]

Meanwhile, the Third Battalion's field return for August 1808 included ten captains, ten lieutenants, eleven ensigns, thirty-nine sergeants, five drummers, and 549 men 'present in the field.' Thirty others were sick, forty-one were absent with leave, and forty were absent without leave. For all these men, there were only seventy-five firearms.[23] In submitting this return, Cull commended the 'orderly behaviour and good conduct' of his charges. The only discordant note was the 'intruding vagabond' who interrupted Captain Glen when he was drawing up the line in Stanstead, but none of the 300 men quit his post, and a small guard took the intruder into custody. Referring to the officers, most of whom had seen experience in the American Revolution, Cull added that 'some of us are too old to improve much, but our exertions shall not be wanting to encourage the youth of the Country to persevere in their fidelity and finally receive their share of the reward and Honor which their country is always ready to bestow.'[24]

Cull soon became less sanguine about local military zeal. Referring to two of his captains from Stanstead in late 1809, he wrote: 'I wish Taplin & Bodwell would adopt the measure that the Democratic Hovey has done; and give in their Resignation, though I firmly believe both of them are well attach'd to the Government (which is no small recommendation these times).' It is quite possible that Captain Ebenezer Hovey, who was the first settler in Hatley, resented Cull as an interloper with whom he had to share the role of township leader.[25] Cull added that the company Hovey had formerly commanded was large enough to be divided in two, 'but I know not whom to recommend from amongst our Sectarians – many of whom have not taken the Oath of Allegiance.'[26] In September 1810 Cull reported that at the latest muster there were no men absent without leave from the cavalry company, but seventy-eight from four of the Stanstead companies failed to make an appearance, as did nine from one of the Barnston companies. Cull added: 'To prevent such neglect of the Law in future (for I do not think it arose from disaffection) I have to request that you will prosecute the Delinquents according to Law.'[27]

Cull proceeded to do so himself without waiting for authorization, summoning the absentees to appear before the magistrates in their respective townships.[28] But this tactic failed to produce the desired result, for a year later Cull's report again complained that a large number were absent without leave, adding that 'many of them are men that a Dollar cannot be recovered from by means of an Execution and the expense of forwarding them to Montreal for a few days would be a great Tax on the well disposed.'[29] Acting in his own capacity as magistrate, however, Cull summoned the delinquents once again, accepting excuses from most of them but fining two in Hatley and three or four in Barnston. By January 1812 he was also losing patience with those militia captains who failed to submit their annual returns, reporting that he had 'waited several days & sent often to the two defaulters [...] but all to no effect.'[30]

The first true test as far as military service was concerned would come with the 1 June muster, shortly before the outbreak of war, when five men were to be balloted from each company to join the active militia.[31] No mention was made of the incentives offered in Upper Canada to join active militia units (known there as flank companies), namely exemption from statute labour, jury duty, and arrest for failure to pay small debts.[32] The result from the companies under Cull's command was a combination of mostly unmarried volunteers and draftees, nearly all in their late teens or early twenties. Two companies produced their quota of five men, three produced four, two produced two (both of whom were absent), and three produced only one each, for a total of twenty-nine, one of whom was later judged to be infirm.[33] Cull assured the adjutant-general that 'such as are defaulters will be prosecuted as the Law directs (or if minors) their Parents,' and he issued orders for their apprehension.[34] Several days later, however, he was mortified to learn that only fourteen of the twenty-nine men were ready to march to the rendezvous at Laprairie. He asked the governor for advice on how to prosecute the delinquents, claiming that his fellow justices would hesitate to pursue the absconders' parents, 'particularly as it will require so large a Portion of their Property to raise twenty dollars in the present scarcity of specie in the country.'[35]

Jesse Pennoyer of the neighbouring Fifth Battalion was also having difficulty, for the entire Hereford company failed to appear at the June muster.[36] Pennoyer explained to the adjutant-general that his battalion was 'so thinly scattered over an extensive country of upwards of One Hundred Miles in length that it was out of my power to carry your orders into Effect in as short a time as I could have wished.' He added, however, that when he did manage to call the various companies together, 'I found them to behave with the utmost propriety and the quotas of each company to turn out voluntarily and with that alacrity which afforded me great pleasure, and I think does them great honors.' There were, admittedly, irregularities with two companies – Kingsey and Shipton – whose captains simply mustered those men they had decided should attend the rendezvous. The Kingsey men were taken to Laprairie without difficulty, but the Shipton captain failed to provide an officer to conduct his men there, leaving them waiting at the company parade ground for nearly three days before they decided to return home.[37] They had still not reported for duty in late July, several weeks after war had broken out.[38]

To the west of Lake Memphremagog, conflict between the senior officers of the Fourth Battalion was coming to a head, as we shall see, and four of the men balloted from the Second Battalion had subsequently deserted. Like Cull, Lieutenant-Colonel Ruiter, who had been a lieutenant in the loyalist Rogers' Rangers during the War of Independence,[39] argued that his men would be much more eager to serve if they were commanded by some of the officers of their own battalion, but the senior command doubted the wisdom of such a strategy. It ordered, instead, that the parents of sons who had deserted be prosecuted,[40] forgetting – it seems – that not all the deserters were minors. There is no evidence that such steps were taken at any point during the war, and, given the proximity of the American border, attempts to make arrests would obviously have been futile. In the meantime, not only were the Eastern Townships militia units poorly trained and equipped on the eve of war, but many of the members clearly had an ambivalent attitude towards active service. Had there been a military fortress inside the region, the story would very likely have been much different, but the colonial authorities had presumably decided that this borderland was neither strategically vital nor defensible.

An 'exposed and defenceless situation': The Outbreak of War

Following the American declaration of war on 18 June a Vermont government committee sent a memorial to the American Secretary of War stressing that the state bordered 'the British province of Lower Canada, having a frontier of ninety miles, exposed to inroads and depredations of the enemy.' If the 'new settlements on and near the Canada line' were in an 'exposed and defenceless situation,'[41] as the state committee pointed out, the same could be said for the settlements north of the border, where residents who may not have felt strong ties to Great Britain nevertheless remembered the violence and destruction of the American Revolution. The names of Henry Cull and Jesse Pennoyer appeared at the head of a petition dated 6 July and signed by 230 men from Compton and Ascot Townships attributing the declaration of war by the United States to a 'hostile coalition against the tranquility, the happiness and liberties of the civilized world of mankind, in obedience to the mandates of the Tyrant of France, to gratify his insatiable pride, and lust of power!' The petitioners expressed confidence that the 'justice of our cause' would prevail, and bring 'ruin and destruction' to the enemy, but they could only

lament the sad, and deplorable situation of our defenceless Frontier settlements, which consist of many thousand worthy loyal subjects! – And we
tremble for their fate! For although the whole of these Townships are men-
aced with immediate invasion, destruction and death, yet it is the unarmed,
and unorganized Inhabitants of these devoted Townships, who alone are to
feel the pressure of American aggressions; – who alone are really in immi-
nent danger of being subjugated and deprived of the peaceable exercise of
their dearest rights, and privileges which they have so long enjoyed under
His Majesty's beneficent administration, and of being placed under a Government, (or rather a Faction) of Demagogues, and not of Laws!

The protests of loyalty to Britain may have been exaggerated as far
as many of the signatories were concerned, but they clearly felt vulnerable. The petition added that 'prowling Bandittis of Marauders'
would soon be crossing the border 'to possess themselves of our
numerous herds of cattle, Horses, and other valuable movables,' yet
there was not 'at this moment a single effective stand of arms, or a
round of ammunition in either the *Second*, *Third*, *Fourth* or *Fifth* Battalions of Royal Eastern Militia belonging to these Frontier Townships, and consisting in the aggregate of about *Fifty Companies*.'
Even if it was unlikely that the Eastern Townships would experience
a large-scale invasion, and even if cross-border relations were generally amicable, the petitioners were well aware that war could disturb
their lives, especially if American soldiers were deployed to seize
livestock that had been smuggled across the line.

The petition made it clear that the settlers of the Eastern Townships
were not asking for regular troops to protect them, though 'a small
force would be of essential service,' but simply for the means to
enable them to defend themselves. While it would obviously not be
feasible to arm every adult male in the region, the petition recommended the formation of a regiment of volunteers from the four battalions. They would be provided with the same pay, clothing, rations,
and so on as other provincial regiments. But, not being professional
soldiers, they would serve under the Militia Act, and not martial law,
and they would be restricted to the southern frontiers of the province
for a maximum of two years. Furthermore, the volunteers would
'possess accurate knowledge of the character, abilities and disposi-
tion of the Officers who are to command them, and consequently
place a greater confidence in them.'[42] Localism was the key note,
then, expressed as a desire to serve in defence of local communities
under the authority of local officers.

The government chose not to form such a regiment, leaving the path open to individual initiative. Because of the Canadian militia's lack of training and its requirement to provide only six months of active service, the colonial authorities had encouraged the formation of volunteer corps of regulars whose members would receive good training while remaining subject to duty only in North America. Incentives included enlistment bounties of £5 and grants of land upon termination of service.[43] Compton's Oliver Barker, whose father had owned an extensive estate in Virginia,[44] did not wait for authorization before proceeding to form such a company after the war broke out. He recruited sixty-two men with the understanding that their primary role would be 'the defence of the Frontiers contiguous to the State of Vermont, & between the Connecticut River & Lake Champlain.' They would, however, march to Saint-Jean, Montreal, or Quebec in the event of an American invasion. But Barker's hasty action brought him into conflict with Captain Glen when the latter attempted to recruit volunteers in the same townships, leaving Barker uncertain as to whether or not the government would recognize his company.[45]

This recognition had still not been granted as of early November 1812, when Lieutenant-Colonel Cull reported that eleven American soldiers had crossed the border to rob an Eaton merchant of a yoke of oxen he was driving home after paying $60 for them on the Canadian side of the border. Referring to other incidents of this nature, Cull stated that 'our neighbors are always ready to steal a march upon us,' and – passing over Barker – he recommended Captain Samuel Heard of Newport to head a company of volunteers.[46] The higher authorities presumably were ambivalent about Barker, who was not a Loyalist and who had been dismissed as justice of the peace in 1808 because of his overly zealous cooperation with American authorities in pursuit of counterfeiters on Canadian soil.[47] In January, Barker expressed his annoyance with the delay, complaining that 'there are none who have raised men for the defence of the Country who have not been cheerfully received, and accepted but myself. Boys without merit and without men are daily promoted & commissioned! I am neglected!'[48]

Two hundred seventy-one inhabitants of Shipton, Melbourne, Brompton, and Kingsey, on the lower St Francis River, had also submitted a loyalty petition after the declaration of war. Drafted by Elmer Cushing, the controversial township leader who had been commissioned to establish a troop of cavalry in 1808,[49] the petition stated that although they previously had been citizens of the United States they were loyal to the British crown. The emphasis was again on self-defence, however, for the petitioners pledged that they would 'assist to the utmost of our abilities, at the risk of our lives and fortunes to repel any enemy whatever who shall attempt to invade our happy land.' To do so, they would need to be supplied with arms and 'an experienced commander' who would preferably be a local resident, presumably referring to Cushing himself.[50] A much shorter petition signed by ninety-one men from Eaton requested arms and ammunition 'to enable them to protect their Families and Property, and to assist in Repelling any attack that may be made by the Enemy against the Peace and Security of His Majesty's Province.'[51]

Finally, from further west, another loyalty petition was submitted by the magistrates, militia officers, and members of what were known as committees of safety in Shefford, Stukely, Bolton, Brome, St Armand, Farnham, Dunham, Potton, and Sutton Townships. In reply, Governor-General Prevost promised to supply them with arms 'as soon as the Exigencies of the other parts of the Province will admit of it,' expressing faith that the inhabitants of the townships 'will successfully employ them in repelling any attempt of Invasion on the Part of the Enemy.'[52] In November 1812 Colonel Johnson did order 400 stand of arms for Lieutenant-Colonel Luke's Fourth Battalion, noting that it was 'chiefly composed of Loyalists' and that they were 'exposed to the Enemy without the means of defending themselves, or aiding in the defence of the Country.'[53] He would not be so generous to the other battalions in the region.

As for the Eastern Townships militiamen, the outbreak of war made them more resistant than ever to service outside the region. After informing five of his captains in August that they would have to draft one man each to go to Saint-Jean 'to make good the casualties in the embodied militia,' Henry Cull complained that 'many of our young men have endeavor'd to screen themselves from being Drafted, by entering into the Cavalry, which causes some confusion in the Returns, and many disputes among the officers commanding Companies.'[54] He hoped, however, that 'the precipitate and inconsiderate conduct of a few Boys of no property' would not tarnish his battalion's reputation for loyalty.[55]

While Jesse Pennoyer sent the required five men from the Fifth Battalion, Philip Luke reported in September that of the nine men recruited from the Fourth Battalion, six had become deserters.[56] Given the proximity of the American border, no attempts were made in the Eastern Townships to make the arrests that had touched off the Lachine Riot in July.[57] Like their French-Canadian counterparts, the Eastern Townships militiamen were opposed to service on distant frontiers but quite willing to defend their home territory. In late

November – following rumours of an American invasion west of Lake Champlain – 300 men volunteered in response to Cull's order that each company of his battalion supply forty recruits plus three commissioned and three non-commissioned officers, one drummer, and one fife player. The volunteers were to carry eight days' provision, but Cull learned that it was a false alarm before they were scheduled to march.[58] Meanwhile, Pennoyer took essentially the same steps as Cull, ordering that all his men who could leave home should be prepared to march on 10 December. He later boasted to the governor-general that, in addition to officers, 300 men – mostly volunteers – had been prepared for the campaign. Such enthusiasm was all the more significant given that Pennoyer's battalion was 'wholly deficient with respect to Field Officers,' and that there were vacancies for other officers as well in some of his companies.[59]

The shortage of officers would persist throughout much of the war, and most of the blame lay with government neglect rather than local apathy. In October 1812 Henry Ruiter complained that two years earlier he had forwarded a list of names to fill officer vacancies in his battalion, but this had not been done, 'which causes a deal of confusion and murmurings.'[60] Several months later Pennoyer reported that the Fifth Battalion still had no adjutant. He also recommended a new captain, lieutenant, and ensign for each of nine companies, and a lieutenant and ensign for a tenth. Some of the former officers had moved, some had resigned, and one had died.[61] Further west, Henry Ruiter reported in November 1813 that the Bolton and Stukely companies of his Second Battalion still did not have a single officer, resulting in considerable confusion when the men turned out in response to an alarm.[62] Officers were finally appointed for Shefford, Stukely, and Farnham in February 1814, but not for the two companies in Bolton, and Lieutenant-Colonel Ruiter remained without either an adjutant or a paymaster.[63] Finally, three of the six companies under Philip Luke's command had no lieutenants as late as October 1813.[64]

Still more serious were the conflicts at the command level resulting from a combination of incompetence on the part of the aging senior officers and independence and perhaps ambition on the part of their subordinates. Only three days after war was declared, Major Joseph Powell – second-in-command of the Fourth Battalion – reported that Lieutenant-Colonel Luke had placed him under house arrest for reasons that were 'frivolous, unjust and unprecedented.' Powell asked for a court of inquiry into his conduct or a court martial based on whatever charges Luke wished to lay against him. He also claimed that Luke was guilty of 'a total neglect of duty, particularly in not causing his Battalion to be assembled and exercised every year as the Law directs or permitting me to do it. In not using due diligence to cause deserters to be apprehended. In ungentleman and unofficer like conduct. In making use of gross, abusive, injurious and insulting language to his officers and particularly to myself. In neglect, in not enrolling the Militia.'[65] Henry Ruiter also came into conflict with his junior officers, reporting in July 1814: 'I gave particular orders to the officers of the 2d Battalion and I am sory to find Some of them pays verry little attention to any orders they receive especially Capt. Moses Elkins who Countenances Deserters and harbors one in his House and has engaged to protect him I think such Officers Does not merit a Commission and I should be glad how to Proceed with such Officers.'[66]

More serious, still, was the conflict within Pennoyer's Fifth Battalion between Elmer Cushing of the Shipton Cavalry and his lieutenant, Gordon Lawrence. Cushing complained in June 1812 that his charge of disobedience against Lawrence had gone unanswered, and he warned that if he did not have the authority to discipline his lieutenant he would resign his commission.[67] A month later, with the outbreak of war, the self-serving Cushing attempted to use the threat of resignation to acquire a sum of money from the government. In 1796, when he was operating an unprofitable Montreal coffee house, Cushing had been granted Shipton Township in return for testifying against the American David McLane, who was subsequently executed on questionable legal grounds for plotting a French invasion of the colony. Cushing now protested to the governor-general that the Shipton patent promised in 1790 (the case actually took place in 1796–7) had not been delivered until 1805, after he had sent an agent to London at the expense of over £150. Cushing also claimed that he alone had assumed the financial burden of developing the township, but the land was now worth less than it had been two years after its initial settlement, and he complained that his moral character had been defamed as a result of McLane's execution.

Cushing's request of an additional 8,000 acres (3,239 hectares) in the vicinity of Shipton was, not surprisingly, greeted with little sympathy by the government. On the margins of his petition is written: 'This is about the most impudent Claim I ever saw. The man it is true did give some information concerning McLane, but not till after he had the promise of being rewarded by the grant of about 45 Thousand acres of Land, which he afterwards obtained.'[68] Cushing finally resigned his commission the following year, explaining that it had cost him a good deal of money and he had no more to spend. He also

referred to the 'base intrigues' of his enemies, hinting that 'dark mis-
teries' would eventually be brought to light.[69] The perennially
aggrieved Cushing was presumably referring to the arrest of his son
for selling liquor without a licence to the mustered cavalrymen, and
to his own arrest on the charge of consorting with the enemy, though
he claimed that the individual in question was simply a visiting
American businessman.[70] As for his rival, Lawrence, he was indicted
for allowing prisoners to escape shortly after he succeeded Cushing
as the cavalry commander.[71]

Though the outbreak of war had caused considerable anxiety north
of the forty-fifth parallel, then, and an eagerness to defend the region
from American invasion, the colonial authorities hesitated to arm the
militia or to authorize local volunteer units and neglected to appoint
officers to the regular units. The fact that the militia companies continued to resist orders to draft a limited number of men for service
outside the region, and that there were conflicts within the higher
ranks, clearly did little to reassure the government about the loyalty
of the region or the competence of its officers. This impasse would
persist throughout the war.

'Delay, backwardness, and want of zeal':
The Conscription Crisis

In response to the rumour that there would be a draft of men from the
region to serve in the Select Embodied Militia, three Loyalist township leaders and magistrates – Samuel Gale of Farnham, Samuel
Willard of Stukely, and John Savage of Shefford – circulated a petition in December 1812 asking that the new townships be exempt due
to the thinness of their settlements. Gale, a leading New York Loyalist, had spent three years in London lobbying to have the government
honour its commitment to those who had invested in land as township
leaders.[72] The other two men, Savage and Willard, were both militia
captains, and the latter would replace Philip Luke as lieutenant-
colonel of the Third Battalion in 1814.[73] The document had thirty-
three signatures, including those of militia officers from various
townships as well as two British-born Anglican ministers, Charles
Stewart of St Armand and Charles Cotton of Dunham. These men
could obviously not be suspected of sympathy for the enemy.

The petition claimed that 'it is not without great Difficulty that the
necessary labour for raising and gathering the Crops for the subsistence of the Families and Cattle, can be performed, even when there
is no other Interruption than the natural one of bad weather; and it is

utterly impossible, until Time shall have rendered them more numerous and compact, for any of them to leave their Families for any considerable length of Time, without actual Ruin, not only to the Families of those who are drawn away, but the settlement at large.' Pointing to the strong voluntary response of the previous month, the petitioners assured the governor-general that the region would always be prepared to do whatever it could to defend the province from invasion.[74] Gale also informed Prevost that the loyalty of Willard and Savage (and obviously himself) was not a matter of doubt and claimed that the small number of signatures was due to the fact that the contemplated draft had been 'countermanded' before the petition was circulated widely.[75]

The military leadership was not pleased. Colonel Murray in Saint-Jean later claimed to have heard that Gale 'went so far as to say that it was all a scheme of General de Rottenburg's & Colonel Murray's,' for 'his Excellency had promised him that no more drafts were to be made from the Townships, nor were they to be called out except in case of actual invasion.'[76] Whether or not this rumour was true, Gale was assured by Governor Prevost that Colonel Johnson's six battalions would require only one hundred men from the region. With twenty recruits from the Sixth Battalion, which lay west of the Eastern Townships, these men were to be formed into two companies that would serve as light troops in the vicinity of Isle aux Noix in Lake Champlain. Prevost added that this proportion, 'as well as the nature of the service,' should be considered light compared with what would be required under the next militia draft from other parts of the province.[77]

Oliver Barker was also finally informed that the services of his volunteer militia would not be required because the two companies that would become known as the Frontier Light Infantry were 'all that His Excellency would require at present from the townships.'[78] To cushion the blow, the message added that the governor-general was 'fully aware from your character and loyalty how usefully you may be employed and that His Exc[y] will not fail to avail himself of any favourable opportunity that may offer of placing you in a situation corresponding to your wishes.'[79] But Barker simply refused to take no for an answer, and in May the adjutant-general authorized the attachment of his company to the Frontier Light Infantry, whose main role would be to facilitate movement of smuggled goods into Lower Canada.[80] Barker later complained that when he arrived in Saint-Jean with half the fifty men he had raised – the others to follow later in the month – the commanding officer took this as justification to flout the terms of his men's enlistment agreement by using them to fill vacancies in the existing companies. Rather than serve with 'hirelings and such as were destitute, or not susceptible of the same loyal principles as glowed in their breasts,' Barker's men had returned to their homes in disappointment and disgust. Needless to say, the other half of the unit did not report for duty.[81]

Meanwhile, the four battalion commanders of the Eastern Townships were each ordered to provide twenty 'of the most able active intelligent & trusty men, well acquainted with the woods to serve on the Frontiers during pleasure or the American War.'[82] The open-ended term would prove to be very unpopular among the region's militiamen, though the process appears to have unfolded quite smoothly as far as Ruiter's Second Battalion was concerned. An officer named J. Jones reported to headquarters in Saint-Jean in late January that he had obtained more than the quota of volunteers from Sutton and Potton and that he did not expect difficulty in the other towns because 'on explaining the requirement & the nature of the service they will readily comply as they acknowledge the number small and also as they are told this will exempt them from the Draft soon to be expected in the Battalions East of the Lake,' meaning Lake Memphremagog.

What Jones meant by the latter phrase is not clear, but he admitted that the members of Missisquoi's Fourth Battalion were more recalcitrant, though he blamed Lieutenant-Colonel Luke for doing all in his power 'to render the Batt.[n] under his command as refractory as possible.' Luke did not order his companies, located in St Armand, Dunham, and Stanbridge, to meet until a fortnight after he had received orders that they should do so, and he had chosen a single location for the entire battalion to rendezvous on the same day![83] An angry Colonel Murray wrote to General de Rottenburg that 'Colonel Luke's conduct borders upon downright disaffection.' He blamed Luke for the fact that two captains at Caldwell's Manor had refused to call out their quota and added that 'a Mr Gale' had also been 'excessively busy.' In Murray's opinion, 'the Generality of the inhabitants of the townships' would be 'highly pleased to serve in this description of corps,' but several agitators were stirring up resistance to the draft. He recommended that Colonel Luke, who was a half-pay officer – having been a captain in Cuyler's refugee volunteers during the American Revolution – be severely fined and have his commission removed.[84]

East of Lake Memphremagog, the two battalion commanders were more conscientious, yet the recruitment process failed there as well.

Lieutenant-Colonel Cull personally attended the selection process for his companies, five of which were ordered to provide three men each, and the other five to provide one each.[85] There being no volunteers from the Hatley company, the captain chose three young men himself, but, when Cull went to Barnston, Captain Joseph Bartlett 'made a long speech ... setting forth the General Order as Partial; a speculation by some interested officers who had imposed on the Governor in procuring such Order.' He then dismissed his company, and Cull had him sign a memorandum recording what he had done. Bartlett later had second thoughts and submitted a list of three names.

The captain of the second company also dismissed his men, but they were recalled by Cull, who selected three draftees. Cull was able to draft six more men from the four companies meeting in Stanstead, but none of the recruits made an appearance on the day they were to march to Saint-Jean.[86] Cull later explained to Colonel Johnson that his men objected to the apparently open-ended term of service (a sharp contrast to the standard six-month period for regular militia), for 'that jealousy which pervades the minds of our militiamen that they are to be made soldiers of during life, is not easily overcome.' He suspected that all the men drafted had left the province.[87]

Jesse Pennoyer met even more resistance in his attempts to recruit his quota of twenty from the Fifth Battalion. When he met the first two companies in Compton, no one stepped forward to volunteer, which Pennoyer claimed 'really surprised me the more so as on all former occasions of a similar nature I had ever found them prompt in showing their Loyalty.' What Pennoyer was forgetting was that there had been no former occasions in which men were asked to serve outside the region for an unspecified period. Asked to explain their behaviour, some of the men stated that under these conditions they felt they would 'be considered as having permanently enlisted as regular soldiers and if it might please their superior officers held as such during life.' Pennoyer attempted to dissuade them, pleading that they not tarnish the good reputation the region had established to that point, but the men insisted on a clearer explanation of the order. Pennoyer then asked their officers to pick draftees but was forced to give them more time to do so. Two of the men subsequently selected fled to the United States. Meanwhile, travelling on to Ascot, where the entire company had volunteered to meet the rumoured American invasion west of Lake Champlain in June, Pennoyer experienced the same resistance, and he would do so again when he met the Eaton and Hereford companies two days later. He then decided that meeting more companies would be pointless.[88]

Succumbing to his men's protests, Cull recommended to Colonel Johnson that the General Order be modified to make clear that men in the Frontier Light Infantry 'are still employed as militiamen.' He added that 'there is also some undue prejudice against the Officers the men are to serve under.'[89] Without waiting for a reply, Cull wrote to his captains stating that in order to convince Prevost 'that it is not from disloyalty to the King or any dislike of the Constitution' that the draft had failed, they should offer the services of a complete company of militia volunteers for one year. Willing to serve as captain of the company was Major Charles Kilborn, the former Loyalist officer who had established a number of industries at Kilborn's Mills, later known as Rock Island, on the Vermont border.[90] Pennoyer had obviously joined Cull in this proposal, for in the Pennoyer archival collection is a document dated 23 February 1813 listing the number of men required from each company in his battalion to create a volunteer company of sixty, which was triple the number of men called for by the official draft notice.[91]

The objection to that notice, Cull and Pennoyer clearly felt, was not so much service outside the region as service under strangers during an undefined period of time. But professional officers were not likely to be satisfied with companies commanded by amateurs. Before the petition was circulated and the two volunteer companies established, Governor-General Prevost succumbed to the popular pressure by reducing the term of service in the Frontier Light Infantry to one year, 'unless the greatest emergency should render the continuance of their services indispensably necessary.'[92] In forwarding Prevost's new orders, Colonel Johnson chastised his battalion commanders, declaring that 'I am greatly disappointed and much concerned to learn that so much delay, backwardness, and want of zeal for the service, has been evinced in a Quarter I thought there was the least reason to expect anything of the kind from. And that any doubts should have arisen as to the authenticity or origin of the order.' In a face-saving gesture of his own, Johnson blamed his senior militia officers for misinterpreting the duration and nature of the service, though the draft order had clearly stated that it would be for the duration of the war or 'during pleasure.'[93]

Johnson ordered that the draft be completed without further delay, but, despite the new conditions, resistance to enlistment in the Frontier Light Infantry persisted. Major Charles Kilborn attempted to persuade twenty men to volunteer under him as captain of one of the companies, but Cull noted that 'the attempt (as I expected) was fruitless, only sixteen men could be *hired* to go out of the whole Batt^n.'[94]

Cull's reference to being hired suggests that militiamen, in some cases at least, received local payments to supplement the meagre salaries provided by the government to those in active service.[95] Presumably to fill the rest of the complement, Cull claimed that his officers had selected twenty men with 'a visible property' which could be seized in case of desertion.[96] This would explain why the ages of four of the eight men who finally did march with Kilborn on 23 March ranged from forty-five to fifty, with only one being under twenty-five.[97] One of these men failed to appear in Saint-Jean, Cull reported, notwithstanding 'the liberality of the neighbours.'[98]

How money was raised to subsidize recruitment is revealed in a document which records the resolution of a meeting of the inhabitants of Stukely Township to hire two men for military service. One 'volunteer' agreed to serve for $10 per month and the other for $12 per month, sums that would be paid to their families after being raised by a local assessment, with the collector to be paid $6.50.[99] Even though the colonial authorities had not instituted the town meeting system, seen to be a leading cause of the War of Independence, it had survived informally in at least one township. Even there it appears to have ended in 1814,[100] but this obviously did not prevent families from continuing to take part in what might be viewed as a form of moral economy. When the state demanded that a sacrifice be made by a few on behalf of the many, the community's response was to share the burden as equitably as possible.

But such payments were not enough incentive to fill the quotas, and Cull issued orders in March that any of the ten remaining men who failed to go to Saint-Jean 'must be apprehended as Deserters & carried before a magistrate to be dealt with as the Law directs.' Only five men obeyed.[101] Two months later Cull informed his captains that if bachelors could not be found, 'married men must absolutely go without any hesitation or excuse whatever.'[102] The local settlers were concerned not only about the possibility that their sons would be killed in action but also about losing manpower on their farms. In one case a Stanstead militia captain was criticized (in Cull's paraphrase) for 'sending a handsome young man "to play the Soldier" who does as much work at husbandry in a day as any man in the Township in which he lived.' Despite the boasted strength of the man in question, he had applied to the medical board for exempt status due to ill health.[103]

The Third Battalion finally met its quota in late May when the Barnston captain balloted three married men, reporting that there were now only five bachelors remaining in his company and they were '*ready* to *run.*'[104] But the married men also refused to march, preferring to face a magistrate instead.[105] They had little to fear from such an alternative, according to Cull, who reported that 'I strongly suspect the magistrates before whom they are ordered will not have the courage to send them on.' Revealing his class prejudices, Cull added that the local men 'have no other Idea of *Honor & Glory* than to work sometimes much harder than the slaves in Virginia & South Carolina & leisurely consume their earnings in Pumpkin Pies & Sweet Cakes, in junketing & whiskey.' His only consolation was that 'our enemies are pretty much of the same description.' The chief problem as far as meeting the quota in Barnston was concerned (aside from the drop in militia members from one hundred to fifty due to the population exodus since the start of the war) was 'the unwillingness or inability of the inhabitants to give a Bounty to such as will undertake *the short twelve months of Honor & Glory* which has been practised in all the Townships notwithstanding substitutes are not allowable.'[106]

With the conscription fiasco reaching an impasse, Lieutenant-Colonel Cull faced a new crisis when, rather than selecting one of his more senior officers, he recommended twenty-year-old Lieutenant Lauren Bangs to serve as his adjutant. Because the young Bangs, unarmed and alone, had faced down an American dragoon who was brandishing a pistol, Cull felt that his promotion would be 'an encouragement to further exertions.' His senior officers declared, however, that they would never appear on the parade ground to take orders from a mere youngster.[107] Cull's response was that 'I never could nor can yet conceive that Grey Hairs are sure signs of merit (if it was I should myself be highly meritorious),' and he added that he had consistently followed Sir John Johnson's instructions to favour 'Old Loyalists.'[108] He acquiesced, however, to the alternate appointment of a middle-aged ensign from the delinquent Barnston company.[109]

Cull was, not surprisingly, becoming increasingly critical of his officers. Having long supported the local distribution of firearms, he now claimed that 'I cannot well account for the Conduct of those Captains who have apply'd for Arms nor can I conceive what they mean to do with them all.' He worried that 'there might be cause for discontent in the Batt.ⁿ if fools & knaves were preferred to carry arms instead of the better informed & honestly disposed.' And Cull had little faith in some of his captains' abilities to make the distinction, for he wrote that while Captain James Ruiter of Stanstead was 'a Loyal man,' he 'wants one grand usefull requisite – Common Sense & consequently the good opinion & confidence of his men.' Captain James Bodwell, also of Stanstead, 'may be Loyal but does not shew it by his frequently allowing Prisoners sent from Capt.ⁿ to Capt.ⁿ to escape.' Captain Johnson Taplin, Stanstead Plain's first settler,[110] 'is Loyal – but has no *command* of himself[,] consequently negligent & careless.' Cull finally had to write to Taplin's lieutenant for the company's last returns, which were then submitted two months late. He also claimed that Captain Issachar Norton of Barnston had 'by his indeterminate & undecisive mode of conducting the business' caused 'a great deal of unnecessary trouble.' As for the two Hatley captains, Joseph Ives and Simon Kezar, they 'are incapable of making out a Return, as well as careless & inattentive to their Duty, & it was my intention to propose that they should be replaced by others.'[111] Cull had more regard for Captain David Curtis of Stanstead, who was 'Loyal and zealous in the glorious cause.' Even Curtis, however, in requesting that his company be furnished with arms, had added that it was '*not for the purpose of being dragged into the Upper Province*, those were his Words.'

Only four captains were left unscathed by Cull, who complained that 'the militia here chiefly continue that revolutionizing spirit of insubordination brought with them from the Country they emigrated from.' The only hope, Cull felt, lay with the 'rising' generation which 'might be improved by Government School-masters and English School-Books & good men to Preach to them that morality which their Hypocritical [illegible] Teachers totally disregard.'[112] This would, indeed, be the strategy adopted by the governing authorities during the following years when more than forty-five Anglican-controlled Royal Institution of Learning schools were established in the region.[113]

Meanwhile, contrary to Major Pennoyer's expectations, no one from his Fifth Battalion marched to Saint-Jean in late March. Clearly frustrated, he asked Colonel Johnson for 'orders and directions' as to how to proceed with respect to the delinquents.[114] The following month Pennoyer ordered those captains whose companies had not contributed their quota to have recruits prepared to march to Saint-Jean on 19 April, but once again no one made an appearance.[115] The conscripts from Ascot and Hereford had left the country, and no one from Compton had answered the order 'owing in great measure to the circumstance of Captain O. Barker's having taken the most of the young men into his Volunteer Company.' Pennoyer expressed hope that the delinquents would be brought to justice, but claimed that most of the blame lay with the officers 'for their want of zeal and even neglect of Duty.' Captain Bishop of Dudswell had gone so far as to claim that 'he has not one man in his Company who will answer the description as required by the Original order.'[116]

The following month, in May, the lone volunteer from Pennoyer's Fifth Battalion, Sergeant Hudson, was sent from Saint-Jean to round up the men required to complete its quota. Pennoyer urged his captains that 'unless this order is promptly complied with disgrace must follow[.] I must therefore hope that you will duly weigh these circumstances and so acquit yourself as to ease my mind from a truly painful anxiety.'[117] But only three of the seven men still owed by his battalion made an appearance. Pennoyer was inclined to accept the excuse of the Hereford company whose commanding officer explained that no man would leave his home because the frontier township was 'entirely under the fear and control of the enemy who are stationed immediately on the line.' But the more distant and populous township of Shipton owed three men, and Pennoyer asked that 'a more active and zealous man' replace its captain.[118] Finally, 'after much trouble and pains,' Ensign Harvel (also spelled Hervil), who was also from the region, managed to recruit three volunteers from Shipton in June, with the result that the Fifth Battalion – unlike the neighbouring Third – could finally claim to have met its quota.[119]

Farther west, Henry Ruiter presumably had little difficulty persuading the companies from the Second Battalion to meet their quotas (judging from the lack of correspondence on the issue), though four of his men would fail to appear in Saint-Jean, as we shall see. But Philip Luke of Missisquoi's Fourth Battalion continued to take an independent stance. He wrote on 15 April that he was sending three volunteers and the remainder would follow in a few days. He insisted, however, that he would not 'send a man but what is willing to turn out of his own accord,' adding that 'there is a number that had gon of but they are a Return bac again and now seam willing to go and serve their King and Country so that I hope by the first of Next week they will al be at Saint Johns.' Luke may have had little respect for outside authority, but his loyalty could not be questioned as he forwarded information concerning American troop movements gleaned by his son who had penetrated enemy lines.[120]

Not surprisingly, Captain Louis Ritter, commanding officer of the Frontier Light Infantry, which entered active service in May 1813, was far from impressed with the effort made by the Townships militia. Each of his two companies was still short eight men despite repeated orders to meet the quota (six men had died in hospital and eight had deserted). Ritter did admit that the recruits 'tho' not of the description as might be expected from the first order for their formation, are in perfect discipline and well behaved in general.'[121] The following month, however, he complained that 'the lawless Militia Officers in the Townships from whom I have with trouble obtained one hundred & ten men have prevented the appointment of Subalterns.'[122] It was actually Ritter who was preventing the appointments of two lieutenants and two ensigns, for he claimed that 'no Subject from the Townships has from *merit* of exertions any *Claim* to a commission' and rejected those recommended by one of his captains, Charles Kilborn (who had been second-in-command of the Third Battalion). He added that James Harvel, who had assisted with recruitment (as we have seen), would be unsuitable as ensign because he was a mere carpenter who had been working as a stage coach driver and waiter in a public house while waiting in Saint-Jean for his appointment. As for Luke's daring son, who had also been recommended as ensign, Ritter simply stated that the irascible lieutenant-colonel could 'by no means expect his son's appointment.'[123]

Ritter's advice backfired on him when his superiors misinterpreted it by assuming that his rejection of Kilborn's recommendations meant that they should also ignore General de Rottenburg's promise that Kilborn would replace the inactive Captain Jones. The consequence would be that Jones would be paid despite devoting all his time to his private business, while Kilborn would not even be compensated for the five months he had been serving in Saint-Jean. Ritter apologized profusely to Kilborn and advised him to petition Prevost to have the decision reversed. He added that even though Kilborn had failed to induce the Townships officers to do their duty, 'yet you have endeavoured as much as lay in your power to have the Drafts Compleat in some way however.' In his subsequent petition, Kilborn claimed that the draftees had initially refused to march to Saint-Jean due to their prejudice against Captain Jones and fear that 'some Snare was laid for them.' They submitted only when he promised to accompany them himself and 'to Remain with them until they were Satisfied.' Kilborn also stated that the people of the Townships would feel slighted if the two recommended subaltern officers, John Savage and James Harvel, were not appointed.[124] To avoid further alienating the region, the commander of the forces shortly afterward did appoint Kilborn and the other two men to the promised positions.[125]

As the one-year anniversary of the conscription for the Frontier Light Infantry approached, Captain Ritter took stock of his declining troop strength. The only men from the Eastern Townships in the First Company, under the command of Captain Mailloux, were from the

Fourth Battalion in the St Armand area. They had been reduced by three hospital deaths, two desertions, and the capture of one man by the Americans.[126] The story was similar for Kilborn's Second Company. Aside from the four conscripts from Ruiter's Second Battalion who had failed to appear, three men from the same battalion had died in hospital, one had been killed in action, and one had deserted. From Cull's Third Battalion two men had died in hospital, one was a prisoner of war, one had been discharged, and one had been shot for deserting. The complement from Pennoyer's Fifth Battalion was more complete, for it was short by only one man, who had been killed in action, though the two volunteers were also counted as non-effectives.[127]

Judging from the number of men killed in action, the Frontier Light Infantry had been quite active even though the Americans had yet to invade Lower Canada, but the hospital deaths reveal that the greatest danger to the men (as in Upper Canada) was disease.[128] Despite the high mortality rate, Ritter was confident that the second year's draft would be successful because the officers of the Second Company (Kilborn and his subordinates) would be in charge of it. He also suggested that if substitutes for draftees were formally allowed, nearly all the men currently serving in the Second Company would remain after the year's term had expired, though he would weed out 'the bad or unserviceable.' Only now had these men become trained sufficiently to be fit for duty, for they knew *every Individual and every part of the Country near the Boundaries.*'[129]

Contrary to Ritter's prediction, few men did volunteer for a second term, and on 24 March 1814 he reported from Lacolle (where his company was evidently now stationed to be closer to the border) that the untrained new recruits, some of whom had never fired a gun, were unfit for piquet duty.[130] The draft had been organized in the same fashion as the previous year, with twenty men balloted from each militia battalion, and each company required to contribute to that quota according to its number of men aged eighteen to thirty years.[131] To cut expenses claimed by officers accompanying the recruits, Ritter decreed that they should not be sent in twos and threes this time, but as a single group from each battalion.[132] But his optimism proved to be misplaced, for the heightened tensions along the border did little to stimulate enthusiasm.

Henry Ruiter of the Second Battalion protested in June that 'I have Don avery thing in my power to heve the orders obade,' but some of those who had been balloted had fled across the border.[133] His neighbouring colleague, Philip Luke, who had hitherto refused to enforce the draft on his companies, was now more compliant, presumably because the Americans had attacked Philipsburg and captured his son (as we shall see). The suddenly enthusiastic Luke chastised one of his captains for his 'Total Neglect' in failing to have his company comply to the order: 'Horried indeed will be our Situation if Such disobediance to the Just and Reasonable Order of Government are to be disregarded or not Complyed with.'[134] The man in question was presumably Jacob Ruiter, for Luke had him arrested, later reporting that he had failed to provide a single man for the Frontier Light Infantry. As commander of a grenadier company recruited from all the units in Dunham Township, Jacob Ruiter (Lieutenant-Colonel Henry Ruiter's nephew) argued that his men were exempt, though he did hire one individual as his contribution to the quota.[135] April found Luke still threatening dire consequences if the 'coto' were not fulfilled at once, but to no avail, and in May he blamed his commanding officers – two of whom were mere sergeants – for the fact that only nine of the twenty required men had been enlisted.[136] In July, after Jacob Ruiter had failed to have his company respond to the muster of the battalion for the selection of conscripts, Luke charged him with causing disaffection among the other officers and demanded that he be dismissed and his company disbanded.[137]

Meanwhile, Jesse Pennoyer was able to forward only nine men from the Fifth Battalion in late February, with one more volunteer appearing in early March. Pennoyer noted that this man was 'considerably older than what was originally ordered' and apologized for the fact that not all twenty men were sent at once, adding darkly that the reasons why his orders had not been obeyed 'must be inquired into ... and the blame placed to the right person.'[138] After repeated orders to his captains to meet their quotas, and a warning from the governor-general to supply the remaining nine recruits, Pennoyer finally forwarded two more men in August. Of the six recruits still owed by five of his companies, Pennoyer noted that two men selected by their captains had absconded, the Hereford company could not provide men because that township was 'in a great degree under the control of the enemy,' and three captains had simply not submitted reports.[139]

As for the Third Battalion, Henry Cull reported in mid-June – after at least four visits to his companies – that some of the captains had still failed to supply their quota of men, and he feared that they never would.[140] A month later, eleven men were delivered from six of his companies, but nine were missing from the four others.[141] Consequently, Captain Ritter could only report that the drafts of the First, Second, and Third Battalions were 'as much neglected as it was the case last year.' The regiment's other three battalions did eventually supply most of their quota,[142] but Ritter noted that the Townships militia was much more resistant to the draft than the 'other good Canadian Battalions of the Province.'[143]

In defence of his men, Lieutenant-Colonel Cull protested in August 1814 that some of the draftees from his battalion had not been discharged after two years' service, giving 'the Domestic enemies of the Province great cause of rejoicing, as tending to fulfill their sly insinuations *"that the militiamen would be held during the War or Life."'* Cull added that 'should any of the young men Desert and return home,' he doubted if the magistrates would commit them to prison. He concluded that he was 'very certain that one half of the loyal part of the militia would rather turn out and do duty' than that the terms under which the draftees had been selected be altered to extend their service.[144] Despite his exasperation with the men in his battalion, then, Cull was still acting as their spokesman to some extent as the war entered its third year and resistance to service outside the region became stiffer than ever.

The conscription process began for the third time in January 1815, when a new militia levy ordered that twenty men once again be furnished by each Eastern Townships battalion by 20 February.[145] Philip Luke reported on 28 February that 'nothing but a totle disobedients to Orders and a want of Subordination prevails Among the officers in my Battalion.' Not one officer aside from the cavalry captain, John Ruiter, had appeared on the muster day, and only two captains had submitted the names of militiamen who had been balloted to serve in the Frontier Light Infantry.[146] There was no response from the other battalions, but, mercifully, the order to march was suspended on 1 March, when the adjutant-general announced officially that a peace treaty had been ratified on 17 February.[147]

Even though the draft had been limited to twenty men per battalion, and even though the service was to be in an infantry unit defending the Lower Canadian border, it had proven nearly impossible to fill the Eastern Townships quota. This was largely due to suspicion about the length of service that would be required and to a strong sense of localism that placed a priority on protecting family and community ahead of participating in an unpopular war. With sometimes recalcitrant militia officers and independent-minded justices of the peace as its only agents in the region, the government had limited means to enforce its will on a population determined to resist orders that it felt were not in its own best interest. A lingering sense of loyalty to the

United States was not the real issue, for American raiding across the border had been resisted, as we shall see.

'Making the fur fly':
Resisting American Invasion

The heightened tension with Vermont and New Hampshire along the Eastern Townships border contributed to the growing resistance to enlistment in the Frontier Light Infantry. Until late in 1813 the Vermont militia was the only armed force defending that state's border with Lower Canada.[148] Anti-war feeling had become so strong in certain Vermont towns that they refused to pay for soldiers or assist enlistment officers, and communities on both sides of the border entered into mutual agreements to refrain from molesting one another.[149] Particularly irritating to the American authorities was the large-scale smuggling trade (examined in the next section) that took place in the borderland region. Major-General Wade Hampton complained to the United States Secretary of War that 'there has been inculcated by the British, a shameful and corrupt neutrality on the lines, for the purpose of gain.' The military focus was also shifting eastward because, with the campaign on the Niagara peninsula at a standstill in the fall of 1813, the Americans had reverted to their original strategy of attacking Kingston or Montreal.[150] The planned avenue of attack on Montreal was via the Châteauguay Valley but, as a diversionary tactic as well as a strike against the smuggling trade, Hampton ordered Colonel Isaac Clark to incite a 'petty war near Lake Champlain.'[151] Clark, commander of the forces stationed at Burlington, was to 'break the truce and, should other means fail, to act the part of mischievous urchin, who, to get two peacable [*sic*] *tabbies* at "*making the fur fly*" holds them together by the tail.'[152]

In mid-October a small fleet of American vessels entered Missisquoi Bay, where Clark and approximately one hundred riflemen plundered Caldwell's Manor on the west side of the bay before proceeding to Philipsburg. All six companies of the Fourth Battalion turned out to repel the invaders despite Lieutenant-Colonel Luke's absence, but they had received so little training that Major Joseph Powell declined to arm any but those detailed for guard duty.[153] Expecting to face a force approaching from the lake, the advance guard was surprised at dawn by a land attack and quickly overpowered. According to Colonel Clark's report, 'ten minutes after the first attack they laid down their arms and surrendered themselves prisoners of war.' Clark then sent an advanced guard to meet the force of 200 men hurrying to the rescue under Lieutenant-Colonel Luke. Clark's men surprised and captured Luke's advance guard, causing him to retreat so hastily that he left seventy-six stand of arms behind. This was hardly a glorious day for the Townships militia! Clark reported that 'our whole force engaged was 102 – the number of prisoners taken is 101; their killed 9, and wounded 14.'[154]

To minimize his own responsibility for the fiasco, Luke claimed that Clark had 150 men, and he neglected to mention the defeat of his own advance guard. He also stated that only one man was killed and eight wounded, but there was no fudging the number of prisoners. In total, Luke reported, they were one major, two captains, two lieutenants, three ensigns, five sergeants, and ninety-one privates. This was a significant proportion of the 500 men who were enlisted in the Fourth Battalion.[155] The main American force of 300 men who had been waiting offshore was now able to enter Philipsburg without opposition. Taking the abandoned arms, they also plundered two stores of $4,540 in goods and drove off many horses and oxen. The Americans left the bay next day, but Luke reported that 'many marauding parties straggled from the troops, committed incessant roberies on the inhabitants contiguous to the Line, by driving off their Cattle, Horses, waggons, etc., etc., and robbing the families of cloaths, provisions, beding, etc., to a very considerable amount.'[156]

Philip Ruiter, a local justice of the peace, later submitted a similar report to the government, noting that two of his brothers had been among the prisoners, though one escaped the third day. Of those robbed of bedding and wearing apparel, two families claimed that they were left with only the clothes on their backs.[157] Colonel Clark crossed the border again two weeks later with fifty cavalry to drive off eighty to a hundred head of cattle that had been smuggled in from Vermont to sell to local contractors for the British army. In this state of alarm, many families carried much of their movable property to the north of St Armand and into Stanbridge and Dunham.[158]

Meanwhile, the Canadian prisoners had been immediately marched to Swanton, and from there to Burlington. Lieutenant-Colonel Ruiter wrote to the Reverend Charles Stewart asking him to urge the governor-general to arrange for a prisoner exchange, noting that many of the men were poorly clothed and had not yet harvested their Indian corn and potatoes.[159] Stewart did as he was asked, pointing out that the families of these men were in different circumstances than if they had been regular soldiers. He also informed Governor Prevost that he had promised Colonel Clark that the two surgeons he had left with the wounded American soldiers would be safe, yet the hot-headed Philip Luke had arrested them and had them marched to Chambly. Stewart added that while they were unskilled, these doctors had been as attentive to the Canadians as to their own men.[160] Finally, the Anglican clergyman worried that the United States military would treat the American-born members of the Missisquoi militia units the same way the British military treated British-born prisoners from American units, namely as traitors.[161] But Stewart still hoped for an early release of the Canadian prisoners, noting that it had been British practice to liberate captured American militiamen on swearing that they would no longer take up arms in the conflict.[162] He asked the commanding officer in Burlington to release those prisoners who had dependent families, and Lieutenant-Colonel Bedel replied that had the letter arrived before they were marched away and their names sent to the War Office, Stewart's 'wishes might have been answered.' Now, however, the Commissary of Prisoners was the proper person to apply to.[163]

The captured militiamen were taken to the prisoner of war camp in Greenbush, Massachusetts, south of Boston, where a reporter for a local newspaper wrote on 16 October: 'I have just seen Colonel Clark's prisoners, who were paraded through this town. They are a motley crew of farmers, citizens, tavern-keepers, etc.; not a regular soldier among them. They were surprised in their beds.'[164] The prisoners were marched back again to Burlington in late November, apparently in preparation for release.[165] Several days later one of them, Private Amos Davis of Stanbridge, informed the governor-general that he had been freed on a $1,000 bond not to leave the town of Burlington, presumably because his wounded son had also been captured. Reporting that he was the only person in a position to support his son's wife and 'infant family,' Davis asked the government for relief.[166]

In early December the Reverend Stewart informed Prevost that he had taken a personal interest in the matter, not only because many of the prisoners were his neighbours, 'but especially because their families & themselves were remarkably ill prepared & fitted for such distressing circumstances.' Noting that 'they have been miserably lodged, & badly treated in several respects,' Stewart added that there were promises of removal to a better building. He had also sent them 'various necessaries,' perhaps supplied in part by the Patriotic Society at Quebec to which he had appealed in October.[167] But it was not until 6 December that Philip Ruiter was given permission to travel to a tavern in Burlington with supplies for the imprisoned British officers.[168] It was not only officers who felt the cold, however, and two days later ten of the prisoners wrote to Ruiter stating that the American government had given permission for him to bring 'Flanels, Casiners, Vestings, Linens, Broad Cloths, Handkerchiefs, and Stockings, all of which we are much in want.'[169]

Finally, after another month had passed, during which the British and Americans hardened their positions over the prisoner of war issue, orders were issued for a prisoner exchange at Odelltown, just north of the border.[170] The senior officer, Major Powell, was valued at eight private soldiers or non-commissioned officers, each of the nine captains represented the equivalent of six ordinary prisoners, and the five lieutenants equalled four each. The proposal of the hard-bargaining Yankees was, however, to exchange the ninety-two Canadian prisoners (a few had presumably escaped, been released, or died) for seventeen American officers, including three brigadier-generals and two lieutenant-colonels, plus sixty-eight ordinary soldiers to make up the difference.[171] These unreasonable terms were presumably accepted, but Major Powell, Lieutenant Luke (who was held hostage in distant Philadelphia), and Lieutenant Rhykert did not return home until 16 May.[172] Inhabitants who had their horses taken in the attack petitioned for compensation in February, but some of them, at least, were still waiting to be paid in June.[173]

Meanwhile, in late 1813, the Americans had erected barracks for 1,200 men (far more than the normal garrison) at Derby, Vermont, as well as a blockhouse and depots at Stewartstown, New Hampshire – villages that lay on the two main routes of entry into Lower Canada east of Lake Memphremagog. The British commander-in-chief responded by giving Oliver Barker, whose half company had deserted the Frontier Light Infantry in Saint-Jean a year earlier, orders to destroy these buildings. Barker recruited officers from the local sedentary units, leading to complaints of poaching by Lieutenant-Colonel Cull,[174] but the campaign was a complete success. Derby was raided at daybreak on 17 December, and, as the adjutant-general later boasted, the barracks were destroyed 'together with the Stables and Store-Houses, and a considerable quantity of valuable Military Stores, have been brought away.' Barker's attack on Stewartstown followed shortly thereafter,[175] but it was obviously less successful because soldiers stationed there were seizing livestock smuggled into Hereford in the fall of 1814, as we shall see.

The ease with which Barker recruited volunteers for his dangerous mission reveals that popular enthusiasm was far from lacking when it came to local defence. In March 1814 four Stanstead residents reported that they had formed a committee of safety after learning that 250 American soldiers had arrived at nearby Barton, Vermont, presumably to continue the operations that had been started at Derby. Having been informed that the Americans' purpose was to 'harrass this frontier,' the committee requested the loan of the seventy-five rifles that had recently been delivered to Ascot and Compton, as well as equipment for the local cavalry.[176] Cull, in turn, requested that Pennoyer's Fifth Battalion, or 'at least that part of it which is armed,' be prepared to provide assistance to his own Third Battalion should an American raid take place.[177] In addition, each of Cull's local companies was ordered to establish alarm posts where eight to ten militiamen 'can be assembled in a few minutes at the Firing of one or more muskets or other signal that the Captain orders.' Each of the small squads was then to march in strict silence to the place designated as the company rendezvous. Those with arms 'are expected to be foremost in the field,' but the others were to assemble as well because they could prove 'very usefull in driving Cattle, removing Goods & other property to a place of greater security.'[178]

Left to their own devices by the British military, the Townships militia prepared itself to resist American attacks, but the shortage of arms would remain a persistent worry throughout the war. As we have seen, Cull's frustration with his companies' resistance to the draft had briefly led him to question the wisdom of supplying them with rifles, but in June 1813 – even before tensions had increased along the local border – he wrote that 'I still think they may be safely intrusted with them & have no doubt but that they will be faithfull through the whole Battn.'[179] The following month Cull asked each captain to report the number of firelocks his company wished to receive.[180] In response, Hatley's Captain Kezar asked for sixty-four stand of arms, stating that supplying them to only some of the men would cause resentment on the part of the others.[181] In October, however, Cull was again forced to complain that only the cavalry troop was armed: 'the very few rusty neglected fowling pieces that some few men (addicted to Hunting) have to snap three or four times probably at a Partridge are not worthy to be reckon'd.'[182]

If Cull could at least report an armed cavalry unit, this was not so of Pennoyer's Fifth Battalion, for the Shipton cavalry did not receive its 'appointments' until March 1814.[183] Paradoxically, despite their vulnerable frontier location, the Eastern Townships militia units were underarmed in comparison with those elsewhere in the province. The official provincial militia report for July 1813 states that the four Eastern Townships battalions included a total of 2,781 men, or 4.9

per cent of the total for the fifty-one battalions in the province, but they had only 337 rifles, or 3.5 per cent of the provincial total. Luke's Fourth Battalion, which had been issued a hundred stand of arms as early as July 1812, as we have seen, reported 176 rifles. Nearly all would, however, soon be captured in Clark's Phillipsburg raid, discussed above. Pennoyer's Fifth Battalion reported 101 rifles, while Cull's Third Battalion reported none whatsoever.[184] As already noted, two of Cull's companies finally received seventy-five stand of arms in February 1814, but they were loaned to Pennoyer's battalion.[185]

These delays in arming the Eastern Townships militia undoubtedly reflect the British preoccupation with protecting Montreal rather than a region with little strategic value,[186] as well as uncertainty about the loyalty of a population that was stubbornly resisting the draft. The neighbouring Vermonters, despite their involvement in supplying the British army, were in a much better situation as far as arms were concerned. At the outbreak of war the American government announced that 1,000 stand of rifles would be distributed where they could provide the greatest protection to the frontier, and the selectmen of at least one town were authorized to borrow muskets and bayonets on the credit of the town, as well as to purchase powder and lead on six months' credit. Other towns furnished and supported their own guards,[187] but, with no official system of local government, Canadians were not in a position to take similar steps to defend themselves, aside from limited volunteer initiatives.

Rather than weakening the resolve of the Missisquoi area settlers, however, Clark's raid appears to have united a militia battalion whose effectiveness had been hampered by the high-handedness of the commanding officer, Philip Luke. Three months after the brief occupation of Philipsburg, the villagers retained enough spirit to supply a volunteer force of twenty – of whom only six were armed – to attack a patrol of fourteen America dragoons at a farm on the boundary. One of the Americans was killed, two were severely wounded, and six were taken prisoner.[188] But the local militia was in no position to resist Colonel Clark when he returned on 22 March with an overwhelming force of 400 men.[189] He was followed the next day by General McComb's 800 infantrymen and eight pieces of artillery. This raid was simply a feint to draw the British eastward while Major-General Wilkinson, whose army had been wintering at Plattsburg after being defeated at Châteauguay, attacked the British outpost on the Lacolle River. When Prevost failed to take the bait, Clark withdrew on 26 March to rejoin the main army of 4,000 men. They failed ignominiously to achieve their objective at the Lacolle mill, even though it was defended by only 340 men, including 40 from Ritter's Frontier Light Infantry.[190] From this point on it would be the British who took the initiative in the Lake Champlain area and the Vermonters who found themselves on the defensive.

No major battles took place in the Eastern Townships during the War of 1812, but Colonel Isaac Clark's attack in October 1813 made a traumatic impact on the Missisquoi Bay settlements, ending what had effectively been a 'phony' war as far as the borderland region was concerned. The imprisonment of local farmers reinforced the perception of the United States as the enemy. Rather than adopting a defeatist attitude, the Eastern Townships militia and volunteer units became more active. The success of the skirmishes they engaged in must have further strengthened local resolve, despite the ongoing failure of the government to provide arms. Clever as the American military command's strategy of bringing the war to the Vermont–Lower Canadian borderland may have been, it failed in its ultimate objective of curtailing the lucrative smuggling trade.

'Like herds of buffalo':
The Smuggling and Counterfeiting Frontier

Western Vermont's natural trading links were along the Lake Champlain–Richelieu River corridor to Montreal. Consequently, Jefferson's Embargo failed to impede the traffic northward into Lower Canada, leading to a virtual rebellion in certain Vermont and New York communities.[191] The outbreak of war with Britain in 1812 also did little to diminish that trade, despite the 170 seizures of smuggled goods in northern Vermont.[192] The Vermont government passed an act in November declaring that no one could pass either way across the border without a permit from the governor and also forbidding anyone from 'driving horses, cattle or conveying any property *towards* Canada, so as to create a reasonable *suspicion* that the same is intended for Canada.' Flouting this law could result in confiscation of property, a $1,000 fine, and seven years' hard labour.[193] But this initial flush of American patriotism soon waned, and, in order to placate Vermonters opposed to the war, the United States government quietly sanctioned the evasion of the law for goods of no obvious military value.[194]

Foodstuffs were presumably not exempt, but, with the price of beef tripling during the war to as much as $12 a hundredweight,[195] little could be done to prevent the smuggling of cattle northward. And not only cattle, for the inhabitants of Alburg, Vermont, entered into a contract in December 1812 to supply 2,000 fat hogs and 2,000 bushels of wheat to the British army.[196] This activity persisted throughout the war. In early September 1813 the militia captain at French Mills, Vermont, reported that the whole countryside was being stripped of provisions. He added that a Canadian agent was openly contracting for supplies, and 'the host of smuglars that hover on our lines is beyond description. Since the first of August to this date there has been from the best calculation more than sixty yoak of oxen besides other beef cattle drove to Canada.'[197] The following summer, the American general, George Izard, complained:

> On the eastern side of Lake Champlain, the high roads are found insufficient for the supplies of cattle which are pouring into Canada; like herds of buffalo they press through the forests, making paths for themselves ... Nothing but a cordon of troops from the French Mills to Lake Memphremagog could effectively check the evil. Were it not for these supplies the British forces in Canada would soon be suffering from famine, or their government subjected to enormous expense for their maintenance.[198]

This statement was corroborated on the British side by Prevost, who declared in 1814 that 'two-thirds of the Army in Canada' were living on 'Beef provided by American Contractors drawn principally from the States of Vermont and New York.'[199]

The border communities of the Eastern Townships benefited enormously from this activity. The Reverend Charles Stewart wrote in November 1814 that 'a great deal of smuggling' was carried on by the merchants at Philipsburg: 'It is surprising how many Cattle for our Army-Contractors are driven in here from Vermont – such is the weakness of the existing Governt there.'[200] A former resident of the Missisquoi Bay area later recalled that 'Phillipsburg was a small hamlet in 1809 but in 1814 it was a place of immense trade, thousands of dollars in a day sometimes, but it was the smugglers that made the trade.'[201] This traffic was not confined to the lake port towns. From the imposition of Jefferson's Embargo to the outbreak of war, Levi Bigelow of Derby Line, Vermont, had been entering for re-export from the port of Quebec up to 4,000 barrels of pearlash and potash a year, as well as cattle, wheat, and other produce. In January 1809, when he learned that American guard units were being stationed along the border, Bigelow had moved as much of his merchandise as he could to the Canadian side of the border.[202] In November 1812, five months after the declaration of war, Bigelow was granted permission to remain in Quebec long enough to sell the sizable quantity of ashes he had accumulated there.[203] Bigelow had also asked to remain in the Townships for a few days in order to settle his personal affairs there, and his nephew, Marcus Child, became his agent on the Canadian side of the border, where he continued to carry on a lucrative smuggling trade.[204] Child would ultimately attain prominent status as a Stanstead druggist and pro-reform member of the Legislative Assembly.

Not all the cross-border traffic was headed north. A strict embargo was declared by the Lower Canadian government in the fall of 1812 against the export of grain, flour, and salt meat to the United States,[205] but Thomas Coffin, the police inspector for the Trois-Riv-ières District, reported in 1813 that a reputable Stanstead farmer had informed him that grain was being taken across the border to Vermont. Coffin was also convinced that other goods passed through the region, explaining that 'many articles have been sent from Quebec and from this Place up the St Francis River which could not have been intended for the consumption of the Townships.' He added that 'from the Character of a great number of the People there, it is to be apprehended that they would willingly supply the Enemy with any *article whatever*, from which they would derive a considerable profit.'[206] A militia captain also complained that American smugglers carried as much Canadian news as they could back to the United States.[207]

In an attempt to exert greater control over the situation, the Lower Canadian government proclaimed on 6 November 1813 that the transfer of restricted goods across the border to the United States was to be prohibited, and a licence would be required by those who purchased American merchandise. The response of St Armand merchant John Jones was to petition the governor-general requesting a permit not only to purchase goods from Americans but to sell them merchandise acquired in Montreal.[208] Only four days later, a committee of the Executive Council recommended that special temporary licences be granted for the export of non-restricted items to Vermont only. But it is doubtful that Eastern Townships merchants would take the trouble to acquire such permits because they had to be collected in person from the police office in Trois-Rivières, and the merchandise would have to be certified by the Saint-Jean customs collector, which would mean first transporting the goods in the opposite direction from the border.[209]

One smuggler from Orleans County, Vermont, to the immediate south of Stanstead, later recalled that 'the goods and merchandise which came from Canada was smuggled in winter when the swamps and rivers were frozen and when the deep snows could be made into a hard road over the roughest ground.' Traffic in the opposite direction took place during the summer when cattle 'could get their sustenance from the leaves of the forrest.' According to this individual, the main challenge was passing through the Vermont countryside because patriotism provided armed gangs with a convenient excuse to rob the smugglers whenever they could, even if it meant crossing the border into Lower Canada.[210] Incursions were also made in the opposite direction, for in June 1814 the commanding officer in Derby complained to Cull that his armed militiamen were entering Vermont to conduct cattle into the Eastern Townships. Cull expressed concern to the governor-general that this activity would 'interrupt the intercourse that actually exists of exchanging money for Cattle, and might eventually draw a force of the enemys regulars nearer the Line to the annoyance of our own settlers.' He also hinted at the American commanding officer's tolerance of the smuggling trade when he noted that the Canadian militiamen's activities would make him unpopular with the Democratic party, 'and not commended by his own.' Cull, therefore, issued an order forbidding his militiamen from crossing the border under arms unless accompanied by their company commander. To reinforce his order, Cull warned that, should they be captured in Vermont, they would not be considered eligible for exchange with American prisoners, and they could be fined for loss of their arms.[211]

According to Muller, American troops stationed along the border actually assisted smugglers to move goods across the line, as well as venturing into commerce on their own.[212] During the spring of 1813, however, American soldiers entered the village of Stanstead and took away two tons of tobacco, claiming it was contraband. They also attempted without success to arrest a deserter. Lieutenant-Colonel Cull asked that the local militia be armed to discourage such incursions, adding that 'with the few old Firelocks, fowling pieces, Pitchforks, etc. that we could muster, it is not very probable that our defence would redound much to our Honor or the advantage of the Country.'[213] Another example of American zealousness took place in the fall of 1814, when Captain Bradford Powell, a Richford, Vermont, merchant who had been assigned to enforce the embargo, seized the goods that a Potton Township resident had purchased in Montreal and was transporting home via Richford. In retaliation, this individual had Powell's own cattle driven across the border to Dunham. Charged with theft, he asserted that Powell had interfered with his right to transport goods through the United States, but local arbitrators rejected this argument and Powell's cattle were restored to him.[214]

Most of the border incidents connected to smuggling took place further east, where mountainous Hereford Township borders on New Hampshire as well as Vermont. Here the settlers were to some extent at the mercy of the American soldiers stationed just south of the border in Stewartstown, though they apparently did not interfere with Canadians who depended on the local grist mill.[215] In February 1813, for example, an American lieutenant and about a dozen troops crossed the border in pursuit of a Canadian who was reportedly transporting smuggled American goods. Pressing ahead of his troops, the lieutenant was briefly made a prisoner by some local militiamen until they learned that his troops were on the way. The lieutenant and his rescuers then helped themselves to drink and food in a Canadian house, according to a local affidavit, before marching 'on towards the line making use of insulting menacing and abusive language as they have frequently done before insomuch that I verily believe the Inhabitants of Hereford and Clifton are really in fear of them.'[216]

The following year a similar incident resulted in the death of a cattle trader from Stanstead. According to two Hereford Township farmers, six armed men led by Samuel Hugh, the United States Deputy Collector of Customs at Maidstone, Vermont, had seized from one of their farms thirteen cattle purchased from the United States by four men from Stanstead and Barnston. In the ensuing fracas David Morrill of Stanstead was shot and killed by Hugh, and his brother was wounded. A bullet meant for yet another brother killed one of the cattle instead. Five weeks later, on 22 November, this brother, Archibald Morrill, and sixteen to eighteen of his friends went to Canaan, Vermont, where they seized Hugh and his cattle and took them to Stanstead. Hugh was then placed in the Montreal jail and subsequently moved to Trois-Rivières for trial on the charge of murder.

Meanwhile, an armed force of Americans had seized five Hereford residents, 'and in a savage manner plundered some of the said houses of many articles of Goods and wearing Apparel, Money, etc., and all of our Barnyards of our Cattle to the number of Twenty-seven head, besides horses and sheep.' The Americans declared that these men would receive the same treatment as Hugh; 'if he was hanged we should also be hanged – if his property was kept, ours should also be kept, and until he, Hugh, was released we should be kept Prisoners.' Fortunately for them, several more friendly residents of Canaan brokered an agreement whereby the Canadians and most of their cattle (but not their other goods) were released in return for a promise to provide forty-eight hours' notice once a decision concerning Hugh had been reached by the Lower Canadian government. Presumably this would give the Americans time to re-imprison them. Indeed, the two Hereford petitioners identified themselves as prisoners even though they were back on their farms when they drafted their document, which they then carried to Quebec. Early in 1815, two Canadian officials and an unofficial group of deputies from Vermont and New Hampshire met at Hereford to arbitrate the matter. While the question of Hugh's release was left unsettled, the United States Congress appointed a commissioner to negotiate the issue with the Lower Canadian government, a process that was soon facilitated by the termination of the war.[217]

If the Eastern Townships economy benefited greatly from the smuggling of American livestock during the war, a somewhat complementary activity had a more problematic impact. Most of the cattle were paid for with legitimate army bills, but there was already an established practice of using counterfeit American bank notes manufactured in the border communities of the Eastern Townships to purchase goods stolen south of the border. The Americans were obviously the greatest losers from this clandestine activity, which was still not illegal in Lower Canada in 1806, when its most notorious practitioner – Stephen Burroughs – was arrested by an American colonel on the authority of a warrant issued by Oliver Barker as justice of the peace.[218] In 1808 Vermont authorities served sixty-one indictments for counterfeiting or passing counterfeit money, and the Vermont legislature requested that the governor of Lower Canada take action against the band of counterfeiters operating within his jurisdiction. But the Vermont authorities also took matters into their own hands by entering Lower Canada to apprehend counterfeiters and take them back across the border for trial.[219]

Pressure to end the counterfeiting activities also came from north of the border, for the magistrates and militia officers of St Armand and the surrounding townships took advantage of the heightened state of alert during the war to launch a campaign against the forgers of American bank notes. A petition to government in late 1813 claimed that the border townships had prospered until 1803, when their tranquility was disturbed, and commerce with the United States endangered, 'by the arrival of a class of profligate and unprincipled men' who took advantage of the milder laws against counterfeiting in Lower Canada. There was now a gang of them in almost every one of the newly settled townships, where they indulged publicly in 'drunkenness and riot,' thereby corrupting 'the morals of the young and old of both sexes.' Furthermore, many innocent settlers had incurred suspicion and 'been brought into danger and difficulty' by unknowingly passing forged bills. The ability of the counterfeiters to evade punishment had also induced 'many of the poorer class of inhabitants who had previously supported good characters' to join them. Many were engaged in passing the counterfeit bills in the United States, and some had been detected and imprisoned for as long as life. As a result, 'more than one hundred families have, within a short space lost their principal dependence and support and are reduced to the most deplorable distress.'[220] But only when a large quantity of counterfeit Lower Canadian army bills forged in Boston was about to be distributed from Derby, Vermont, did the Canadian authorities take active measures. The intrepid Oliver Barker seized the bills and ringleader Dr Benjamin Dolbear in December 1813, narrowly escaping when forty Americans pursued his party of twenty poorly armed men on their way to Montreal with the prisoner.[221]

While the war only stimulated the smuggling and counterfeiting that had already been taking place in this borderland region, enriching a number of Eastern Townships residents in the process, it also heightened tensions along the border as American civil and military authorities attempted to staunch the flow of livestock northward and bogus bank notes southward. Townships farmers may also have resented the American competition, though prices would not decline until after the war ended, and law-abiding citizens were concerned about the corrupting influence of illicitly gained wealth. But whatever the feelings of the majority may have been about these cross-border activities, they did, paradoxically, make the rather porous international boundary more tangible, for smuggling, counterfeiting, and the related tensions were obviously corollories of the border.

'Improper communication': Policing Cross-Border Migration

Of much greater to concern to the Canadian authorities than counterfeiting was the threat of American spies and agitators. The government warned local magistrates shortly after the outbreak of war to be on the lookout for emissaries distributing proclamations aimed at inducing the inhabitants 'either to remain inactive, whilst an American Army invades this Country; or framed with the more hostile view to make the peaceful Inhabitants of Canada facilitate the plans of their enemies, and thus render them the instruments of their own destruction.'[222] The following year, the Montreal Police Office complained that 'subjects of the United States are permitted to come into the Province through the Townships without being noticed or reported & that every protection and countenance is given them and that many are permitted to remain.' The militia colonels were instructed to 'keep a strict Eye over people of that description and prevent any improper communication between our people and the Enemy.' Given that all able-bodied male residents were militiamen, the instructions stated, 'there can be little difficulty in ascertaining the arrival of strangers.'[223]

In some cases, Americans such as the Derby, Vermont, tanner and currier Isaac W. Richards were given character references by prominent officials in the border townships in order to transact business in the province.[224] Recent American arrivals also found local support, as when eighteen Hatley petitioners reported that a young man from Vermont 'has been living here about three months and appears to be an industrious labouring Man' whose conduct had been 'such as becometh a good inhabitant so far as we have had any information.'[225] One surviving letter illustrates how families divided by the war attempted to negotiate the border in a time of personal crisis. Abraham Channel, Jr, of Bolton Township wrote in June 1813 to his brother Robert somewhere in New England asking that he return to visit their elderly father who was then on the point of death. Abraham advised Robert to seek permission from the commanding officer on the Vermont side of the border to cross into Canada, assuring him that there would be 'no difficulty this side of the line in a man's coming in and seeing his friends [illegible] and returning in safety.'[226]

Jesse Pennoyer did issue an arrest warrant against a Vermonter who claimed to be visiting his father in Melbourne and another against a man who had lived in Compton until just after the war broke out and now wished to return from the United States with his family.[227] But Henry Cull took offence at the Montreal police missive that put the loyalty of the Townships into question. He wrote in June 1813 'that some of the neighbors in Derby and Stanstead (the same as the right & Left of the street of St Paul in Montreal) Pay and receive visits cannot be denied – and if they pass through the Townships unnoticed it is because the Magistrates have no knowledge of it, and I am persuaded you do not expect them to stand as Centinels at different Ports.' Cull himself supported the petition of a man named Levi Noble who had been jailed in Montpelier, Vermont, for 'Trading from Montreal' and who had escaped to Barnston, where he had taken up farming, joined the militia, and requested to take the oath of allegiance.[228]

Police Inspector Coffin was inclined to be less sympathetic in such cases. In late December 1813 an Ascot justice of the peace informed Coffin that he had required a bond for good behaviour from Luther Baker, who had recently returned home after four years' absence in the United States. The justice had seized the young man's 'fine fleet Horse' until the sheriff's 'pleasure should be known,' but he noted that Baker was 'a likely young man, his Character always good while he formerly resided here, his connections respectable, & I recommend him to your clemency.'[229] Coffin, however, had heard another report, one to the effect that Baker had recently served in General Hampton's army, and so he issued a warrant for his arrest. The same week Coffin arrested another young man whom he identified as 'an Alien Enemy' from New Hampshire who had travelled through the Townships 'under the pretence of going to his Father, who, he says, resides in some part of the District of Montreal.'[230]

Two deserters from the American army who wished to join their father in Shipton in May 1814 were also greeted with suspicion, but in July another deserter was given a pass by Lieutenant-Colonel Cull and employment in Shipton by Elmer Cushing.[231] According to Oliver Barker's complaint in February, the cross-border traffic remained essentially unchecked. He reported that some Americans 'have been very improperly and injudiciously furnished with Certificates, Letter, etc. to facilitate their passage thro' the Country, by some of our Magistrates, and Officers of Militia. At other times they pass on, and no one takes the trouble to stop them, or even bring them to a superficial examination. – Not infrequently it happens that some of our Inhabitants, for a liberal reward, undertake to carry them to Montreal, and other places in their carriages, etc.' Some went so far as to borrow certificates of the oath of allegiance. The local magistrates and militia officers claimed, according to Barker, that since their positions brought no remuneration, most of their efforts had to be devoted to acquiring a subsistence for themselves and their families 'in this new country.' They also claimed that 'the extreme difficulty and expense attending the conveyance of prisoners from hence to Head Quarters, under existing circumstances are embarrassments so discouraging as to render it next to impossible for them to accomplish it.'[232]

The continuing divergence between the policies of provincial authorities on the one hand and the more local authorities on the other is illustrated by the case of an American shoemaker named Lowell Fowler, who travelled to Shipton in July 1814 to join his parents and two siblings. Fowler, who had attempted to ease his way into the province by bringing a model of the horse-propelled boat he had invented, had been given a pass by Henry Cull and another magistrate. But he was rumoured to be a spy simply on the basis that he had boarded in Shipton with the former counterfeiter Stephen Burroughs, though the latter fashioned himself a British spy.[233] Fowler was subsequently ordered deported by the governor-general, who asked Sheriff Coffin to remind the Townships magistrates about the policy 'to be observed towards Alien Enemies coming into this Province.' Coffin remained uncertain, however, as to whether he should arrest such individuals, immediately send them back, or, in certain cases, permit them to remain at large until the governor-general's pleasure was made known.[234]

Traffic also continued in the opposite direction, and in January 1814 the Reverend Stewart asked that the son of one of his parishioners be granted a licence to travel to Albany to marry a woman he had met before the war broke out.[235] The following May, Ephraim Knight of Bolton petitioned to visit Vermont in order to settle his recently deceased brother's estate.[236] Even the militia captain, John Savage, was given a pass to travel to his former residence of Alburg, where he would serve as witness in a court case.[237] Oliver Barker objected to such visits, claiming that some Townships residents who retained strong attachments to the American government frequently visited Quebec, Montreal, and other garrisons 'under pretence of marketing their produce,' then, 'whenever they please, go into the United States to visit their connections, as they pretend, or to transact business of an indispensable nature.' As a result, the enemy received information 'of the greatest importance and advantage to them.'[238]

Whether or not Barker was exaggerating, Henry Cull reported that some settlers crossed the line expressly to be made prisoners by the force stationed in Derby so that they could be paroled on swearing not to take up arms against the Americans. This was a widespread practice in Upper Canada, but Cull advised that, 'as they are not worth exchanging,' these individuals should be obliged to leave the country with their families. He hesitated, however, to take such steps without authorization to do so, claiming to be 'more afraid of Chastisement and expense from the Goose quills in Montreal than from the Bayonetts of the King's declared enemies.'[239] Cull did, nonetheless, issue a warrant for the arrest of a militia draftee who refused to serve on the basis of such a parole.[240]

Other settlers followed the example of their Orleans County, Vermont, neighbours by fleeing southward to avoid being caught up in a battle zone.[241] The Reverend Charles Stewart reported such a panic in St Armand in May 1813, and, further east, Henry Cull wrote the same month that 'more than one half of the people from Barnston are gone from the Township and those that remain are mostly very poor and indigent.'[242] Militia officers had stopped some of those who were leaving behind debts, but Cull admitted that he knew of no law authorizing them or magistrates to do so.[243] The following summer, the Reverend Charles Cotton of Dunham wrote to his sister that more than a hundred local inhabitants had moved away since the war began, '& there has been much depopulation in several of the other Townships. This has been owing to disaffection to our excellent Government in many, & to the dread of being drafted into the standing Militia, in many others.'[244]

Easier for the authorities to control than the movements of local residents on either side of the border were those of the travelling American preachers appointed to serve circuits that lay either partially or wholly in the Eastern Townships. As a consequence, the Episcopal Methodists' Stanstead and St Francis circuits remained vacant during the war. One of the two Methodist preachers appointed for the Dunham circuit was given permission to enter Lower Canada in 1813, but his colleague was forced to leave after some local Baptists claimed, incorrectly it appears, that he was preaching sedition. In July 1814 Elmer Cushing sought official sanction to take steps against Methodist clergymen who 'reciprocally visit the two Countries which are at war.'[245] The governor's response was that their conduct should be observed, 'and should you have cause to suspect that the intrusion is prejudicial to the interests of H.M.G. you will, with the assistance of the other Magistrates of the Townships, take measures to prevent it.'[246] But the Dunham circuit, like the other two, remained vacant in 1814, and, even though the Episcopal Methodists were rapidly becoming the most popular denomination in Vermont, the church would never recover in the Eastern Townships.[247]

The circuit riders were replaced to some extent during the war by American-born preachers who resided in the region, but they, too, were harassed by the authorities. The memoirs of Joseph Badger – whose brother was charged in October 1813 with aiding a prisoner to escape[248] – claim that three local justices of the peace, including Major Jesse Pennoyer, arrested six leading lay members and three local preachers after Ascot's Baptists and Methodists held a joint prayer meeting that same month. Badger added that Pennoyer was found drunk in a ditch the following morning and that the suit was dismissed on the advice of a local militia captain, though this seems unlikely given that Pennoyer was the commanding officer.[249] The following year, Lieutenant-Colonel Cull examined Badger's mentor, Freewill Baptist minister Avery Moulton, who was accused of sedition, but no formal charge appears to have been laid.[250]

The end of the war posed a dilemma when many of those who had fled to the United States began to return. Badger, who had begun preaching in New England in the spring of 1814, was arrested when he returned for a visit to his parental family the following year. Philip Luke, nevertheless, reported to the adjutant-general that returnees, including draft dodgers and militia deserters, 'are actually residing with us perfectly at ease and as unconcerned as though the Event had not happened.' Claiming that he was responding to local complaints, Luke asked whether he was to 'Execute the law in its utmost Rigor or would some other corse with them be better, and if any what – or is it best to leave them at Rest.'[251] After Luke had sent essentially the same letter to the government again three months later, he was finally ordered to submit the names of all those who had deserted from his battalion during the war.[252] Whether or not any charges were laid, the war made a lasting impact on the Eastern Townships by sharply reducing the New England influx. After 1815 the region would become more reliant on natural increase and British immigration, limited though the latter was, as the New Englanders turned to their own country's western frontier. American missionary efforts would follow the same channels, leaving a vacuum that would be filled by the London-based Anglican and Methodist missionary societies. As a result, the cultural identity of the Eastern Townships became less American in character even before the French-Canadian colonization process began in earnest during the 1840s.

Conclusion

According to Sahlins, 'the idea of territorial sovereignty and the inviolability of political boundaries owes much to modern political nationalism.'[253] Any sense of American nationalism was obviously still weak in Vermont during the early nineteenth century, when the state's residents bitterly opposed Jefferson's Embargo and did not hesitate to smuggle livestock to the British enemy after the war broke out. On the northern side of the border, the largely American-born non-Loyalist population certainly did not identify strongly with the British empire or with the French-speaking Catholic majority of their province. As Taylor has noted of Upper Canada's 'Late Loyalists,' they 'cared much for their families, farms, and communities but little for the empire, which they regarded as an absence of any demands

MAP of the EASTERN TOWNSHIPS of LOWER CANADA. From "BRITISH AMERICAN LAND COMPANY," by W. J. Duffy, London, 1833.

Col. Joseph Bouchette, *Isle aux Noix in the River Richelieu*
(Quebec), pre-1815 (National Archives of Canada, C-3293).
Originally published in Joseph Bouchette's *A Topographical
Description of Lower Canada* (1815), this painting illustrates where
the men from the Eastern Townships who were drafted into Lower
Canada's Frontier Light Infantry were based during much of the
War of 1812. Befitting their status as highly mobile border troops,

they evidently had little in the way of fortifications to protect them. Because this painting was produced for military purposes, the only drama in the scene appears in the sky. The black and white clouds presumably symbolize the clash between the American and the British forces, with the sun's rays just managing to penetrate the dark clouds to illuminate the encampment.

Col. Joseph Bouchette, *Kilborn's Mills, Stanstead*, QC, 1827 (McCord Museum, Montreal, M354). When this watercolour was made by the surveyor-general of Lower Canada in 1827, the international border was clearly of little significance to the people clustered around the mills on the Tomifobia River. In fact, the margins of the lithograph produced from this painting in 1832 reveal that the border had recently been shifted south by a few feet. Named for Charles Kilborn, the local Loyalist entrepreneur who played a prominent role in the Eastern Townships militia during the War

of 1812, Kilborn's Mills – just south of the village of Stanstead – would become known as Rock Island, while the settlement on the Vermont side of the border was known as Derby Line. Robert Shore Milnes Bouchette accompanied his father in 1827, making some of the sketches that would join this one in a promotional brochure published by the British American Land Company in 1836. Two years later he would be captured while leading a rebel attack across the border near Moore's Corner in Missisquoi County.

Lake Memphremagog (near Georgeville), 1838 (Bishop's University
Archives, FC 72.W5, from W.H. Bartlett, *Canadian Scenery
Illustrated* [London, 1842]). The well-known English painter, W.H.
Bartlett, visited the Eastern Townships in 1838, where he painted
several scenes on picturesque Lake Memphremagog. On the left
side of this one, the lake is shown stretching southward towards
Vermont, making it a popular smuggling route. The village of
Georgeville, where the ferry was taken to cross the lake, was on
the stage coach route from Montreal to Stanstead and points south.
Perhaps these outside links help to explain why the village was a
centre of political radicalism.

Methodist Church, Philipsburg, QC, about 1910 (McCord Museum, Montreal, MP-0000.1042.3). Begun in 1819, Philipsburg's Methodist church was the first of this denomination to be built in the Eastern Townships. The white marble stones were provided by Lieutenant-Colonel Philip Ruiter, and the architecture – modelled on the first Methodist chapel in New York City – reflects the fact that it was built by the local German Palatine Loyalists. During the Rebellions of 1837–8, the church was barricaded as an emergency arsenal. A number of other churches in the region served as temporary military barracks.

Block House at Philipsburg, QC, ca. 1895 (McCord Museum,
Montreal, MP-0000.2). The photograph of this blockhouse on
Missisquoi Bay, constructed in 1838, is one of the few remaining
reminders that there ever was a military presence in the Eastern
Townships during the early nineteenth century.

upon their imagination, emotions, or pockets.'[254] Resistance in the Eastern Townships to service in the active militia stands in marked contrast to the more positive response of the French Canadians, who were neither enamoured of Napoleon nor anxious to exchange British rule for the uncertainties of American annexation.[255] But the habitants were, themselves, still not interested in fighting in the name of religion or nation, despite the rhetoric of loyalty and patriotism issuing from their bourgeoisie and clergy. The loyalties of rural people were primarily to kinfolk and neighbours even when – as in the case of the Eastern Townships – many of those individuals lived on the other side of the international border.

But the War of 1812 did help to make this rather artificial boundary more real as far as the borderland communities were concerned. Even though cross-border contacts persisted, and even though the inhabitants of the Lower Canadian townships were reluctant to serve outside their region, at least for an indefinite period, the fact remains that they were prepared to defend their homes against invasion from the south. Thus, the Reverend Charles Stewart wrote in the pamphlet he published for a British audience just as the war was drawing to a close:

> Some persons have entertained an opinion that it would have tended to the security of the Province not to have suffered the Frontier Townships to have been settled, but that it would have been advisable to have kept them in a state of nature, that they might serve as a barrier between the Province and the United States. And some have been averse to their being settled by people from the United States, considering settlers from that country as dangerous subjects. Neither of these questions need now to be discussed. They are over-ruled by circumstances; and they are answered in some measure by late events, as the settlement of them has not proved detrimental but beneficial to us in the present war.[256]

The American attack on Philipsburg in 1813, and the smaller raids into the border townships, may not have produced a sudden outpouring of pro-British sentiment, but they did make the boundary line more tangible simply because families and local communities now felt threatened. Admittedly, a small number of Townships residents were accused of being American collaborators or sympathizers,[257] and many fled southward to escape the war, but the evidence does not suggest a broad-based desire to return to life under the American flag. For the militia in this region, as in Vermont, there was very little willingness to join the fight elsewhere, but also no hesitation as far as protecting their home territory was concerned. The attitude would quite likely have changed had there been a full-scale American invasion, as in Upper Canada where the population showed little inclination to resist, but the people of the Eastern Townships could claim that they had passed the test of loyalty presented by the war. British authorities would remain sceptical, as we shall see, and close cross-border ties persisted. But, by the time the Rebellion of 1837 broke out, a strong sense of regional identity had developed, one that was quite distinct from that on the other side of the border.

The Rebellions of 1837–8

Historians have debated whether the Rebellions in Lower Canada represent a failed national liberation movement or a class conflict between the English-speaking merchants tied to the British market and the French-Canadian liberal professionals with close links to the rural parishes.[1] The second group is divided as to whether or not the liberal professionals represented a progressive force, but the general understanding of both groups is that the colony's English-speaking minority was overwhelmingly opposed to the constitutional reform movement.[2] Given such an assumption, historians of Lower Canada have seen little reason to include the Eastern Townships in their studies,[3] even though Patriot leaders such as Louis-Joseph Papineau and Edmund B. O'Callaghan devoted considerable time to wooing a people who were, after all, immigrants from the very country upon which their revolutionary program was modelled.[4] In fact, there had been strong support in the Eastern Townships for the *Parti patriote* after constituencies for the Legislative Assembly were finally established in the region in 1829. That support began to evaporate as the threat of rebellion intensified,[5] but the people of the Eastern Townships did not suddenly become devoted to the British monarchy or the political status quo, and they should not be labelled as tories simply because most of them opposed an armed uprising.

Postwar Developments

In 1815, shortly after the War of 1812 had ended, Surveyor-General Joseph Bouchette reported that the farms of the Eastern Townships were prospering, with those in Compton Township, for example, 'generally producing crops of wheat of excellent quality, and quantity far beyond the home consumption.' Unfortunately, during the next four years the region was hit by the same summer frosts that destroyed much of the harvests elsewhere in Lower Canada as well as northern New England, causing many settlers to abandon their homesteads to move west. The influx of New Englanders would remain small, especially after the opening of the Erie Canal in 1825, and, in contrast to Upper Canada, relatively few British immigrants were attracted to the region. As a result, the population of roughly 26,500 in 1819 had fallen to 25,000 by 1825.[6]

Crop yields during the pre-Rebellion era were, nevertheless, considerably higher in the Eastern Townships than in the rest of the province, and the lack of dependency on wheat meant that the region's farmers avoided the agricultural crisis of the 1830s. Their main handicap was their reliance on snow-packed winter trails to drive their cattle or haul their surplus produce to the distant markets of Montreal and Quebec. Barges did ply the St Francis River below Sherbrooke, but the various portages drove the cost of shipping up to $20 a ton, the same price as from Stanstead to Montreal by sled. Apart from cattle, which lost up to a quarter of their weight on the long road to market, the principal exports were butter and cheese, pork and beef, and distilled products such as potash and potato whiskey. More than half the province's alcohol distilleries were located in the Eastern Townships in 1831, just before the local temperance movement became a significant force. Even in the longer-settled townships, three-quarters of the farms still had only four to twenty improved hectares in 1831.

That same year the region's farmers were hit hard by the removal of import duties on American agricultural produce, though increased sales of cattle to American drovers did help to compensate for losses in Montreal and Quebec.[7] The opening of the Champlain Canal in 1823 had also greatly benefited the sawmill industry of Missisquoi and Shefford counties, with the result that the population of the Eastern Townships shot up to 37,600 in 1831, though only 3,000 were listed as immigrants to Lower Canada since 1825. The region's roads remained in poor condition, and the population's growth rate failed to exceed its natural increase during the next decade or so despite the massive influx of British immigrants to the port of Quebec.[8]

Still a highly localized society at the time of the War of 1812, the Eastern Townships began to develop what Jeffrey McNairn refers to as a civic culture during the postwar era. In his study on Upper Canada, McNairn stresses the role of voluntary societies such as the

Masonic and temperance lodges, as well as the rise of the local press (examined in the next subsection) in creating a 'public.' Freemasonry, McNairn notes, 'offered membership in a fraternity and cosmopolitan fellowship cemented by ritual, friendship, and benevolence.'[9] It was certainly the first significant voluntary society in the Eastern Townships, where four lodges were established prior to the 1820s.[10] The roots of Stanstead's lodge, the only one to have left a record from the pre-Rebellion era, lie in the Lively Stone Lodge chartered by the Grand Lodge of Vermont in 1803. Its meeting hall was located on the border so that an entrance was available from both the Canadian and American sides. Because the authorities frowned on this arrangement after the outbreak of the war, Stanstead established its own chapter, known as Golden Rule, in 1813. The two lodges reportedly cooperated with each other, however, by appointing peace committees that held regular joint meetings in an attempt to prevent border hostilities from breaking out.[11]

While Freemasonry represented a link with Enlightenment thought, the main role of the Golden Rule Lodge in the postwar era was to foster a degree of harmony and order on a rather lawless frontier. The lodge's historian claims that it took a strong stand against gambling, expelled members 'who had contracted the habit of intemperance,' and twice prevented armed mobs from clashing with authorities who were attempting to suppress cross-border smuggling. Certainly, the lodge's officers included the most prominent members of the community, most of whom were political conservatives.[12] But Golden Rule went into decline in the 1820s when economic depression made the payment of dues, some of which went to England, particularly burdensome. The attempt in 1823 to rejuvenate the society by moving the meeting to Georgeville caused a split in the ranks, and the anti-Masonic fervour south of the border following the mysterious disappearance in 1826 of the apostate Mason, William Morgan, also took its toll. Golden Rule dissolved early in 1829, not to re-emerge until 1847, and the region's other lodges all experienced the same fate. This may have been a shared cross-border experience, but the conspiratorial hysteria that placed a member of the anti-Mason party in the Vermont governor's chair from 1831 to 1836 had no discernible impact on Eastern Townships politics.[13]

Coincidentally or not, the temperance movement emerged in the Eastern Townships just as the Masonic Lodge was going into decline. With a wider popular base than Freemasonry, it made a profound impact on attitudes towards alcohol consumption in an era when many of the region's communities relied on the distilling of potato whiskey as an important source of external revenue. While the temperance movement had American origins, it was the local churches that were the driving force behind the first phase of the movement in the 1830s. The thirteen Eastern Townships societies that submitted reports to the Montreal Temperance Convention in February 1836 claimed to have 2,871 members, two-thirds of the convention total. Taverns were now vastly outnumbered by temperance houses, but the enthusiasm had already begun to wane in 1836 due largely to the heightening of political tensions in the province. In Stanstead the number of temperance adherents declined from a peak of nearly 1,000 to only 60 by 1838, when people had more pressing issues to worry about.[14] Like the Masonic Lodge, the temperance movement was hardly radical in a political sense, supported as it was by several of the region's Church of England clergymen, but it did instill a sense of common purpose and impose a set of rules, thereby fostering the development of a civic consciousness.[15]

In contrast to Upper Canada, urbanization and social life had still not developed sufficiently in the Eastern Townships to sustain a debating or literary society, a mechanics' institute, or a public library, and the Irish population was too small to support many Orange Lodges.[16] But there were numerous public spaces such as the Royal Institution of Learning schools and others that were built and funded by volunteers long before grants from the Legislative Assembly became available in 1829.[17] As we have seen, the lack of a formal local government system did not prevent communities from holding public meetings and imposing unofficial levies. Finally, overlooked by McNairn, was the role played by religion in breaking down social isolation. There was little in the way of institutional religion prior to the War of 1812, when the border townships were served largely by itinerant American preachers, but entire communities flocked to hear them when they passed through. After the war, when churches and meeting houses were built, some of these buildings were shared by several denominations on a rotating basis. Considerable local input was required even for the construction of Anglican churches, which were largely funded by outside sources. Furthermore, the temperance societies were not the only church-supported organizations that operated on an interdenominational level, for people defended their community-based Sunday schools against the efforts of the Methodist and Anglican clergy to assert control over them.[18] Worth noting is the fact that these social institutions were locally or regionally based, with few cross-border connections.

Civic consciousness was transformed into political activism by the increasing desire to break free of the restraints that were hindering the region's economic development. A political history of the pre-Rebellion period in the Eastern Townships remains to be written, but during the 1820s and 1830s mass petitions were submitted to the government demanding road subsidies to improve their transportation links to the St Lawrence, registry offices to enable them to raise capital by recording land sales and mortgages, a more accessible court system to enforce the collection of small debts in an economy based on credit, and, above all, seats in the Legislative Assembly to help gain these economic benefits.[19] The French-Canadian nationalists who dominated the Assembly had little interest in promoting the development of a region that had been colonized by English-speaking Protestants, so, in frustration, a widely circulated petition from the Eastern Townships in 1828 demanded the union of Lower and Upper Canada.[20] The hostile attitude of the *Parti patriote* changed suddenly, however, when the Eastern Townships was finally subdivided into six constituencies the following year. The Legislative Assembly then began to provide generous road grants and it established a few land registry offices in the region.[21] The result was that the candidates returned in the following elections were all Papineau supporters.

There was, in fact, little reason for the people of the Eastern Townships to identify with the Montreal merchants whose demands that the Legislative Assembly provide public funds to develop the St Lawrence canals lay at the base of the constitutional impasse.[22] These canals would do nothing for the Eastern Townships, and the fact that much of the region's land was either mortgaged to, or in the hands of, those same merchants inevitably caused local resentment. Another grievance was the crown and clergy reserves that were scattered throughout each township, interfering with road construction and maintenance.[23] But what appears to have rankled most of all was the imposition of a British office-holding clique over the region.

In Upper Canada, members of the Family Compact, generally of Loyalist background, had played prominent roles in the War of 1812, but the Eastern Townships was not in a position to foster the Upper Canadian myth of popular resistance to American invasion, except in a very limited sense, as we have seen.[24] There was no move by the government to declare non-Loyalist Americans to be resident aliens, as in Upper Canada,[25] but the colonial authorities continued to mistrust the region's local notables. In 1826 a correspondent to Stanstead's *British Colonist* complained that the government, after having invited Americans to settle in the Eastern Townships, had treated them 'with distrust; with a cold reserve, and a freezing indifference bordering on contempt.' Once they had cleared the forests and surmounted 'all embarrassments, both natural and artificial, so as to compose a population of forty thousand souls,' the settlers needed 'internal regulations by which to conduct and manage our little concerns. – To carry such a purpose into effect, there have uniformly been sent among us foreigners, unacquainted with our habits, manners and customs, to fill and execute every official function, thereby declaring, in language too unequivocal to be misunderstood, that no confidence was to be placed in a native born American.'[26]

There is a distant echo here of the bitter resentment that American colonists felt towards British assumptions of superiority leading up to the American Revolution.[27] Certainly, the British gentility who were attracted to the Eastern Townships by its picturesque landscape did not hesitate to express that sense of superiority in response to the Yankee settlers' refusal to demonstrate suitable deference. For example, they were described by the leading member of the Sherbrooke oligarchy, William Bowman Felton, as 'a horde of disaffected and disloyal squatters.'[28] A wealthy naval veteran of the Napoleonic Wars, Felton had acquired over 10,000 hectares of crown land in the heart of the Eastern Townships, while his two brothers and two brothers-in-law also received substantial grants. Felton became a justice of the peace and lieutenant-colonel of the province's Fifth Battalion in 1821 and was appointed to the Legislative Council the following year. He was thereby able to ensure that the future town of Sherbrooke, whose promising mill sites he had purchased, became the seat of the newly established St Francis Judicial District in 1823. Needless to say, his family members all received important patronage positions, including those of district sheriff and court clerk.

Felton had taken advantage of the destruction of the first customs officer's house soon after his arrival in Sherbrooke in 1822 to argue that the region was essentially a lawless American frontier. In expressing his gratitude to the government for assigning preventative officers to the main border crossing points of Hereford and Stanstead, and sending a detachment of troops to Sherbrooke, Felton stated that 'many idle and abandoned characters, formidable in numbers and atrocities,' had fled back to the United States. He added that 'the more remote but not less important effects of this measure will be the improved tone of public opinion, political and moral, by which the almost exclusively American population, feeling the immediate presence of Government, will become familiarized to the respectful observance of British Laws and manners.'[29]

Felton had attracted the ire of one of these Americans, the irascible Elmer Cushing (whom we met in the previous chapter) by mishandling much of the £6,400 granted in 1817 to build a leading road alongside the St Francis River to the St Lawrence. Resorting to satire, Cushing complained that the local Americans had been overlooked for an Englishman whose wealth proved that he was 'a man of sound calculation, and shrewd discernment on subjects with which he was *acquainted*. Yet the analogy between nautical and mercantile concerns, and those of a new country, was not very striking.'[30] When no further government subsidies were forthcoming, Felton attempted in 1825 to establish a London-based land company to build arterial roads and establish an industrial infrastructure in return for most of the region's crown land. The Colonial Office refused to cooperate, but it did appoint Felton as the province's first Commissioner of Crown Lands in 1827. Although he attempted to activate the Escheats Court against absentee proprietors who were doing nothing to develop their properties, Felton stood accused of rushing crown land sales by auctioning large blocks to outside investors in order to increase his own commission.[31]

The Crown Land Office's role in the Eastern Townships became somewhat redundant after 1833, when the Legislative Assembly's repeated blocking of money bills led the British government to sell much of the public land in the region to the London-based British American Land Company. As well as representing a significant source of funds for the colonial administration, the company's role would be to build the much-needed transportation arteries and attract British settlers, thereby orienting the Eastern Townships more towards the St Lawrence and Great Britain. Local farmers were concerned, however, that their sons would not be able to afford to settle in the region, and the company wasted much of its resources on a road to its own port at the mouth of the St Francis River and on attempting to develop its remote and mountainous St Francis Tract.[32]

But the consequences of these economic blunders would only materialize when the Rebellions curtailed the influx of British immigrants, thereby effectively destroying the company's colonization program. In the shorter term, the region's economy was sustained by this artificial stimulus through a period of international economic downturn, a period when northern New Englanders were abandoning their exhausted land and the habitants in many parishes were facing hunger.[33] Eastern Townships farmers not only were offered high prices for their farms, they also found a ready market for their produce among the several thousand British settlers attracted by the land company.[34] Despite the protests that followed its establishment, then, the British American Land Company undoubtedly played a role in the sudden dampening of pro-Patriot enthusiasm as political tensions heightened in the mid-1830s.

The Political Culture

Standard political terminology poses a problem when one tries to identify the two sides during this increasingly polarized era. Even though the people of the Eastern Townships became sharply divided between the competing political movements after 1834, most of them shared essentially the same ideology. Neither British tories nor American republicans, most were political pragmatists who valued property ownership, economic development, and liberal political institutions. The basic division expressed in the region's press was between those who were willing to risk the increased French-Canadian political power that would result from democratic reforms and those who argued that such reforms would result in government by a nationalist autocracy eager to drive the English-speaking Protestants from the province. This francophobia was fomented by conservative newspaper editors in order to weaken popular support for the liberalizaton of government, but even the self-styled constitutionalists favoured some fundamental reforms, as we shall see. On the other side, it would be less accurate to refer to 'Patriot' politicians in the Townships than to liberal reformers who allied strategically with this party up to the point of rebellion, but not beyond.[35] This chapter will refer to 'conservatives,' 'constitutionalists,' 'government supporters,' and 'anti-Patriots,' on the one hand, and to 'reformers', 'liberals,' and even 'radicals,' on the other, but it will avoid applying the terms 'tory' and 'Patriot' to residents of the Eastern Townships, except in the few cases where they do apply.

Jean-Pierre Kesteman has noted a fundamental political division between tory Sherbrooke, with its British office holders and American-born entrepreneurs, and the more reform-oriented rural townships, notably Stanstead. Indeed, Sherbrooke's main economic rival, Stanstead Plain, was the political centre of the district's reform movement.[36] As we shall see, however, a political rift was developing between the British office holders and American merchants of Sherbrooke, though the latter were certainly anti-Patriots, and Stanstead Plain was becoming increasingly conservative in the pre-Rebellion era. Stanstead County's radicals were mostly to be found in the countryside and in small villages such as Georgeville.[37]

To the west, in Missisquoi County, the political division again followed socioeconomic lines to a considerable extent. Denyse Beaugrand-Champagne has found that of those individuals in Missisquoi who could be identified as supporting one side or the other and who could be linked to the 1831 and/or 1842 census, eighteen merchants and manufacturers and seven liberal professionals were constitutionalists, while only five of the former and four of the latter were reformers. Tradesmen were more likely to be reformers, at a ratio of seventeen to seven. In comparison to Stanstead, however, Missisquoi was a conservative county, for eighty-six of its farmers were identified as government supporters and only fifty-eight as opponents. To some extent, this political division reflected the socioeconomic cleavage within the farming population, for the average reformer owned smaller acreages, grew less wheat, had fewer livestock, and was less likely to be a proprietor than his conservative counterpart. Beaugrand-Champagne assumes that differences in economic well-being also explain why the more recently settled Dunham and Stanbridge Townships were much more reform-oriented than was the older parish of St Armand on Missisquoi Bay. More important factors in determining this geographic divide, however, may have been that the later arrivals neither were obviously of Loyalist origin (as many were in St Armand) nor had they experienced the dramatic impact of the American raids during the War of 1812. Even religious affiliation made little difference, for the St Armand Anglicans were strongly pro-government while those in Dunham and Stanbridge favoured the reformers. The same dividing line can be observed among the Methodists and Baptists,[38] reflecting how important localism remained in the late 1830s.

Both parties relied to a considerable extent on the press to express support for their causes, for newspapers, McNairn notes, 'were at the centre of the emergent public sphere.'[39] The first newspaper established in the region, and a strong voice for political reform, was Silas Horton Dickerson's *British Colonist and St Francis Gazette*, founded in 1823. It was silenced in 1834, however, when – burdened with debt as a result of repeated prosecution by Judge John Fletcher – it was purchased by a group of anti-Patriot entrepreneurs from Sherbrooke.[40] Sherbooke's *St Francis Courier and Sherbrooke Gazette*, which also supported the reform cause, was acquired as well by local conservatives in the spring of 1834. The original publisher, Calvin W. Tolford, nevertheless managed to produce a newspaper in Stanstead for another year with a press provided by Edmund B. O'Callaghan of the pro-Patriot Montreal *Vindicator*.[41]

Farther west, the radical *Missiskoui Post and Canada Record* was launched in Stanbridge East in 1834. Beaugrand-Champagne suggests that it ceased publication in 1836, but the press was thrown in the local mill pond by the militia shortly after the outbreak of the Rebellion when the editor, Hiram J. Thomas, fled to Vermont. Thomas was allowed to return briefly to be with his dying wife as she gave birth to their second child, and from April 1839 to August 1841 he published Swanton, Vermont's, *North American*, which sported the motto, 'Canadian Rights and Canadian Independence.'[42]

Another pro-Patriot newspaper, the *Township Reformer*, appeared in Stanbridge East in November 1836. Editor Elkanah Phelps, the most active reform leader in Missisquoi, continued to produce issues after a tory mob damaged his printing press in early August 1837, but he ceased publishing after the outbreak of rebellion in November. In his last editorial, Phelps defended the Patriots and wrote that he expected to be 'shortly visited with a pair of hand-cuffs and a loathsome prison,' but he counselled that the people of the Townships should not become involved in the conflict 'inasmuch as they are divided in sentiment in such ratios as would not add or diminish essentially the strength of either party.'[43]

Finally, 1838 saw the brief appearance of the radical *Canadian Patriot* with Stanstead on the masthead, though it was published in neighbouring Derby, Vermont. The publisher, Hiram F. Blanchard, was producing another newspaper, the *Democrat*, by July, but it was also seized at the border by the Stanstead postmaster. After launching the *Montreal Express* later in the fall, Blanchard would spend November and part of December 1838 in jail.[44]

The pro-government forces clearly had the advantage of deeper pockets in financing newspapers, and the press that had printed Dickerson's *British Colonist* from 1823 to 1834 thereafter turned out copies of the anti-Patriot *Farmer's Advocate and Townships Gazette*, edited by Joseph Walton. Though it was supported heavily by the British American Land Company, the *Advocate* ceased publication in July 1837, to be succeeded by the *Sherbrooke Gazette and Townships Advertiser* with probable ties to the *Montreal Gazette*.[45] To counter the influence of the *Missiskoui Post*, Stanbridge-area conservatives began in April 1835 to publish the *Missiskoui Standard and Farmers' Advocate*, edited by the rabidly francophobe Scot, James Moir Ferres. Ferres became the main force behind the county's anti-Patriot movement until he departed for the *Montreal Herald* in December 1836 when the *Standard*'s co-founder, Joseph D. Gilman, took over. The *Standard* later claimed somewhat immodestly to have saved the county's loyalty.[46] Prior to the Rebellions, then, the people of the Eastern Townships had access to local newspapers that engaged fully in the political debate, but there was little opportunity for dissenting opinion to be heard during the hostilities.

'Incurably cursed with Radicalism': Prelude to Rebellion

Following the adoption by the Legislative Assembly of the 92 Resolutions in February 1834, the Patriots sustained their political initiative throughout the province by organizing local committees to circulate a petition to the imperial Parliament supporting the demand for reform. The formation of such committees, yet another step in the development of a civic culture, came naturally to the people of the Eastern Townships, who had a tradition of local political meetings stemming from effective lack of representation in the Legislative Assembly prior to 1829.[47] As noted above, the reformers held a firm upper hand in the region's most prosperous county, Stanstead, which had a population of 10,306 in 1831, nearly half of whom were in Stanstead Township. Stanstead's Marcus Child was one of only two MLAs from the Eastern Townships to vote in favour of the 92 Resolutions, though he was careful not to present himself as an American-style republican but as a supporter of British rights and liberties. Without referring directly to the governing elite's mistrust of the Americans in the Eastern Townships, the Massachusetts-born Child declared to a public meeting in April 1834 that 'this is the land of our adoption and choice, and as properly ours as though it were the land of our birth; its chartered rights are ours, and it is to our political happiness and prosperity to join its ancient inhabitants in supporting and improving what they have obtained by their birth and blood, "civil and religious liberty."'[48]

After expressing their support for the 92 Resolutions, the reformers from Hatley, Stanstead, and Barnston who attended this same meeting organized a correspondence committee of six for each of these three townships. In addition to circulating the petition destined for the imperial Parliament (signed by 800, according to the *Vindicator*), each township committee's tasks were to correspond with the county committee and suggest reform candidates for the upcoming election. The county committee would in turn correspond with the Permanent Central Committees of Montreal and Quebec.[49] According to S.D. Clark, these committees were intended 'to act continuously as local bodies mobilizing and directing the collective efforts of the population.'[50]

In May a meeting of residents from Stanstead County's two other townships, Bolton and Potton, also supported the 92 Resolutions despite the attempts of their recently deposed MLA, Wright Chamberlin, to convince them that the Patriots' aim was to foment a revolution.[51] Among the local meeting's resolutions was one vowing support for Papineau and the Assembly in the struggle against 'self-interested individuals, high-minded Tories, cringing sycophants, and overbearing aristocrats, bent upon despoiling the people, and aggrandizing themselves.'[52] But Stanstead County was not entirely pro-Patriot, for approximately 200 opponents did hold a meeting in Georgeville, where they denounced the 92 Resolutions.[53]

Missisquoi County, with a population of 10,736 in 1831, was much more evenly divided politically than was Stanstead, with the result that intense organization on both sides took place between 1834 and 1837. According to Gilles Laporte, not less than thirty-six public events were held by the constitutionalists and thirty-two events by the reformers during this period, making Missisquoi the most active rural county in the province.[54] The pro-government forces took the initiative by holding the first public meeting in Frelighsburg in April 1834. Participants selected a committee of twenty-three to obtain signatures in support of the Montreal loyalty petition.[55] The conservatives also seized the upper hand in Sherbrooke, where they took over a reform meeting scheduled for 28 April and passed resolutions favourable to the governor-general.[56]

To the north, where the less economically developed Shefford County had scarcely 5,000 inhabitants in 1831, a public meeting held in the village of Waterloo in May also resolved to support the Montreal petition.[57] Finally, still farther north, in Megantic County, most of whose approximately 4,000 settlers were Irish and Scots Protestants who had arrived within the previous five years, a pro-government meeting was held in Ireland Township in March 1834. It denounced the 92 Resolutions while admitting 'that in them there is much to which this County, and it is believed, the Province, would have yielded a willing consent ... had they not been interwoven with other objectionable matters ... at utter variance with the sentiments and feelings of all true and loyal British Subjects.'[58] As McNairn has pointed out, the very concept of public meetings and constitutional associations was a liberal one, for the government could not always control the agenda.[59]

In the fall election, only Stanstead fielded candidates who supported the *Parti patriote*, though Drummond County's Edward Toomy had voted for the 92 Resolutions.[60] Stanstead's Marcus Child and his running mate, a Hatley farmer named John Grannis, received 449 votes to only 166 for their opponents.[61] In Shefford and Missisquoi the reformers took some comfort in the fact that the pro-administration incumbents either did not contest the election or were defeated by newcomers. Their optimism was not entirely misplaced, for shortly after the election Ephraim Knight switched sides to the Patriots.[62]

The Stanstead reform victory attracted a good deal of attention in Montreal, where Patriot spokesmen presented this constituency as the model to follow, irrefutable proof that the liberal and nationalist movement transcended linguistic cultural barriers.[63] To celebrate their victory in Stanstead, the reformers hosted a public dinner in January 1835 attended by Louis-Joseph Papineau, Edmund O'Callaghan, Jacques Viger (mayor of Montreal), and other leading Patriots as well as American observers. More than 500 people took part, toasting to unity between the French Canadians of the seigneuries and the English-speaking inhabitants of the Eastern Townships, as well as to the reformers of Upper Canada, a free press, agricultural development, and manufactures and commerce. More partisan toasts included: 'THE TORIES. May they ride backwards on Balaam's Ass, and be confounded.' In the eyes of both Kesteman and Clark, such toasts were a reflection of American republicanism with a strong support for the elective principle, including for the Legislative Council.[64] Included, however, was a toast to a more solid link with the mother country.[65]

In response to their crushing defeat at the provincial polls, having returned only eleven candidates to the Patriots' seventy-seven, the leading tories of the colony decided to follow their opponents' example by establishing locally based associations, though initially these were restricted largely to the county level. The Quebec Constitutional Association declared itself in opposition to an elected Legislative Council but in favour of an improved system of representation in the Assembly, judicial reform, a more effective Executive Council, continued ties to Great Britain, and the maintenance of peace and order with equal rights to all classes of Her Majesty's subjects.[66] Envoys were sent to the Eastern Townships to form sister associations,[67] and a meeting of 1,200 in Frelighsburg in February 1835 established the Missisquoi Branch Constitutional Association, 'the object of which shall be to maintain, by all lawful means, our connexion with the Empire, and to preserve inviolate the present Constitution.'[68] The ten members of the resolutions committee decided to adopt the regulations of the Quebec Constitutional Association, pro tem.

The St Francis Branch, with an executive of thirteen members, had already been established by a meeting held in Richmond in late January 1835,[69] and another was founded in Drummond County as well as one in Megantic County's Leeds Township. There was some opposition to the latter organization, for Robert Layfield – who had narrowly lost the previous election to the Quebec resident, John Greaves Clapham – declared that the meeting was unconstitutional. By January 1836, however, there were close to 300 members of the Leeds association, and four other branches had been formed in the county.[70] The Quebec emissaries proved less successful in Shefford County, where it was decided not to hold a meeting because of the strength of the local reformers. In Stanstead County the only constitutional association to be formed was in deeply divided Potton Township.[71]

Even the reformers displayed little activity in Stanstead, probably because of their position of strength, for the most politically active counties were those that were most evenly divided. The only pro-reform association in Stanstead was established in Hatley Township in July 1835, and it appears to have been rather short-lived.[72] In politically polarized Missisquoi, however, prominent Patriots from Montreal, including Thomas Storrow Brown, Augustin-Norbert Morin, and Edmund O'Callaghan, met local sympathizers in Stanbridge Upper Mills in February 1835 to form a correspondence committee linked to that of Montreal.[73]

The following July, 900 people congregated in Dunham Flat, where T.S. Brown, in a fiery speech, demanded:

What right have those who have left Britain yesterday to any privileges above ourselves? Have we not with themselves an equal inheritance in all the by-gone greatness, and by-gone glory of the nation? And does not the blood of a Wallace, or a Hampden, or a Milton, a Shakespeare, and of all the mighty dead who have made the name of Britain famous in his history, flow as purely through the veins of native born Americans, as through those of the proudest Baron of the British realm? ... I see around me many whose hairs have grown grey in reducing the wild forests into these cultivated farms, and do their sons find favor with the Government? No; – but any whipper-snapper of a month's residence, by bowing lowly at Quebec, may be sent out to rule over you.[74]

The resolutions supported at this meeting – which established the Missiskoui Reform Association – included opposition to the interference of the Colonial Office in colonial affairs, opposition to all monopolies including the British American Land Company, and support for a general system of public education as well as freedom from church taxes, even though these did not apply to Protestants. Commenting on these resolutions, Quebec's pro-Patriot *Le Canadien* suggested that 'la population britannique' might take the Canadian reformers 'un peu plus loin que ceux-ci ne se proposent d'aller.'[75]

Reacting to the increased activity of the local reform movement, and to Gosford's conciliatory gestures towards the majority party in the Assembly, the *Missiskoui Standard* warned repeatedly that the constitutionalists would resort to arms if the governor acceded to the *Parti patriote*'s demands. It proclaimed in June 1835, for example, that 'if the British government give us up, we must rise for life and liberty; and we are possessed of power enough to secure both.'[76] The following December, editor Ferres advised that the county constitutional associations follow the example of their urban counterparts by forming bodies 'under prudent, but resolute leaders' and preparing 'with arms in their hands to repel force by force.'[77] Soon afterward, Missisquoi's constitutional association, guided by the incendiary Ferres, decided to establish township committees which would in turn divide each township into districts under their direction. One of the tasks of these committees would be to submit a list of members 'in order that in time of need, friends should know on whom to depend for accurate information, etc.'[78]

Shefford County's anti-Patriots also held a meeting in early 1836, when 300 participants voted to affiliate with the Montreal Constitutional Association, but their resolutions were relatively mild in comparison with those of Missisquoi.[79] The same was true of the resolutions passed by a meeting of 400 Megantic freeholders on 25 March 1836. While protesting the inadequate British and Irish representation in the Legislative Assembly, saluting the formation of Montreal's British Rifle Corps, and opposing further concessions to the Assembly's demands, it also declared itself 'earnestly desirous of the reform of all abuses which may exist in the different departments of Government, as well as in the present composition of the Legislative

Council.' In addition, the Megantic meeting proposed a radical revision of the land granting system as well as easier credit for colonists and more generous grants for local schools. The latter resolutions reflected the fact that the county's settlers, most of whom had been directed to the isolated and mountainous area as they arrived in Quebec in 1829–31, were facing considerable hardship. A local physician claimed in the spring of 1837 that the county 'is now forsaken by all who had means enough left to permit them to do so.'[80] The March meeting declared, nonetheless, that there were only about three local individuals who supported the Patriots and who were therefore capable 'of repudiating those principles which are implanted in mankind by nature, and from which they cannot swerve without becoming traitors to their birth and origin.' One of the three was clearly Robert Layfield, who would later be arrested for political reasons.[81]

Plans were made by Lower Canada's constitutional leaders to hold a provincial congress in the spring of 1836, but the conservatives of the Eastern Townships felt abandoned when the Montreal Association declared its support for the union of that city – and not the rest of the province – with Upper Canada.[82] When the provincial congress failed to take place, the *Missiskoui Standard* suggested that the Eastern Townships associations secede from those of Montreal and Quebec and form their own grand association.[83] The *Standard* did not support union with Upper Canada, arguing that the French-Canadian and Upper Canadian radicals would control the Legislative Assembly. Other options were broached by the two Constitutional Associations of Sherbrooke County when they reported to the Gosford Commission in May 1836. They declared that if union with the French Canadians were to become 'incompatible with peace, unanimity, and good Government' (a phrase that would be closely echoed in the British North America Act), they would prefer 'a dependency in some other form upon the Mother Country ... whether as a distinct province, or connected with some other, or all of the British Colonies of North America.'[84]

Such proposals reflected the prevailing despair among the conservatives with the Gosford Commission's reform mandate. The anti-Patriot *Farmer's Advocate* of Sherbrooke lamented in May 1836:

Stanstead and Drummond counties appear to be incurably cursed with Radicalism. Missiskoui notwithstanding it can boast of one of the most ably conducted and loyal Journals in the province, is at present but half and half (...) nothing can save the cause here – Radicalism will reign triumphant. The abuses of our Officials have generated the disease, and while the cause is suffered to exist a cure is hopeless.[85]

The latter reference was clearly to the Felton clique in Sherbrooke. While Laporte claims that the constitutional crisis caused a coalition to form between the leading Montreal and Quebec merchants, on the one hand, and the colonization agents, speculators, and large proprietors, on the other, it actually resulted in the dismissal of the once-powerful William Bowman Felton as Commissioner of Crown Lands after the local constitutionalist MLA B.C.A. Gugy headed a grievance committee to investigate him. In addition, Marcus Child chaired the committee to inquire into the activities of Felton's brother-in-law, Sheriff Charles Whitcher, and the chronically debt-ridden and scandal-plagued Charles Felton resigned as court clerk in order to avoid similar scrutiny. The result was the political entrenchment of Sherbrooke's American-born entrepreneurs, who had once been on the Patriot side.[86]

Meanwhile, the wind was still in the reformers' sails in the border townships, where Potton's Patriot supporters held their first meeting in February 1836, attracting 800 people and creating a vigilance committee of fourteen. A noisy assembly held in Dunham Flat the following July went as far as to support the boycott of British goods and the encouragement of smuggling from the United States.[87] But sentiment had begun to turn with the conservative newspapers' repeated assertion that Papineau's threat to abolish the Tenures Act would mean the extension of the seigneurial system into the Eastern Townships. Popular concerns would obviously not be much allayed by the Patriot leader's explanation that he was referring only to crown land (which in the Eastern Townships would largely mean land purchased by the British American Land Company). In addition, the pro-government press did its best to spread alarm by predicting, should the Patriots prevail, the seizure of mill sites by seigneurs as well as the levy of seigneurial dues and ecclesiastical tithes upon Anglo-Protestant farmers.[88]

The campaign was effective, for in early 1837 the conservatives won an upset victory in the Stanstead by-election that followed the resignation of ailing Stanstead MLA John Grannis.[89] The contest was between the constitutionalist Dr Moses Colby, who had arrived from nearby Derby, Vermont, only five years earlier, and the reformer Elias Lee, farmer and older brother of the famous Methodist missionary Jason Lee, known as the prophet of Oregon.[90] Colby, who named his eldest son after the only-surviving signatory to the American constitution,[91] was an enthusiastic promoter of economic progress and a sharp critic of what he felt was the archaic legal system of Lower Canada, a system that 'foreclosed every avenue to public enterprise.' By sustaining the constitution, he argued, electors could 'find in the concentration of foreign capital among us increased means for accomplishing those projects of internal improvement we so ardently desire. Our lakes and rivers will soon be chained together by Railways, and our vallies intersected by Canals. The invincible power of steam will impart a new life and vigor to every department of labor and every enterprise of trade, and thus an incalculable benefit will accrue to the agricultural, commercial and mechanical interests of the community.'[92]

Following Colby's victory, the jubilant *Farmer's Advocate* declared that 'the people have, by a noble effort, wiped off the stain which for a time shaded their political character, and the tie which was supposed to link them to the enemies of British institutions has been severed forever. Stanstead can no longer bear the name of being the strong hold of disaffection, nor can her people submit to be dictated to by French charlatans.'[93] While historians interpret the basic political contest in the United States during this era as one between those who supported integration into the market and those who resisted it,[94] most farmers of the Eastern Townships would have welcomed easier access to outside markets. They would also have questioned, however, whether the imposition of a land monopoly was in their best economic interest. Colby won the election by the relatively narrow margin of 267 to 195, and the small number of votes cast reflected the inability of many farmers who might have voted against him to reach the polls during the stormy winter weather.[95]

Expressions of discontent continued to be heard. The government had stirred up opposition by threatening to dispossess the tenants of crown and clergy reserves who were in arrears (726 of whom were in the Eastern Townships) and to sell their lots to the British American Land Company.[96] 'A Backwoodsman' from Shefford wrote that 'no one cause has operated so powerfully to alienate the affections of his Majesty's heretofore, faithful and loyal subjects in the Townships, as this.' He argued that the tenants had been compelled to pay, on average, more than double the price demanded for unoccupied lands of equal quality.[97] From Inverness Township in Megantic County, the quit rent settlers – 148 of whom were in arrears by two to seven years – protested that crop failures had rendered them indigent and asked that the governor renew the road-building project that had been providing them with the necessary income to make payments before the constitutional conflict had terminated public works grants.[98]

Rather than quelling dissent, Lord Russell's Ten Resolutions were greeted with defiance by the Townships radicals during the summer of 1837. Preparations were made to celebrate American Independence Day in Stanbridge Upper Mills, whose Union Free Church tower flew a flag featuring a white eagle clutching six arrows and surrounded by six stars for the six provinces. Closely patterned on the American Great Seal, the fact that the stripes representing the states of the Union were missing may have meant that the flag represented British North American independence, but presumably as a first step towards joining the Union. Excitement ran high as a result of the threat by fifty militiamen from Missisquoi Bay to tear down any American emblem in Stanbridge and the counter-threat by the captain of a United States company of riflemen that he would intervene if anyone attacked his country's flag. He presumably meant to include any flag modelled on American symbols. On 4 July the small village witnessed a procession of a thousand people carrying banners with political slogans led by a corps of musicians from an American militia company accompanied by two veterans of the American Revolution.

The celebratory crowd was addressed by the fiery Thomas Storrow Brown, who condemned the conduct of Lord Gosford and called for the boycott of British imports. The local Baptist preacher then compared the French Canadians to black slaves, and the county's MLA, Ephraim Knight, asked rhetorically: 'Are we not told by the conduct, if not the words of the grumbling and haughty officials, that the working classes, to wit, the farmers, mechanics, and artisans from whom they obtain all their necessary supplies of food and clothing, may continue in their slavish employment, to procure them those necessaries, as they are only fit for such dirty work.'[99] The meeting, said by a recent historian to be one of the most important held in Lower Canada,[100] also supported stronger ties with the Americans, declaring that the support of these natural allies could be relied upon in case of a struggle to defend their rights. Following the example of the constitutionalists, a vigilance committee of twelve was established to discuss the interests of the community and correspond with the central county committee. Finally, after the British flag was burned, the meeting selected delegates to represent Missisquoi at the Assembly of Six Counties to be held at Saint-Charles in Richelieu County.[101]

Two weeks later, a meeting in nearby Bolton and Potton also denounced the Russell Resolutions as well as advocating the purchase of smuggled goods in order to avoid contributing taxes to the government. A permanent vigilance committee was selected, in addition to delegates to a future convention of counties, but this was the last pro-Patriot manifestation to take place in the region prior to the outbreak of rebellion.[102] In contrast to Upper Canada, where the Rebellion was to a considerable degree an expression of frustration with the tory mobs' campaign of violence against reform meetings,[103] such meetings in the Eastern Townships were relatively peaceable, probably because the Orange Lodge had not taken root in the region.

As noted above, the short-term economic causes of the Rebellion were also weaker in the Eastern Townships than elsewhere because the region escaped the worst effects of the international financial crisis as a result of the British American Land Company's large investments. And, even though the French-Canadian and Irish settlers of Grantham, Wickham, Durham, and Kingsey Townships on the lower St Francis River were facing starvation in the spring of 1837 after early frost had hit the entire region for two succeeding years, crops were generally very good in the ensuing summer.[104]

Finally, the conservative press was outdoing itself in stirring up ethnic prejudices (the *Missiskoui Standard* repeatedly referred to the French Canadians as illiterate and backward 'children of the dirt,' a sarcastic reference to the nationalistic motto 'les enfants du sol'), and the increasingly radical posture of the Patriots appeared to be leading inevitably to armed conflict. In his report, Lord Gosford observed astutely that the pro-reform deputies of the Eastern Townships had not been elected to defend the feudal system, protect the French language, or oppose the establishment of registry offices, but 'to lend their aid to the assertors of public rights, and to oppose a Government by which, in their opinion, settlers from the United States had been neglected, or regarded with disfavor.'[105] Thus, the local conservative press and constitutional associations stressed the Assembly's refusal to provide a subsidy for railway construction into the region (even though Marcus Child was a leading promoter),[106] to support reciprocal tariffs against the import of American livestock and produce, or to improve the land registry act, which was about to expire. It also demanded the permanent establishment of the St Francis District Court and argued that if the *Parti patriote* were truly interested in reform rather than protecting the interests of the seigneurs, it would support a tax on privately owned wild land.[107] More generally, in

September 1837 the newly established constitutionalist mouthpiece, the *Sherbrooke Gazette*, declared itself in favour of a modified Executive Council, a more representative Legislative Council, a more efficient judicial system, the abolition of the seigneurial system, and 'greater facilities in the granting of waste Lands of the Crown to actual settlers.'[108]

In short, while the pro-government side was more effectively organized than its opponents in the Eastern Townships prior to the outbreak of rebellion, it was not so strongly in favour of the status quo as has been assumed.[109] Nor was it unreservedly loyal to the imperial connection so much as it was concerned that increased French-Canadian political power would have negative consequences for the province's English-speaking minority. Still anticipating that the British government would submit to the Patriot demands even after the Rebellion broke out, a letter in the 5 December issue of the *Missiskoui Standard* declared that 'when a mandate from the *Mother Country* shall have invested Britain's enemies with supreme control; and the French Seignior walks rough shod upon the necks of his vassals; then will you grasp the well worn sword, and bid defiance to the craven crowd.'[110]

'I shall die defending my home and family': Rebellion

The outbreak of rebellion in November was followed by the arrest of several prominent Eastern Townships reformers, including the Missisquoi justice of the peace Dr Leonard Brown. A search of his house discovered $900 in counterfeit bills, though Brown claimed they had been seized by him seven years earlier and he had been holding them as evidence.[111] In February Brown admitted under examination that he had helped organize the 4 July demonstration at Stanbridge, where there had been a flag 'more calculated to represent the American flag than the British flag,' and he confessed that the meeting date 'was incorrect and improper,' adding that 'if such a thing were to take place again I should stand forth and oppose it.'[112] Ephraim Knight, the MLA who had spoken at the same meeting (as we have seen), was also arrested, though he would serve as an unofficial informant during the second rebellion.[113]

Alarmed by these events, Marcus Child summoned a meeting of his political supporters in Georgeville on 5 December 'to consider the best means' of dissociating themselves from 'those deluded men who are exciting and leading the Rebellion in this Province.'[114] The per-

sonal journal kept by Papineau's son Amédée records how Child
spoke out on his behalf when he was stopped for questioning while
attempting to cross the border at Stanstead, but it appears that Child
was unaware of the young man's identity.[115] One of the rebel organizers wrote in January 1838, when plans were being made for cross-
border raids from the United States, that Child 'worships his property
too much to jeopardize his safety by doing anything to advance the
interest of the sacred cause.'[116] After being dismissed as postmaster,[117] however, Child refused to take the oath of loyalty on the
grounds that he had already done so. Pride undoubtedly played a role
in this act of defiance for the oaths commissioner was William
Ritchie, who, as returning officer in the 1834 election, had succeeded
in depriving Child of his seat for a time despite the fact that he had
obtained the most votes. When Child was also dismissed as commissioner of the peace in 1837, he took the precaution of fleeing across
the border to Vermont.[118]

Ritchie had recommended that oaths be administered locally
because 'many of the Inhabitants, and some of considerable property,
are undecided, looking on, as the Yankee says *on the fence* ready to
step down as best suits their convenience.' He feared that 'should the
Rebel party have a partial triumph' there would be local disturbances
before the winter ended.[119] Indeed, Child was far from alone in refus-
ing to take the oath, for Ritchie reported in late January that 'I meet
with a good deal of opposition and many refusals.' Blaming the influence of the *Canadian Patriot*, Ritchie added: 'I am very sorry to say
that prospects are darker than what I first anticipated.' He concluded
that, judging from 'the public prints,' Stanstead County was 'the most
disaffected and restless in the province.'[120] Ritchie's observations are
supported to some extent by the reports of Stanstead's Wesleyan
Methodist minister, Thomas Turner, who claimed that he had to be
very careful not to go too far in expressing support for the efforts to
suppress the Rebellion, for 'such has been the high state of excitement we have been in that I have reason to fear some of our Societies
would have been torn to pieces.'[121]

Like Ritchie, Dr Joshua Chamberlin, the postmaster of Frelighsburg in St Armand East, pursued his task as oaths commissioner
enthusiastically, keeping a register of names which he claimed 'will
have the very best effect in the country, more especially over the
lukewarm and disaffected.' Chamberlin added that 'the granting of
certificates will give an idea of importance which otherwise could not
be created.'[122] Even the Quaker settlement in Farnham Township was
not to be exempt.[123] As late as April 1838, however, one complainant

reported that no oaths had been administered in Compton Township, 'although a considerable number of People of American origin here are represented, I believe upon good Authority as disaffected to the Government of the Queen.'[124]

Ritchie and Chamberlin may have been overly sanguine about how the oath was interpreted by those who did take it, for Ralph Merry of the Outlet (today's Magog) reasoned to himself that the requirement 'to make known all treasons and traterous [sic] conspiracies and attempts that I shall know to be against her majesty or her successors' did not include stories that he did not positively know to be true.[125] Lieutenant-Colonel Head, commanding officer of the Shefford and Brome district, nevertheless feared that individuals living close to the border who swore allegiance would be subject to molestation by their disloyal neighbours, who tended to flee to Vermont on the slightest alarm from the authorities. Furthermore, the government failed to provide instructions as to what steps to take against individuals such as the Megantic sergeant of militia Thomas Sheridan, who, with a number of recent arrivals in the largely Irish-settled county, had refused to comply.[126]

In addition to complaining about the lack of support for administering the oath of allegiance, Ritchie noted that there were few justices of the peace in the district,[127] and the outbreak of rebellion had also found many militia units in the Eastern Townships without commissioned or non-commissioned officers. The leading men of Sherbrooke, anticipating that the militia would be required to suppress riots and provide local defence, requested that the vacancies in the Fifth Battalion be filled as soon as possible.[128] But the authorities were slow to respond, and in June 1838 a list of nine recommended names was submitted by Major Charles Whitcher, the officer in command since his brother-in-law, the disgraced Lieutenant-Colonel William Felton, had died during the summer of 1837. Ten of the companies saw duty soon afterwards, but new officers had still not been formally appointed as late as June 1839.[129]

Instead, steps were taken throughout the region to establish volunteer units which the government felt would be more trustworthy than the militia.[130] In mid-November Attorney-General C.R. Ogden offered to form such a company to assist the militia, survey the movements of 'insurrectionalists,' and maintain links with areas inhabited by British settlers as well as the military posts on the Richelieu.[131] Nothing came of this proposal, but on 21 November Lord Gosford recommended to Sir John Colborne that 500 to 800 men be selected to form a paid corps of Eastern Townships volunteers under the command of Colonel Frederick G. Heriot. The Swiss-born Heriot had become the commanding officer of the Voltigeurs Canadiens in 1814 and founder of the military settlement of Drummondville after the war.[132] By late December, the Eastern Townships Loyal Volunteers, apparently limited to Sherbrooke and Drummond Counties, consisted of 600 rank and file under Heriot's command (see Appendix A).[133]

Three local companies had been established in the Sherbrooke area: the Sherbrooke Dragoons, the Loyal American Rifle Company, and the Queen's Mounted Rangers. When three weeks passed without approval of the three men whom the local MLA, John Moore, had recommended as officers of the rifle company, he complained that the delay might 'create an opinion that there is a want of confidence – on the part of the Government – in relation to the American part of this community, a thing very much to be deprecated at this present time.'[134] Moore was right about the government's feelings, for the company was criticized for drilling before being officially sanctioned and for recommending its own officers.

But it did have an influential defender in Sherbrooke's Edward Hale, grandson of one of Wolfe's senior officers on the Plains of Abraham and nephew of the Governor-General of India, under whom he had recently served. Hale pointed out to Colonel Heriot that he and the other company members had purchased arms, ammunition, and uniforms at their own expense.[135] Consequently, Hale wrote, 'I for one thought that in time of emergency such irregularities would be overlooked,' and he cautioned that 'any measure which would check the zeal they have displayed would not only be grating to their feelings but might in the end tend to damp their Constitutional principles.' Hale felt certain that the rifle company would do its duty 'in the event of any Rebel force approaching us whether French or American,' though he was less confident about what the response would be in the event of war with the United States. In the final analysis, the most important role of the company, Hale felt, would not be a military one, since the Eastern Townships was unlikely to become a major centre of conflict. Rather it would reinforce a sense of loyalty, thereby securing 'the feelings of the Individuals in civil matters, and future Elections.' At Colonel Heriot's suggestion, Colborne complied with Hale's wishes.[136]

Compton Township was overlooked, however, and a meeting on 18 December protested the inhabitants' loyalty and recommended the organization of four militia units of one hundred men each, in addition to a cavalry company.[137] But this meeting had exaggerated the local pro-government enthusiasm, for, eleven months later, Compton's J.S. Jones (a retired major) reported to Colborne that 'the forming of the Volunteer Corps you gave me authority for in March last is in progress, but I fear (nearly two thirds of the people being hostile to our Government) will not be successful.'[138]

In distinct contrast, a late November 1837 meeting in nearby Stanstead did not wait for official sanction before selecting ten men to organize a volunteer unit to guard the roads along which arms were being smuggled in from Vermont and to prevent the escape of 'fugitives from Justice.' The meeting also declared that 'we stand ready to proceed to the assistance of our fellow Loyal subjects in any part of the Province.'[139] Reporting that no fewer than 500 armed rebels were awaiting the signal to attack, Stanstead's justices of the peace had already recommended that Lieutenant-Colonel Wright Chamberlin be placed on full pay to recruit a militia corps.[140]

A group of self-styled reformers from Shefford, a county which had shown little enthusiasm for the constitutionalists, also offered their services in defence of the government, promising Sir John Colborne 1,100 men.[141] In addition, 437 militiamen from St Armand signed a loyalty petition, and three militia captains from Missisquoi County formed what they called 'a volunteer association to aid the government in the defense of the rights of persons and property in this county.' This phrasing suggests that the *Township Reformer* may have had a point when it claimed that the volunteers did not realize that they would be 'compelled to march at a moment's notice to put down the French Rebellion,' but were led to believe that the aim was simply 'to form a combination to protect property from destruction by mobs.'[142]

Whether or not this was true, the government hesitated to arm these men. According to the *Missiskoui Standard*, Lieutenant-Colonel Robert Jones's request for rifles and ammunition for the three volunteer units was met with the statement by the deputy adjutant-general that 'your companies must be embodied; we can give no arms except to men regularly enrolled.' Complaining that the government obviously did not trust the Townships militia, the *Standard* pointed out that only the governor had the power to embody militia units.[143] A resident of Frelighsburg nevertheless claimed on 20 November that there were eighty well-armed men prepared to capture the Patriots fleeing south through the village should they be authorized to do so.[144] By mid-December Missisquoi was more organized from a military perspective than any other part of the region (see Appendix A).

To the north, in Megantic County, the MLA John Greaves Clapham expressed the fear that French-Canadian insurgents from nearby seigneuries would resort to plundering the farms of his constituents during the winter. As a precaution, he recommended the arming of at least 200 of the county's 'yeomanry.'[145] Clapham also advised completion of the Gosford Road as a more secure (though certainly circuitous) communications route between Quebec and Montreal, noting that the project would provide much-needed wage labour for the aggrieved quit rent settlers.[146] According to the *Quebec Mercury* in December 1837, the Megantic settlers were anxious to organize 'more against the predatory incursions of a half-starved population in the seigniories ... than from any organized hostile invasion' of this isolated territory.[147] Clapham reported that the Irish Protestants 'shudder at the remembrances of the rebellion' in their home country,[148] but this did not prevent men from Inverness and Ireland Townships, some of whom were former soldiers, from volunteering to form a paid corps to assist the Quebec garrison until 1 May 1838. Commanded by Archibald McKillop, who was the leader of the Highland settlers from the Isle of Arran, sixty-nine members of the Loyal Megantic Volunteers spent the winter in Quebec, as did the wives and 105 children of the thirty-one who were married, even though they were not entitled to rations.[149] Much to Clapham's chagrin, the government refused to reimburse him for the expenses incurred by the volunteers in travelling to Quebec and while waiting for their barrack to be completed.[150]

Meanwhile, in Shefford County, Lieutenant-Colonel Paul Holland Knowlton was asked to raise a corps of 400 infantry and 60 cavalry.[151] For reasons that are not clear, weapons were sent to Knowlton's Loyal Volunteers in December, before the more exposed Missisquoi Volunteers were armed, even though Philipsburg was under threat of destruction by the rebels who had fled across the border to Vermont after the British had secured the Richelieu Valley.[152] The local Wesleyan Methodist minister, William Squire, reported that he had twice removed his family's furniture and buried some of their possessions, and three times they had 'fled to the woods with our little ones for protection, in the frost and snow of December.'[153]

Fortunately for them, fifty of the Missisquoi Volunteers happened to be escorting the Montreal shipment of guns and ammunition to Lieutenant-Colonel Knowlton in Brome when they learned that eighty-four Patriot cavalrymen recruited from L'Acadie had passed southward on 5 December. Their aim was to transport arms acquired in Swanton, Vermont, to the camp being formed under Robert Nelson at Saint-Césaire, and they apparently made the mistake of parading drunkenly through Philipsburg (where their leader, Lucien Gagnon, reportedly struck a man with his musket and broke some windows) and announcing that they would return to burn it to the ground the following day. This gave Missisquoi's Captain Oren Kemp enough time to distribute arms from the Montreal shipment to some 300 volunteers, approximately 100 of whom surprised the returning Patriots' advance guard at Moore's Corner, near Philipsburg. As darkness was falling, the Volunteers killed one Patriot and wounded five others, causing the main body of invaders, which had been augmented by thirty to forty men in Swanton, to retreat. They left behind five kegs of gunpowder, six boxes of ball cartridges, seventy muskets, and two brass field pieces, all of which they had 'liberated' from the cooperative Vermont militia company at Stowe. Even more of a moral defeat was the fact that their slightly wounded commander, Robert Shore Milnes Bouchette (son of the surveyor-general), had been taken prisoner. Colborne was very pleased with the results of the encounter, even if the volunteers had fired prematurely, thereby allowing most of the invaders to escape. He informed Gosford that 'the good spirits in Missisquoi will enable us to withdraw part of the force ... at St. John's and turn towards St. Eustache.'[154]

The *Missiskoui Standard* expressed outrage that the people of Swanton and St Albans, Vermont, had provided the invaders with weapons. Even when the two countries had been at war in 1812–14, the indignant *Standard* noted, there had been an agreement 'that means should be used to apprehend any and every private depredator, on whatever side.'[155] The Americans would not have considered the rebels 'private depredators,' but the following day a meeting in Lennoxville appointed a committee of seven to draft a petition to the citizens of the United States disabusing them of the idea that the situation was comparable to that of 1776.[156] A week later, however, over 2,000 'freemen' met in St Albans to pass resolutions expressing fear that 'a gang of marauders' from across the border might 'make some petty invasion into our territory, disturbing the public peace and committing acts of outrage.' They also objected that the declaration of martial law in Lower Canada hampered trading because of restrictions placed on Americans entering the province. Finally, they declared that the Patriots were engaged in 'just such a cause as our fathers were engaged in the war of revolution and that they are entitled to the same sympathy and assistance from us that our fathers were from theirs.'[157] Given the stance taken by the French Canadians during the American War of Independence and the War of 1812, those who drafted the resolution were indulging in a considerable amount of historical revisionism.

Similar resolutions were drafted by leading citizens in many other Vermont towns, and, in return, a public meeting in St Armand West denied that there had been any threat of invasion from Lower Canada. The *Missiskoui Standard* declared: 'Henceforth, they may keep their revivals ... their religious tracts – antimasonic – missionary – moral reform – temperance, and all, to themselves. They have sent in a band of robbers upon us, and they are yet contriving and swearing more vengeance.'[158] The American urge for vengeance became very real after the Navy Island incident in Upper Canada, as illustrated by the aggressive wording of the resolutions passed in a late January meeting held in Newport, Vermont, on Lake Memphremagog. Drafted by several leading citizens of the town, they declared 'that for nearly fifty years Canada has been withered under the blighting influence of Military Despots, ruled by tyrants and broken down politicians of John Bull, not according to the laws of their own choice, but by the whimsical dictates of their arbitrary power, and, in our view, becoming weary of oppression, we deem it their bounden duty, to throw off the old despotic yoke of John Bull.' The meeting also resolved that the 'tyrannical officers must hold themselves Responsible before the "Tribunal of the Great Jehovah," for the amount of blood which they have unnecessarily caused to be shed, the lives lost, the crimes they have committed in consigning those who were lawfully (and morally right, too) found resisting the despotism of Her Beautiful Majesty, a tyrant and its laws, – all that may now be wearing the chains of slavery in Dungeons.' It was a moral imperative, therefore, that the assistance Americans had provided Greece when at war with Turkey, and Texas when at war with Mexico, must not be denied the patriots of Canada. Consequently, the Newport meeting proclaimed, 'we will not lay down our arms until we effectually teach them, again, how to bow the knee to American artillery, and that the proud spirit of these Green Mountains are ready prepared to teach them the true value of American steel.'[159]

In reply, the *Missiskoui Standard* reached new heights of outrage: 'Their conduct is inexplicable ... it is insane – the spirit of wild fanaticism. A whip for the slave in one hand, and a gun in the other to give freedom, or rather licentiousness, to people in the enjoyment of a liberty more rational than they ever knew.'[160] The threat was real, for Robert Nelson and the other exiled radicals who had assumed control of the Patriot movement in the United States had decided to launch raids across the border in order to provoke incidents that would lead to ruptured relations between the United States and Britain.[161] To meet this threat, Lieutenant-Colonel Knowlton's Loyal Volunteers were administered the 'Soldiers' Oath' in late January and ordered to remain in full service until 1 May, unless disbanded earlier.[162] Ironically, Knowlton was himself soon criticized for fomenting a mutinous spirit among these volunteers, who had assumed the temporary status of professionals, for his officers threatened to resign their commissions if they and their men did not receive full pay, even when not on active service. According to the local paymaster, Knowlton was responsible for suggesting, mistakenly, that such a promise had been made.[163] As we shall see, this would not be the last time during the Rebellions that the irascible Knowlton would stand accused of encouraging his volunteers to defy constituted authority.

Sherbrooke's Irish-born Catholic curé, John Baptist McMahon, was also a loose cannon, to some extent. Having written a lengthy newspaper column advocating loyalty in November, he now reported a general state of alarm and asked for an *exeat* because he feared assassination in the event of an attack by the Patriots or local American sympathizers. After Archbishop Joseph Signay replied that there was nothing to fear in Sherbrooke, McMahon proceeded to campaign energetically during the Christmas season among the Catholics, whom he claimed to be disaffected in Shipton, Tingwick, and Kingsey Townships.[164] McMahon's rather alarmist claim most likely was based largely on the fact that the Kingsey merchant François-Benjamin Blanchard had been a Montreal business associate of the radical Patriot leader Thomas Storrow Brown. Blanchard was briefly arrested in December for distributing bulletins from Brown's 'Grande armée,' as well as in February, when Papineau's brother, André-Augustin, was discovered in his house.[165]

Meanwhile, Levi Spalding, a Stanstead merchant who visited the Vermont state capital in late December, reported that the Patriots had accumulated 300 guns, with plans to double that number, in addition to acquiring four cannons. Several French-Canadian exiles had already used ten kegs of powder to make cartridges, all of which would be sent to Swanton in preparation for an invasion in three to four weeks' time.[166] Spalding's prediction was not far off, for on 25 February Robert Nelson wrote from Plattsburg to J.B. Ryan in Stanstead informing him that, with Mackenzie on the march in Upper Canada, Colborne had sent a large number of troops up the St Lawrence. Nelson felt that the American General, John E. Wool, who had been guarding the border would also shift his forces westward under the impression that the Lower Canadian Patriots had joined forces with Mackenzie. The Patriot leader concluded that the way was clear for him to enter Lower Canada in the next day or so, and he asked Ryan – who had fled to Vermont from Quebec City the previous year – to proceed as quickly as possible with his men to Trois-Rivières. Nelson would join him there, after taking Montreal. If Ryan did not have enough men for this purpose, he was to go to Saint-Hyacinthe or, failing that, to head for Missisquoi Bay, Saint-Jean, and Laprairie.[167]

Nelson made no reference to the fact that plans were already unfolding to attack border settlements in the Eastern Townships. On the evening of 26 February, one day after Nelson penned his letter, Asa Lillie of Georgeville witnessed a public meeting in Derby Line, Vermont, at which plans were made to seize the arms and the leading men of Stanstead Plain, but 'not to burn or kill without resistance was made.' Lillie named seventeen men, claiming that there were 'a number of others' whom he did not recognize and that he had heard the names Hiram Francis Blanchard and Dr McKeech. Blanchard, publisher of the *Canadian Patriot*, was apparently to lead the raid, and other informants identified leaders to be C.W. Tolford, former publisher of the *St Francis Courier*, and Lewis Hanson of Barnston.[168] Rather curiously, there was no mention of J.B. Ryan.[169]

The raid failed to materialize, apparently because the expected reinforcements and arms from Troy, Vermont, did not arrive on time,[170] but the forty-two members of Sherbrooke's Loyal American Rifle Company, anxious for some action, departed for Stanstead Plain soon afterward. Serving as a lowly private, albeit one 'with a nice soft bed' who was in charge of the commanding officer's correspondence, Edward Hale wrote to his wife that they would be remaining in Stanstead a few days 'because the People cannot consent to let us go and entre nous our Captain being a Stanstead man has no objection to remain.' He added that the Yankees, who were 'constantly driving in from Derby to look at us, ... seem to be surprised that there is so much loyal feeling among the people as they thought that a feeling in favor of being joined to the States prevailed.' While the village of Stanstead had been completely unprepared for an attack, Hale felt that the 150 local men then under arms, in addition to the township's volunteers, would be more than a match for the 150 to 200 armed men congregated in Derby. He assured his wife that 'notwithstanding a variety of wants which in other times I should call nuisances I never enjoyed any frolic more for we are a jolly set of fellows, and there was no end to the fun and romping and joking going on.'[171]

If the organizers in Derby Line were expecting support from Troy, there had obviously been a communications breakdown, for fifty to sixty men in that town had attacked Potton the same evening, reportedly with the aim of seizing arms from the local volunteers. Organized by Captain Ira A. Bailey, who was Troy's first constable and a justice of the peace, the raiding party was apparently not expecting resistance. The former Stanstead resident Hazen Hadlock was shot and killed, however, while climbing the stairs of a house where several defenders had taken refuge. The invaders then hastily retreated, vowing to return and burn down 'every building occupied by a government man.'[172]

A sense of the ensuing panic is reflected in a private letter written several days later by the Potton militia officer Henry Woods to an American correspondent: 'We are in trouble! War has made its appearance among us. Father has risen against son, brother against brother.' His own brother Charles, having been 'led away by a few unprinicipled characters,' was 'numbered among the Rebels. I tell him it is a hard case but shall fight for my country, my home, & property till the last.' Woods expected an attack by 800 invaders from Vermont even though volunteer units from elsewhere in the region as well as Montreal's 63rd Regiment were on their way to Potton to reinforce the sixty local volunteers (there being only sixty guns available). This small local force had already rejected terms of surrender that demanded they give up their arms and not take them up again. Woods added that the town 'is pretty equally divided,' though the local rebels were unarmed. Unless reinforcements arrived the following day, Woods concluded, 'my buildings must be in ashes,' but 'if they go, I go with them. I shall die defending my home & family.'[173]

Fortunately for Woods, 400 volunteers from neighbouring border townships as well as Sherbrooke did soon arrive at what Edward Hale described as 'a miserable place of scattered houses – no more like a village than Wilcox's farm.' He was very enthusiastic about the 'fine loyal fellows from Brome and Potton and Shefford,' however, exclaiming that 'I never saw such warm loyalty it beats the British hollow.'[174] There would be no further attacks on Potton, but the settlement did remain on edge. Harvey Elkins, one of the men who had fired on Hadlock, complained that during the ensuing month he was shot at and repeatedly threatened with death.[175]

As he had indicated in his letter to Ryan two days after the Stanstead and Potton fiascos, Nelson led a force of 600 to 700 well-armed men across the border near Caldwell's Manor, on the western side of Missisquoi Bay, where he declared the province to be a republic with himself as president and commander-in-chief of the Patriot army. Many features of Nelson's declaration of independence would have appealed to the American-origin population of the Eastern Townships – for example, abolition of the seigneurial system and church tithes, public education for all children, and universal suffrage with the secret ballot. Furthermore, allegiances were divided even in this most loyal corner of the region, for the Church of England's Reverend William Squire of Philipsburg noted in May 1838: 'The majority around us are doubtless loyal but there are many who would rebel could they see any probability of success. As it is, we are treated only with a little reviling, a few false reports have been circulated concerning us, and a few individuals have left the place of worship when we have prayed for the Queen, and the Authorities of the Country.'[176] But Nelson's foray across the border was short-lived, for all the Americans deserted overnight, leaving him with only 160 men. Facing approximately 1,000 Missisquoi Volunteers under the command of a British major, Nelson withdrew to Vermont, where he was met by General Wool, who had not moved westward as Nelson had anticipated. As a result, Nelson and his second-in-command were arrested and all their weapons were confiscated.[177]

Realizing that the American authorities were anxious not to alienate the British, but that there was widespread sympathy for the Rebellion in the border states, Nelson – who had been quickly acquitted by an American jury – now adopted the strategy of forming an underground movement known as the Frères Chasseurs or Hunters' Lodges. The goal of these lodges was to supply armed troops within the province during an invasion from the United States.[178] The Hunters' Lodge movement was also launched south of the border, where it proved to be remarkably popular, especially in northern Vermont, where, according to Duffy and Muller, it included 'some of the most substantial elements of society.'[179] Belicose as their pronouncements were, the American Hunters were not in a position to invade. Over 5,000 seasoned British troops had poured into Lower Canada by July 1838, and the United States government issued an official declaration of neutrality as well as expanding the army by approximately 50 per cent to deal with the border situation.[180] But these developments did not prevent the rather deluded Nelson from planning a major Chasseur uprising to be commanded from Napierville, south of Montreal, on 3 November.

Meanwhile, the people of the border townships spent an anxious summer and fall filled with rumours of impending attacks by Patriot exiles and American sympathizers.[181] Silas Dickerson and Hiram Blanchard boasted in June that there were still three radicals for every loyalist in the region, and Dr Cyrille Côté later claimed that there were Hunters' Lodges in Brome, Potton, Sutton, Stanstead, Milton, Barnston, and Shipton Townships.[182] These reports were clearly exaggerated, however, for there appears to have been only one small lodge in Potton and Bolton, and another in the Shefford, Granby, and Stukeley area. According to Major Head, Nelson's attempt to establish lodges in the border townships had been cut short by the arrest of one of the members who had been authorized to administer the secret oath. He had revealed the names of all the initiates with the result that most of the leaders had fled to the United States and the most influential members of the 'Radical' party in Potton and Bolton had been imprisoned.[183]

The local leaders referred to were clearly William Hayden and Dr Enoch Jacquay, who were both charged with high treason in April 1838.[184] But these arrests did not put an end to the local Hunters' Lodge movement, for Robert Manson of Potton, Dr Amos W. Lay of Bolton, and Calvin Harvey of Shefford were imprisoned in the fall for administering the Hunters' oath. Witnesses also claimed that Artemus Newton of Shefford and William Brock of Sutton were two of the principal organizers of the plan to support Nelson's uprising in early November.[185] According to the story of Daniel Miltmore of Potton, he went to the house of B.W. Gilman of the same township on 5 November, where he and sixteen men from Potton, one from Sutton, and five from Troy, Vermont (all of whom were named), were each given one of the thirty to forty guns brought there by Levi Parkhurst and Ira Bailey of Troy. Their aim, Miltmore claimed, was to assist the rebels 'in over turning the British Government in the Province of Lower Canada & to defend themselves against any of Her Majesty's Forces that might be dispersed thro the Country to put down the rebellion' that was supposed to take place that day. Their immediate task would be to disarm the Shefford Dragoons stationed in two Bolton houses. Another witness reported that they had been promised that they could sell the confiscated horses and arms in Vermont, sharing the proceeds among themselves.[186] But the armed confrontations took place to the immediate west of the Eastern Townships, where the Patriot defeats at the battles of Lacolle and Odelltown prevented Nelson from keeping open the line of communications to his source of supplies and reinforcements on the other side of the border. Facing overwhelming British military superiority, the rebels had all dispersed by 13 November.[187]

Megantic and Drummond counties on the northern edge of the region were far removed from danger during the second rebellion, but John Ployart – the Durham Township half-pay officer and justice of the peace who was disappointed not to receive a military commission[188] – did his best to make the local situation seem critical. He reported on 5 November that large herds of cattle were being driven to the United States and that more American peddlers than ever seen before were crossing the border without being searched for hidden ammunition. He also complained that the loyal subjects of the area remained unarmed, but he only managed to identify and arrest one 'rebel.' The man in question, Charles Charpentier, was confined to the Sherbrooke jail on the charge of fomenting rebellion by singing revolutionary songs and distributing seditious materials provided by his pro-Patriot brother, a former militia captain from Baie-du-Fèvre near Trois-Rivières. In response, a petition drafted by the local priest, Hugh Robson, claimed in December that Charpentier had not been politically involved in any way since settling in the township and that Ployart had simply wanted to nip any possible anti-government activity in the bud by making an example of him. Charpentier was finally released on £400 bail in April 1839. Meanwhile, the Reverend Robson insisted that 'la population de ce quartier est des plus loyales,' and Colonel Heriot of Drummondville also noted in December 1838 that 'all is quiet in this part of the Country.'[189]

But all was not so quiet in Stanstead County, where Colonel Robert Nickle had been appointed by the governor to superintend the operations of the frontier forces, including a newly formed infantry company and a cavalry company.[190] Taking advantage of the extension of martial law to the St Francis District with the second outbreak of rebellion, their first duty was to arrest those who had been identified as rebel sympathizers. This time, however, there was some resistance. On the night of 12 or 13 November, Captain Alexander Kilborn of the infantry and Lieutenant J.W. Martin of the cavalry were fired upon in the dark while returning home after a failed attempt to arrest Dr Lovell McKeech and Asa Hollister, who were said to be drilling a party of disaffected Canadians and their American sympathizers in Barnston. Kilborn, whose father had commanded one of the two Frontier Light Infantry companies during the War of 1812, was wounded and Lieutenant Martin's horse was shot in the head, but they managed to reach safety.

Panic ensued, with the local magistrates claiming to have trust-worthy information 'that nearly 500 rebels are armed in this county, and that an attack is intended to be made on Stanstead Plain.'[191] As a result, the local Methodist minister reported, several 'of the most respectable families' were moving to 'places of greater safety,' and 'even our places of worship are being put into a state of preparation for defending the place.'[192] According to the local historian B.F. Hubbard, 'such a panic as that caused by the arrival of Capt. Kilborn on that eventful night has never before or since been witnessed in Stanstead. An attack was hourly expected; messengers were despatched to Hatley, Compton, Lennoxville and Sherbrooke, and before ten o'clock the next morning a military force of 1000 men was on the ground.'[193]

There is no evidence that any attack on Stanstead was planned, but the authorities took advantage of this opportunity to repress political dissent. Linked in their minds with the anticipated raid was the sinking of the ferry at Georgeville, presumably to cut off communication with the other side of Lake Memphremagog, with the result that three of the village's citizens were arrested.[194] The three were Leon Channell, the young son of the local innkeeper; John Carty Tuck, Channell's brother-in-law; and Roswell Bates, the blacksmith. Tuck and Bates had been identified in Derby Line the night of the planned March attack on Stanstead Plain, and Bates had been quoted as boasting in a Derby tavern that if he could not convince enough men to follow him, 'he would come to Georgeville himself alone, armed with Sword, Pistols or Rifles, or both, and challenge for a single combat, in the field.'[195]

The prominent village merchant and postmaster Chauncey Bullock also fled to Vermont with local farmer Julius Ives. Whether or not any or all of these men were involved in a pro-rebellion conspiracy is not clear, for the three who were arrested were never tried despite being held in Sherbrooke for five months before they were released on the sizable bail of £400 each. It is clear, however, that Georgeville was not the loyalist stronghold that Laporte assumes it to have been based on the several anti-Patriot meetings held there.[196] Julius Ives and his wife certainly made their allegiance clear when they gave the name Wolfred Nelson to the son who was born as they fled across the Vermont border.[197] The tory notary and oaths commissioner, William Ritchie, also suggested that Georgeville's deputy registrar, Increase Bullock (brother of Chauncey), was disloyal and that the registry records should be removed to Stanstead Plain, where, as Bullock had pointed out earlier, the official registrar was being paid for doing nothing.[198]

Also apprehended in the first sweep was Elias Lee, Jr, son of the defeated pro-Patriot candidate of 1836, and reported to be 'a leader of the Rebel party' in Stanstead Township.[199] Due to the climate of panic, the less defiant Marcus Child and Silas Dickerson fled to Vermont once again, leaving William Ritchie to lament that they had not been arrested. Ritchie also complained of the loss of the prominent local merchant Ichabod Smith, who left Stanstead because he believed he was 'one of the intended Victims marked by the Rebels.' Finally, Ritchie requested that the local commanding officer be ordered to search 'all suspected persons and places for arms and ammunition' and to 'rid Barnston of those lawless ruffians and nightly assassins, persons who have no quiet residence anywhere.'[200] According to the *Montreal Gazette*, Barnston was full of 'snaggers' (the local name for counterfeiters), horse thieves, and 'every other description of border trash.'[201]

Following Ritchie's advice, there were fifteen more arrests in Barnston the week after the incident, six of whom were sent to the Sherbrooke jail, while six were held in Stanstead for questioning and three were quickly released.[202] Those jailed included John Sanborn, Jr, and Jared F. Blanchard, who may well have been Sanborn's stepbrother since John Sanborn, Sr, had married the widow Blanchard.[203] Jared Blanchard was probably also closely related to radical newspaper publisher Hiram Francis Blanchard, who was originally from Barnston. The marriage partners of three other offspring of John Sanborn and the widow Blanchard suggest that the Barnston radicals formed a tight kin network, for George and Carlisle Sanborn (both identified as having been at Derby Line the night of the aborted raid) were married to a McKeech and to the sister of Andrew Hoeg, respectively. Dr Lovell McKeech, as already noted, was reputed to be a local rebel leader, and Andrew Hoeg was among those arrested in Barnston. Finally, Nancy Sanborn – sister of John, Jr, George, and Carlisle – was married to Hiram Aldrich, another of those identified at Derby Line.[204]

Eleven more men, the only French Canadian being the Charles Charpentier referred to above, were incarcerated in the Sherbrooke jail for 'treasonable practices' between 24 November and 15 December (see Appendix B). Jacob Bachelder was accused of perjury rather than treasonable practices, but Whitcher added him to his list of political prisoners because he assumed that Bachelder was somehow involved with Baruch Burpee, who was arrested at the same time on the latter charge. Bachelder had another link to this group because the prisoner named Jonas Kent (whose brothers Jacob and Blaisdell were also arrested) was married to his niece. Whether these prisoners were of a significantly different socioeconomic background than the general population is not clear, but they were clearly not a gang of marginalized criminals or disaffected youths. The Barnston kin networks, only a hint of which can be detected from the genealogical information provided by Hubbard's nineteenth-century history of the county, suggest that they came from well-established families.[205]

The arrests extended beyond Barnston and Georgeville to include two prominent men who were obviously not rebel conspirators. Captain Taylor Wadleigh of Hatley – who had penned some of the reform candidates' speeches – was jailed for using seditious language to the men of his company when they were on parade on 27 November. Wadleigh admitted that he had said that 'he had no objection to taking the oath of allegiance except that it would gratify some scoundrels,' but he denied that he meant to 'implicate the Government.' He explained that even though he was a 'radical reformer,' he was also 'loyal and a friend to the British Government under which he lives from choice and nothing would give him greater satisfaction than the total failure of the Rebels in this province.' After more than a month's confinement in the Stanstead garrison, Wadleigh was transferred to the Montreal jail in January. He was released on bail eighteen days later after a petition of support was submitted by fifteen of the most prominent men in the counties of Stanstead and Sherbrooke – including five justices of the peace, five militia officers (one of whom was also a JP), the Wesleyan Methodist missionary, and even noted government supporters such as William Ritchie, Samuel Brooks, and Dr Moses Colby.[206] Finally, charged with high treason on 14 December for reasons that are not clear, was George Washington Brooks, brother of Sherbrooke's most influential merchant and politician, Samuel Brooks. This family connection did not save Brooks from being denied bail for another ten months.[207]

The reaction to the Barnston shooting even reached Megantic County, where in January 1839 the magistrates of Leeds Township arrested a man named Jonathan Nelson on suspicion that he knew who had shot at Captain Kilborn. Nelson had reportedly fled to Bangor, Maine, the day after the incident and was on his way to his Hatley home when apprehended. But the careful steps taken by the Leeds magistrates to entrap him were in vain, for Nelson was apparently allowed to escape after he was taken to the Quebec jail.[208]

It appears that none of these prisoners faced trial for treason,[209] but the Barnston incident – minor as it may have been in comparison with events elsewhere in the province – had a galvanizing effect on the region. Stanstead's Congregational minister, R.V. Hall, had been complaining about the soldiers using his meeting house as a barrack and the 'sacred desk' as a card table, but his report of January 1839 adopted a different tone. It stated that 'almost all classes who desire the civil, moral, & religious welfare of this county have rallied round the standard of their country & girded on their armour, with a determination to defend their property, their wives and their children from a hoard of robers [sic] who fear not God nor regard the rights of man.'[210]

But this defensive response to a perceived threat did not mean that the Rebellions were a unifying experience in the Eastern Townships. The Reverend Hall reported in March 1838 that approximately 150 rebel sympathizers had fled the country 'for the country's good.' The Canadian-born clergyman added, sarcastically, that the Americans would probably provide 'as much sympathy for them as though they were poor Polanders just escaped from Siberian slavery.'[211] Further from the border, reform sympathizers felt less pressure to flee, for Shefford's Wesleyan Methodist minister, John Tomkins, reported in early 1839 that 'the community being made up of persons from different countries and political sentiments, unanimity of feelings and desires could not be expected; neither do they exist, and the consequence is that friendly intercourse has been interrupted, and friendly feeling in many instances destroyed.'[212] In Granby and Shefford Townships, the Congregationalist Reverend H.B. Chapin, who had recently arrived from the United States, reported in October 1838 that 'I scarcely know of an American near me [who] from his heart does not wish he was well out of the Country.'[213] The trial of a number of local residents at a court martial in Frost Village sheds light on why the Americans may have felt intimidated.

In September 1838, Shefford's magistrates complained that armed volunteers were engaged in a conspiracy to resist the orders of the commissioners' court by preventing bailiffs from serving warrants and preparing secretly to thwart arrests. The volunteers, who were effectively acting as a vigilante force, argued that the court had no authority under martial law and that they were exempt from the jurisdiction of the civil courts in any case. One volunteer, arrested for ignoring a court order, had been rescued by several others armed with rifles and bayonets. The local militia captain had refused to interfere on the grounds that he had no men under his command because volunteers were under the authority of other officers. In a subsequent dispatch, one of the Shefford Township magistrates forwarded affidavits describing the resistance of four more individuals to court orders. He claimed further that he could 'furnish proof' against a number of others who had declared publicly that they would resist the enforcement of such orders by force of arms, having been authorized to do so by their commanding officer, Lieutenant-Colonel Knowlton. Knowlton was criticized for encouraging this 'shameful spirit of resistance to the Civil laws which now disgraces so many in this county who have hereto sustained the character of loyal and peaceable subjects.' Finally, on 1 October, the commissioners' court reported that several volunteer officers were involved in the conspiracy and that secret meetings had been held to organize active resistance against arrests. The only solution, it argued, was to dispatch a regular force of sufficient strength to 'put down the combination at once.'[214]

Such actions on the part of 'loyalists' suggests that the defiance demonstrated by the Patriots was somewhat infectious. The Reverend Chapin reported with some relief, however, that Colonel Head had disposed of the affair in the December court martial 'far better than our fears.' Chapin's brief sense of optimism had, nevertheless, disappeared again by May 1839, when he wrote that his church in the village of Waterloo was 'breaking up, its members on whom I depended for support leaving the Province. The political disturbances have fallen on my society here with a heavy hand, & connected with our unbelief & unfaithfulness, ruined & dispersed us.'[215] Two years later Stanstead's Wesleyan Methodist minister attributed the decline in his own circuit's income to 'the removal of our most liberal supporters during the rebellion of 1838, and who did not return when peace was restored.'[216]

The Rebellions did not have the dramatic impact on the Eastern Townships that they did in the areas of armed conflict southeast and northwest of Montreal, but they exacted a price as far as the social cohesiveness and economic development of many local communities were concerned. Numerous families moved back to the United States, as did a number of community spokesmen who feared arrest, though the more prominent ones eventually returned. Men such as Marcus Child would adopt a more pragmatic political stance thereafter, and politics would centre around economic development more than constitutional issues at the dawn of the railway era as the region finally saw an opportunity to emerge from its economic isolation.

'These dreadful frontiers':
Post-Rebellion Conflict

Contributing to the public disillusionment with radical politics after the defeat of the Rebellion in November 1838 was the ongoing threat from south of the border. The presence of provincial troops who replaced the desertion-prone British regulars at Hemmingford, Odelltown, and Philipsburg failed to prevent gangs of Canadian exiles – many of whose homes had been torched by British or volunteer troops – from terrorizing those who were identified as loyalists.[217] And, while Vermonters' interest in the Rebellion had generally flagged by the summer of 1838, these gangs also included Americans; it is not clear whether they acted from political motivation or simply because they were outlaws. In short, the situation was similar to that in Upper Canada, where, according to G.M. Craig, the post-Rebellion border raids caused 'far more alarm, expense and bloodshed than the rebellion itself produced.'[218]

In December 1838, for example, John Gibson of Caldwell's Manor was severely wounded and his home burned down. The following February his neighbour, Abraham Vosburgh, suffered the same fate, in addition to losing his barn and livestock.[219] The cautious Vermont governor hesitated to interfere, claiming in early January that 'any attempt on my part to exercise a power ... not conferred on me, would only add to the excitement and increase the difficulties.'[220] A few days later, Lower Canada's governor and commanding officer, John Colborne, reported to the Colonial Office that armed Canadian refugees were planning to enter the province from Swanton and Alburg in order to raze Philipsburg and make scattered attacks west of the Richelieu. Brigadier-General Eustis, in command at Plattsburg, New York, had assured Colborne that there were no preparations to 'disturb the Province,' but he felt that the rebel leaders would likely try to keep up the excitement level 'and encourage the hopes of the disaffected that they will be able to obtain assistance from their friends in the United States.' To be on the safe side, Colborne had advanced a number of troops closer to the border in order to support the volunteers, should that prove necessary. A committee of the Executive Council also recommended in February the appointment of deputy commanding officers at Philipsburg and Frelighsburg.[221]

But the violent border raids continued, albeit on a limited scale, even though they now provoked negative reactions in the United States.[222] In February 1839, the Reverend James Reid reported from St Armand to the Anglican bishop:

Since the beginning of our Provincial troubles, our situation on these exposed frontiers has been very trying. This winter in particular is dreary, gloomy, full of fears and alarms. Our men are on guard on all the roads which lead to the States by night and day. The men are almost worn out with fatigue and exposure. Should this state of things continue long, I am afraid that more than the half of our lands will be untilled, unsowed and unplanted, for want of men to labour. The dire necessity of guarding the country from evil men requires all hands.

Reid then asked to be transferred 'from scenes of plunder and burning to some more peaceful shades,' far removed from 'these dreadful frontiers.'[223]

While Reid focused on the economic consequences of the raids, his Wesleyan Methodist counterpart, William Squire, stressed the moral and religious effects:

As the circuit embraces a large proportion of the most disturbed part of the frontier, we have been called to suffer the painful consequences of the rebellion by frequent alarms and invasions, mid-night burnings, and attempted assassinations. The mental excitement, the constant military occupation of our people, and the harassing nature of the duty, have had a most unfriendly influence upon their character and our work, too plainly evinced in their frequent backsliding and general apathy in respect of religion.[224]

The exact nature of the raids in the early months of 1839 is not known, for there are no surviving issues of the *Missiskoui Standard* from 25 September 1838 to 2 April 1839. On the latter date, however, the editorial – titled 'More Incendiarism' in large block capitals – described how the barn and shed of Captain Charles Miller had been burned to the ground with all their contents, including eight horses, seventeen cattle, and a large quantity of hay. Miller was unfortunate in that his St Armand West farm was close to the border, for it had also been seized by invaders in December 1837. The *Standard* demanded to know: '*How* long are the quiet and peaceable inhabitants on this frontier to be burned and plundered with impunity? If the American government will not take care of these villains, how long can it be supposed that our fellow subjects will submit to be robbed of their property & their lives, by gangs of pirates and freebooters, without visiting them with that retribution which they so justly merit.' In fact, two barns in Highgate, Vermont, were burned soon afterward, though the *Standard* suggested that it was the same gang that was responsible.[225]

Depredations also continued to the east, in Stanstead County, where Captain William Burroughs was visited after midnight on 25 June 1839 by approximately a dozen men seeking the rifles of the Barnston Volunteers. According to Burroughs, one of the men shouted from outside not to be rash: 'We have done up the business at Stanstead and we are going to do it up here.' But the raiders either lost courage or were not prepared to engage in bloodshed, for when Burroughs and his son stepped outside, each holding a gun, there was no one to be seen. Their barn was on fire, however, and while they were extinguishing the blaze a shot was fired at the house, narrowly missing Burroughs's wife. The next morning, Burroughs managed to capture one of the men who had become disoriented in the dark. While the prisoner was an American, Colonel Nickle reported that 'it appears that the majority of the party concerned consisted of the most profligate description of characters that disgraced this part of the country during the last winter, and who escaped justice by crossing the line.'[226]

These 'profligate characters' included a number of counterfeiters, and in December 1839 Sheriff W.L. Coffin was appointed to supervise an operation against the gang of forgers in Barnston and Barford. At his disposal were some men from Colonel Nickle's cavalry, as well as from Lieutenant-Colonel B.C.A. Gugy's rural mounted police force, plus several local men sworn in as special constables. They arrested six suspects from Barnston as well as two from Barford, and Nickle also had two of his volunteer troopers from Stanstead arrested on the same charges. Information gathered in the process led to the apprehension of a third Stanstead resident, in addition to four from Eaton, and, ironically, the two sons of Compton's Oliver Barker, the former magistrate who had been so zealous in pursuing the notorious counterfeiter Stephen Burroughs some thirty-five years earlier. None of these men were among those arrested as rebels in 1838, though warrants were issued against two Bachelders, a name associated (as we have seen) with the arrest of an alleged Patriot sympathizer in Barnston. After being confined to jail for four months, the prisoners were finally released because the American banks whose notes had been forged claimed that they did not have the funds to send an agent to act as a witness in Lower Canada.[227]

Colonel Nickle was finally removed from Stanstead in March 1840, by which time the homesick Patriot leaders in the United States were denouncing the border raids as 'individual private acts.'[228] There were 1,778 signatures on the address thanking Nickle for 'the protection of our Properties, our Families, and our Homes,'[229] but considerable tension had developed between his counterpart in Missisquoi, Lieutenant-Colonel Williams, and the volunteers of that county. In January 1839 a petition headed by the Reverend James Reid and Captain Kemp demanded Williams's removal because of his parsimonious and heavy-handed behaviour. In his own defence, Williams reported that 'I trust I am too much of soldier not to know the value of having men in spirits and fresh for their work.' While the volunteers claimed that their counterparts in other districts were receiving pay for doing nothing, Williams insisted that he could not 'lend myself to plunder,'[230] presumably meaning excessive charges to the government. Williams may also have become the target for local resentment against the restrictions on smuggling. He had reported in December 1838 that the local population had for many years been supplied with tea, tobacco, cotton, silks, and so on without paying duty, and that the interruption of trains with contraband goods by his border picquets was causing local unrest. He recommended the appointment of customs officers at Philipsburg and Frelighsburg, leaving 'the mounted Police' to act as supporters by forwarding confiscated items to the proper authorities rather than making seizures themselves.[231]

Lieutenant-Colonel Williams also asked to remain long enough to end the excitement and threats from the other side of the border, but relations with his men did not improve. The tory *Missisquoi Standard* claimed in early April that he had made himself very obnoxious to 'the great body of the people' and should be removed because the unanimity of feeling had quickly evaporated after his arrival.[232] Williams was evidently unconcerned with this lack of popularity for later in the month he ordered the volunteers to compensate for all loss or damage to military arms and accoutrements as well as buildings used as barracks.[233] The captains were to assume responsibility for these costs, but Henry Baker and Oren Kemp resigned their commissions in June, citing the ill-treatment that they and their companies had received from Williams the previous winter. Expressing regret at these resignations, Lieutenant-Colonel Robert Jones of the Missisquoi militia reported that the two men had faithfully discharged their duties during the Rebellions. He added that 'through their example much good has been effected, especially by Captain Kemp who is deservedly very popular in this county, and one of the most efficient officers of the Battalion.' Due to the local sense of grievance, Jones suggested, the standing order that the Lower Canadian militia muster on 29 June should be rescinded as far as Missisquoi was concerned.[234] Williams was finally replaced in October.[235]

Local notables may have been ready to denounce those who were perceived to be abusive of their authority, as in the case of Williams and the Felton clan, but they were not inclined to receive with open arms the radicals who had fled the region during the conflict. In May 1839 nine magistrates from Stanstead County complained that with the expiration of martial law in the St Francis District, 'several of the Refugees who had left this Province on account of political offences of a very agravated [sic] nature ... have lately returned to it, and are pursuing their usual avocations without molestation.' Pointing out that these men were confident that no jury would convict them 'in consequence of the present divided and irritated state of public feeling,' the magistrates asked the civil secretary how they could demonstrate to the public that the law 'cannot be violated without suffering in some degree from its penal enactments.'[236]

The response is unknown, but the following August, Edward Hale, as justice of the peace for Sherbrooke, sought advice from the attorney-general concerning three returned farmers who, fearing arrest, were offering to provide bail in case they should be brought to trial. Hale noted that, 'together with others in their immediate neighbourhood,' the three men 'have always supposed to be [sic] inimical to Her Majesty's Government, and to have entertained strong Radical opinions, and I have but little doubt that proof might be obtained of their having committed themselves in language or threats – at the same time nothing I believe of the nature of participating in open rebellion can be charged against them.'[237] The attorney-general advised, in reply, that it would be best 'to keep those suspicious characters "in terrorem" for some time longer as admitting them to Bail would make them feel too secure' and complicate possible future actions against them.[238] There is no evidence that any such actions took place against individuals returning from self-imposed exile, and political wounds appear to have healed relatively quickly in the region, but the post-Rebellion raids certainly made the border a more tangible and accepted dividing line. As the Colonel Williams case reveals, however, there was little inclination even in the most Loyalist corner of the region to defer to manifestations of British authority that were considered oppressive in any way.

Conclusion

When asked to submit a list of recommended names to be appointed militia officers in 1839, the acerbic Lieutenant-Colonel Paul Holland Knowlton of Brome replied that it would be difficult to find enough qualified gentlemen because that class upon this frontier consist of ... a few Loyal from principal, many who have come to the country for some years passed who are in nature and education perfectly hostile to British Institutions and who have many of them run away to escape punishment for their crimes or to evade paying their debts or because they could do better here than in the States – None of these have any gratitude for the protection they have enjoyed under this Government, and are notwithstanding abundant Loyal professions, daily plotting with sympathizers and Rebels.[239]

This assessment is somewhat ironic, given that – as we have seen – Knowlton had stood accused of encouraging his men to flout authority at least twice during the Rebellions; ten years later, he would be relieved of his own commission after signing a manifesto supporting annexation to the United States, as would Lieutenant-Colonel Robert Jones.[240] But the fact remains that neither of the twin pillars supporting Family Compact domination and imperial loyalty in Upper Canada was particularly effective in the Eastern Townships. Firstly, most of the region lacked a strong Loyalist tradition, and it had not been the focus of major American attacks during the War of 1812. Secondly, the restriction of patronage appointments to Loyalists and the British-born in a region largely peopled by post-Loyalists meant that, in contrast to Upper Canada, the government had not established strong ties with many of the notables in the local communities.[241]

But if Knowlton's assessment was accurate, what prevented the Eastern Townships from joining the Rebellions? Fear of minority status in a French-Canadian nationalist republic was clearly a very important factor. Also, there was a distinct difference between the political cultures on either side of the forty-fifth parallel. One might find 'the same people, having the same native energy, the same origin, and speaking the same language,' as William Lyon Mackenzie said of Upper Canada and the neighbouring states,[242] but Vermont was characterized during the 1830s by anti-Masonic politics, mob violence, and waves of religious mania, as well as very active temperance and anti-slavery movements.[243] Elements of a civic culture certainly had developed in the Eastern Townships, as had a strong political reform movement, but there was little evidence of the social tumult that was taking place south of the border.

One reason, presumably, was that British missionaries had succeeded in converting the majority of the American-origin inhabitants to the Church of England or the Wesleyan Methodist Society. It was no accident that the most radical communities politically, such as Barnston, Georgeville, and Potton, were also centres of religious sectarianism.[244] Due to their proselytizing efforts, the Universalists and other once-radical sects began making inroads into the Eastern Townships during the early 1830s, but the political unrest and popular anxieties leading up to the Rebellions caused deep divisions within the religious denominations that had originated in the United States.[245] The Anglican clergy, on the other hand, could take advantage of the economic and political crisis by exploiting the psychological need for stability and security. The Reverend James Reid transferred his journalistic efforts from denunciations of the reformers to a less politically partisan series of articles on the family,[246] but he also interpreted the conflict as God's punishment, declaring in November 1837 that 'War, Pestilence, and Famine, have always been viewed as the scourges of God's wrath on a guilty people.' Reid declared that those who had turned to religion as a result of the cholera epidemic had since 'forgot their prayers, and their solemn vows of amendment, together with their fears,' and they had also failed to be suitably grateful to God for the bountiful harvest of the past year.[247] When invasion from the south began to appear likely, however, Reid assured his readers that God 'may for our sins afflict us, but he will not give us over to our enemies. In such a defence as ours, Moses himself, were he alive, would hold up his aged hands on the mount in prayer.'[248]

The fear of an invasion from Vermont undoubtedly stirred memories of the War of 1812, and Reid's comment about the harvest points to an immediate and concrete explanation for the limited nature of unrest in the Eastern Townships during the Rebellions. The crop failures of 1835 and 1836 and the widespread financial crisis of 1837–8 aside, the Eastern Townships presented a sharp contrast to Vermont insofar as the economy north of the border was improving and its population growing after years of stagnation. The border townships now boasted some of the most productive farms in the province, and Sherbrooke was beginning to industrialize as the prospect of railway construction promised much better access to external markets.[249] The economic transition, stimulated by the large influx of capital from the British American Land Company, would admittedly benefit the local bourgeoisie much more than the small farmers whose sons would have to pay higher prices for land. The program of the more radical Patriots might, therefore, have had considerable appeal to these farmers if their opponents had not been able to capitalize so effectively on Papineau's policy concerning the expansion of seigneurial tenure.[250]

Without the movement towards French-Canadian insurrection,

the rural population of the Eastern Townships might well have remained quite radical in political orientation, and many clearly did so, but the majority were essentially frightened into supporting the colonial administration. The Rebellions also intensified the region's conservative shift by stimulating the exodus of those who remained republican-minded, by fostering a defensive reaction against the terrifying night raids from across the border, and by weakening the American religious sects. Dunham's Anglican minister, Charles Cotton, reported in 1839 that one benefit of the continuing military presence was that it had stopped 'the influence of Universalist itinerant Teachers.'[251] There would be a general religious revival fostered by the economic gloom of the early 1840s, but the short-lived millenarian hysteria of the Millerite movement would effectively wipe out the burgeoning Free Will Baptist sect, among others.[252] Knowlton was clearly exaggerating, therefore, when he hinted at plots with rebels as late as the summer of 1839. Loyalties in the Eastern Townships might have remained essentially local or regional in nature, but the region was not willing to gamble its economic and political future on the advent of an independent nationalist republic. That did not mean, however, that it was opposed to fundamental modernizing reforms.

Many Canadian historians have argued that the Rebellions simply delayed the inexorable move towards Responsible Government, finally achieved in 1848.[253] From a different perspective, however, Allan Greer argues that they were 'a turning-point of the first magnitude,' and Michael Cross claims that they were a 'necessary failure' because they cleared the way for the bourgeois hegemony that had been delayed by political polarization.[254] The fact is that the Rebellions set the stage for Durham's Report, which in turn resulted in a more powerful role for the executive as well as fundamental state-forming legislation with the creation of the modern tax-supported school and municipal systems. In short, power became both more centralized and decentralized as it shifted from the popularly elected Legislative Assembly to the Executive Council, on the one hand, and to school and municipal councils, on the other. That this pragmatic model for promoting economic development was not the one envisioned by the Patriots, who instead wished to strengthen the powers of the Legislative Assembly and the liberal professional class, tends to be forgotten by the Quebec nationalist historians who associate the goal of the Rebellions with the drive to capitalism and 'modernity.'[255] In 1832, for example, the municipal bill introduced in the Assembly by Sherbrooke's Ebenezer Peck was defeated by the

Patriot majority, which claimed that it was not compatible with the traditional grand-voyer system.[256]

The constitutional associations of the Eastern Townships did more than pass motions expressing loyalty to Great Britain and hostility to the 92 Resolutions. For example, the two branches of the Sherbrooke Constitutional Association petitioned Lord Gosford in March 1836 for a division of the county into two constituencies, the establishment of a permanent judicial district, registry offices, a railway subsidy, and so on.[257] While historians such as Laporte state that the constitutionalists were imbued with a profoundly anti-democratic ideology,[258] the most prominent members of the Eastern Townships bourgeoisie took advantage of the atmosphere of crisis, as well as the Durham Commission, to demand reforms that would distribute more political power to the local level. Thus, a meeting of the residents of the St Francis District in 1838, chaired by Lieutenant-Colonel William Morris with Samuel Brooks as secretary, demanded that internal communications 'should be under the charge of local commissioners elected periodically by the proprietors, and that absentee as well as resident landholders should be compelled to contribute to the support of those roads.' Even a large proprietor such as Lieutenant-Colonel Knowlton spoke out in favour of abolishing the ineffective grand-voyer system and giving each township the power 'to alter and execute everything pertaining to highways.' His report to Lord Durham added that the people of the Eastern Townships 'are perfectly competent to manage their own affairs, and all road business might be left to them with great advantage.'[259]

In short, in the Eastern Townships – as in the rest of Lower Canada and in Upper Canada – the Rebellions of 1837–8 marked the end of ideological polarization between the toryism of the landed and office-holding elite, on one hand, and the radical agrarianism of much of the rest of the population, on the other. The very threat of rebellion was enough for the Sherbrooke clique of British-born officials to be ousted by the American-born capitalist bourgeoisie, and the politics of the 1840s would be the politics of economic development, with Eastern Townships votes swinging behind whichever party promised the highest subsidies to the region.[260] While the Act of Union would strengthen the sense of being Canadian, the growing political influence of Lower Canada's French-speaking population, combined with the onset of French-Canadian settlement in the region, would also stimulate the English-Canadian exodus. The ultimate result was that the Eastern Townships soon became an integral part of the province of Quebec, culturally as well as economically.

Perhaps none of this matters in the context of the long-standing historical debates about the underlying causes and nature of the Lower Canadian Rebellions. The Eastern Townships did not, after all, play a particularly important role in these events. But the same can be said of most of the province, and a recent detailed study argues that what historians have assumed to be a national movement was actually the sum of various local tensions.[261] Certainly, the Patriot leaders were quite aware of the strategic position occupied by a largely American-origin population living close to the New England border, though Papineau mishandled the situation. Finally, by adding to the larger picture the story of a region whose English-speaking population of more than 40,000 nearly equalled the total population of Montreal, we have undermined Lord Durham's argument that tensions between the two major linguistic groups lay at the root of the Lower Canadian Rebellions.[262] It appears, rather, that class conflict and colonialism were the fundamental issues, even though nationalism took over as the two sides became increasingly intransigent. One can only speculate on the path history would have taken had the fear of intensifying French-Canadian nationalism not driven much of the Eastern Townships into the government camp.

Contrary to the assumption of many historians, not all English-speaking Lower Canadians were members of, or identified with, the economic and social elite.[263] The majority in the largely American-settled Eastern Townships favoured constitutional reforms and resented the selective distribution of patronage to a small British elite, as their support for Reform politicians in the early 1830s demonstrates. Durham's thesis also fails to account for the anxiety of the conservative spokesmen as late as 1837 about the loyalty of the Eastern Townships, or the imprisonment or exile of locally prominent political figures such as Ephraim Knight, Marcus Child, Taylor Wadleigh, Robert Layfield, and several newspaper publishers. Uncompromising radicals may have been relatively few in number, but a good many families did move to the United States. The foregoing examination of the Eastern Townships during the Rebellion era therefore supports the argument by Bernier and Salée that these uprisings were essentially the culmination of a political struggle for greater autonomy in which the colonial forces were British and the majority of the colonized – but by no means all – were French Canadians.[264] In short, the incorporation of the Eastern Townships into the story situates the Lower Canadian reform movement more firmly where it belongs, within the broader historical framework of the transition towards increased political autonomy and capitalist expansion in North America. Nationalist historians such as Gérard Bouchard, who see the defeat of the Rebellions as the key event in perpetuating colonialism in Quebec,[265] might consider the paradoxical role that Papineau's rather conservative and intransigent ethnic nationalism played in alienating what might have been a powerful source of support. It is not difficult to imagine that if outbreaks of civil unrest had taken place in just a few border communities, Americans would have been drawn into the conflict with very dramatic consequences. Whether French Canada would have thrived, or even survived, within the political orbit of the United States is, of course, another question.

Afterword

On 27 June 1797, Moses Elkins of Peacham in central Vermont set out for the Missisquoi Valley with his family, two hired men, and a cart drawn by two oxen . He had heard favourable accounts of this northern frontier from his brother Josiah, who had been trading with those Abenakis who were still living at Lake Memphremagog. Ten days later, having been joined by two other prospective settlers who helped cut the way through dense woods from the last Vermont settlements, Elkins became a squatter in what would become known the following October as Potton Township. Elkins's name does not appear among the seventy-seven associates granted patents in 1803,[1] but he was a militia captain during the War of 1812, when, as we have seen, he was accused of harbouring deserters. Isolated by some of the highest mountains in the Eastern Townships, Potton continued to have closer links with Troy, Vermont, than with the rest of Lower Canada. In contrast to the region as a whole, most settlers in this thinly settled area were either Baptists or members of the radical Protestant Methodist sect.[2] Yet, during the Rebellion of 1838, as we have again seen, a member of a raiding party from Troy was shot and killed in the house of Elkins's neighbouring brother, Salmon. Moses would pay the price in the spring of 1840, two months after the British military commander had been removed from the border. Unseen arsonists burned his house, four barns, and two sheds, as well as livestock and other contents to a reported value of £765. As of 1846, the government had still not given Elkins's widow any compensation, based on the argument that the attack had taken place too long after the Rebellions had ended.[3]

107

Historians have generally assumed that the Eastern Townships was little affected by either the War of 1812 or the Rebellions of 1837–8,[4] but settlers such as Moses Elkins would obviously not have agreed. While he was closer to the front line than most residents of the region, the sense of vulnerability to attack from the powerful neighbour south of the border would have been widely shared. It was only natural, then, that these settlers would begin to perceive themselves as other than American, as reflected in the trajectory of Elkins's own story. From being a squatter who probably had little awareness of the international boundary and whose loyalty, even as a captain of militia, was questioned during the War of 1812, he became firmly linked to the loyalist cause through his family's resistance to invaders from Vermont in 1838.

This act of resistance was, perhaps, an instinctive response to an external threat, and one should not underestimate the persistent sense of localism, for it would strongly manifest itself with the reaction to school and municipal reforms in the 1840s. But the people of Potton, and of the region as a whole, had been forced to choose sides in the broader political struggle. Upper Canadians marked themselves as distinct from Americans by virtue of their Loyalist origins, the myth of their resistance to American invasion during the War of 1812, and the postwar British influx, none of which was experienced to the same degree in the Eastern Townships. Why, then, despite obvious divisions in the region did the people of the Eastern Townships appear to be more uniformly 'loyal' than their Upper Canadian counterparts?

One should not ignore the closer proximity of British troops to the Eastern Townships, the repression of the reform-oriented press, or the vulnerability felt by Anglo-Protestants as French-Canadian nationalism intensified. These factors, and the improved economic conditions of 1837, certainly go a long way to explaining the sudden dampening of radical enthusiasm in the region upon the outbreak of rebellion. But there were also longer-term forces at play. The War of 1812, distant as most of the fighting may have been, represented the first significant step toward transforming the borderland on either side of the forty-fifth parallel into a distinctively bordered land. This process was subsequently furthered by the divergent trajectories of religious culture in northern New England and the Eastern Townships. Despite their American origins, the Masonic Lodge and the temperance societies became independent institutions north of the border. The Rebellions themselves, followed by several years of incendiary raids from south of the border, would contribute to a conservative reaction. The

Eastern Townships did experience a brief surge of annexationist sentiment in 1849–50, but largely as a protest movement against the indemnification of French Canadians whose property had been destroyed during the Rebellions and, more importantly, as a means of gaining access to the protected American market.[5] Like the Millerite hysteria that had preceded it earlier in the decade, the annexationist movement would die quickly in the Eastern Townships, for the political and social values of the region were becoming less American and more British in character as the population adopted the ever-elusive identity of English Canadians.

Appendix A: Volunteer Corps in the Eastern Townships as of 29 December 1837

Missisquoi Borderers, Dec. 14
    Raised for general service and paid at 1s. per diem, with a ration.
    50 rank and file, Captain Botham
First Company of St Armand Loyal Volunteers, Dec. 14
    Unpaid, 64 rank and file, Captain Thomas
Second Company of St Armand Loyal Volunteers, Dec. 14
    Unpaid, 78 rank and file, Captain Kemp
Third Company of St Armand Loyal Volunteers, Dec. 14
    Unpaid, 81 rank and file, Captain Baker
Frelighsburg Light Infantry, Dec. 29
    50 men at 1s. per diem and a ration, one captain and two
    subalterns
St Armand East Loyal Volunteers, Dec. 14
    Unpaid, 200 rank and file
St Armand West Loyal Volunteers, Dec. 14
    Unpaid, 250 rank and file, Colonel the Hon. Robert Jones
Missisquoi Loyal Volunteers, Dec. 14
    Unpaid, 60 rank and file, Captain May
Shefford Loyal Volunteers, Dec. 1
    Unpaid, 400 rank and file, and 50 cavalry, Colonel Knowlton
Granby Loyal Volunteers, Dec. 13
    Unpaid, 50 rank and file, Captain Lyman
Eastern Townships Loyal Volunteers, Dec. 13
    To be paid as soldiers, 600 rank and file
    To be raised in the Townships to defend the frontier and act in
    rear of the Seigniories, Colonel Heriot

Lennoxville Queen's Mounted Rangers, Dec. 21
   Unpaid, one troop light cavalry, Captain Austin

Source: AN, RG4 A1, vol. 528, 168–9, Volunteer corps which have
been authorized to be raised in the Lower Province, Head Quarters,
Montreal, 29 December 1837.

Appendix B: List of Prisoners Confined in the Common Gaol at Sherbrooke Charged with Political Offences, 21 December 1838

Names	When Committed	Offence	By Whom Committed
Roswell Bates	13 Nov. 1838	treasonable pract's	Morris & Hale, JPs
Elias Lee, Jr	″	″	Pomroy, Smith, Pierce, JPs
Leon. Channel	″	″	″
John C. Tuck	″	″	″
John Sanborn	22 Nov. 1838	″	Colonel Nickle
Andrew Hoeg	″	″	″
Jared* Blanchard	″	″	″
George W. Nouns*	″	″	″
Horatio Bullard	24 Nov. 1838	treason	Colonel Nickle and JPs
John Berry*	″	″	″
Charles Charpentier	28 Nov. 1838	treasonable pract's	Lt Col. W. Morris
Jacob L. Kent	2 Dec. 1838	″	″
Blandel* Kent	″	″	″
Jones* Kent	″	″	″
John Lissod	″	″	″
Jacob Bacheldor*	15 Dec. 1838	accused of perjury	Pomroy & Pierce, JPs
Barack* Burpee	″	treasonable pract's	″

Chas. Whitcher, Sheriff, 21 Dec. 1838

Source: NA, RG4 A1, vol. 562, 19.

Note: The names Robert McCrellis and James Dinsunheath, both arrested on 6 December, are added to the above list in 'Return of the Names ... of

the several Persons arrested in the District of St Francis, and placed in confinement in the Common Gaol, on a charge of treason or treasonable practices.' Finally, Hiram F. Blanchard, Taylor Wadleigh, and Patrick Barry, trader,
were jailed in Montreal, though the latter was discharged only a day later.
Journals of the Legislative Assembly, 23 April 1839.

* 'Jared' is crossed out and replaced with 'Gerard' in Sheriff Whitcher's hand-
writing; 'Nouns' should be spelled 'Nownes'; 'Berry' should be 'Barry'; 'Blandel'
should be 'Blaisdell'; 'Jones' should be 'Jonas'; 'Bacheldor' was normally
spelled 'Bachelder'; and 'Barack' should be 'Baruch.' I am grateful to John
Scott for providing the *JLA* reference and the correct spellings of these
names, most of whose identities he has been able to establish.

Notes

Preface

1 See Louis-Georges Harvey, *Le printemps de l'Amérique française: Américanité, anticolonialisme et républicanisme dans le discours politique québécois, 1805–1837* (Montreal, 2004); and Jocelyn Létourneau, 'Going from Heirs to Founders: The Great Collective Narrative of Quebecers as Revisited by Gérard Bouchard,' in *A History for the Future: Rewriting Memory and Identity in Quebec* (Montreal and Kingston, 2004). In his recent popular book on the Canadian–American border, James Laxer essentially ignores the forty-fifth parallel between Quebec and Vermont as well as New York. As a result, his supposedly national study misses the opportunity to inform us about the relationship between French Canadians and Americans living close to the border. James Laxer, *The Border: Canada, the U.S. and Dispatches from the 49th Parallel* (Toronto, 2001), 54–7.

2 Peter Sahlins, *Boundaries: The Making of France and Spain in the Pyrenees* (Berkeley, 1989), 9.

3 J.I. Little, *Borderland Religion: The Emergence of an English-Canadian Identity, 1792–1852* (Toronto, 2005).

4 For one of the first articulations of the concept, see J.M.S. Careless, '"Limited Identities" in Canada,' *Canadian Historical Review* 50 (1969): 1–10. For a critique see Michael Bliss, 'Privatizing the Mind: The Sundering of Canadian History, the Sundering of Canada,' *Journal of Canadian Studies* 26, no. 4 (1991–2): 5–17.

5 For an appreciation of the work done by Marion Phelps, see Louise Abbott, 'Marion Phelps: A Guardian of Townships History,' *Journal of Eastern Townships Studies* 16 (2000): 5–16.

Introduction

1 Jean-Pierre Kesteman, Peter Southam, and Diane Saint-Pierre, *Histoire des Cantons de l'Est* (Sainte-Foy, 1998), 60–75; Colin G. Calloway, *The Western Abenakis of Vermont, 1600–1800: War, Migration, and the Survival of an Indian People* (Norman and London, 1990), 94–5; and Gordon M. Day, *The Identity of the St Francis Indians* (Ottawa, 1981).

2 The terms boundary and border will be used interchangeably in this study, though the former generally has a more precise meaning because it refers to lines on maps or the dividing lines between different peoples and cultures. Michiel Baud and Willem Van Schendel, 'Toward a Comparative History of Borderlands,' *Journal of World History* 8, no. 2 (1997): 213.

3 Also moving north to Odanak were the Abenakis who had taken refuge at Lake Memphremagog during the American Revolution. Calloway, *Western Abenakis*, chap. 12.

4 Alan Taylor, '"The Late Loyalists": Northern Reflections of the Early American Republic,' *Journal of the Early Republic* 27, no. 1 (2007): 5.

5 Gerald F. McGuigan, 'Land Policy and Land Disposal under Tenure of Free and Common Socage, Quebec and Lower Canada' (PhD dissertation, Laval University, 1962), vol. 1: 96–8, 402, 406; vol. 3: 252.

6 F. Murray Greenwood, *Legacies of Fear: Law and Politics in Quebec in the Era of the French Revolution* (Toronto, 1993).

7 Alan Taylor, *The Divided Ground: Indians, Settlers, and the Northern Borderland of the American Revolution* (New York, 2006), 9.

8 The foregoing summary of early Eastern Townships history is taken largely from Jimmy W. Manson, *The Loyal Americans of New England and New York: Founders of the Townships of Lower Canada* ([Knowlton, QC], 2001), 7–36; and J.I. Little, *Ethno-Cultural Transition and Regional Identity in the Eastern Townships of Quebec* (Ottawa, 1989), 5–8. For more details, see Gerald F. McGuigan, 'Administration of Land Policy and the Growth of Corporate Economic Organization in Lower Canada, 1791–1809,' Canadian Historical Association, *Report*, 1963, 65–73; A.J.H. Richardson, 'Captain John Savage and the Settlement of Shefford: From 1740 to 1793,' *Journal of Eastern Townships Studies* 24 (2004): 5–30; 'Captain John Savage and the Settlement of Shefford: From 1792 to 1801,' *Journal of Eastern Townships Studies* 25 (2004): 45–78; Kesteman et al., *Histoire des Cantons de l'Est*, 83–92, 97–9, 108–11, 119–21; Mario Gendron et al., *Histoire du Piémont-des-Appalaches: La Montérégie* ([Sainte-Foy], 1999), 43–52, 63–4, 106–7; and J.I. Little, 'Gale, Samuel,' *Dictionary of Canadian Biography*, vol. 6: 269–70.

9 Taylor, '"Late Loyalists,"' 5–8, 19, 26–9.
10 Little, *Ethno-Cultural Transition*, 8–27.
11 Jane Errington, however, stresses the strong links between early Upper Canada and the United States. *The Lion, the Eagle, and Upper Canada: A Developing Canadian Ideology* (Kingston and Montreal, 1987), chap. 3.
12 Donald Fyson, *Magistrates, Police and People: Everyday Criminal Justice in Quebec and Lower Canada, 1764–1837* (Toronto, 2006), 58; J.I. Little, *State and Society in Transition: The Politics of Institutional Reform in the Eastern Townships, 1838–1852* (Montreal and Kingston, 1997), 48–9.
13 J.I. Little, *Borderland Religion: The Emergence of an English-Canadian Identity, 1792–1852* (Toronto, 2004), 13.
14 Little, *State and Society*, 50–1.
15 See the useful discussion of the contrasting Canadian and American approaches to history in Donald Worster, 'Two Faces West: The Development Myth in Canada and the United States,' in Carol Higham and Robert Thacker, eds, *One West, Two Myths* (Calgary, 2004). Strongly influenced by Turner, but placing more emphasis on the lack of markets, is Cole Harris's simplification thesis. See, for example, R.C. Harris, 'The Historical Geography of North American Regions,' *American Behavioral Scientist* 22, no. 1 (1978): 115–30.
16 See David M. Ludlum, *Social Ferment in Vermont* (New York, 1966), 17; Stephen Marini, *Radical Sects of Revolutionary New England* (Cambridge, MA, 1982), 5–6; Randolph A. Roth, *The Democratic Dilemma: Religion, Reform, and the Social Order in the Connecticut River Valley of Vermont, 1791–1850* (Cambridge, MA, 1987), 1–2, 12.
17 See Jere R. Daniell, *Experiment in Republicanism: New Hampshire Politics and the American Revolution, 1741–1794* (Cambridge, MA, 1970); and Alan Taylor, *Liberty Men and Great Proprietors: The Revolutionary Settlement on the Maine Frontier, 1760–1820* (Chapel Hill, NC, 1990).
18 See Little, *State and Society*, chaps 6–7, and *Borderland Religion*, chaps 7–10.
19 L. McKinsey and V. Konrad, *Borderlands Reflections: The United States and Canada* (Orono, ME, 1989), 4. They note, however, that some scholars feel that 'the essence of the borderlands lies in the working out of tension between two dissimilar cultures' (27).
20 Baud and Van Schendel, 'Toward a Comparative History,' 225. Most detailed studies of the Canadian–American borderland have focused on the impact of the boundary on the Native population. See, for example, Taylor, *The Divided Ground*; Beth LaDow, *The Medicine Line: Life*

and Death on North American Borderland (New York and London, 2001); and Sheila McManus, *The Line Which Separates: Race, Gender, and the Making of the Alberta–Montana Borderlands* (Edmonton, 2005).

21 Evidence of an increasingly self-conscious Canadian identity in the post-Rebellion era can be found in Andrew C. Holman, 'The Fourth of July in Eastern Canada: Negotiating the Identity of the Anglo-American Borderlands, 1837–1870' (unpublished paper presented to the annual meeting of the Canadian Historical Association, 2001).

22 Jeremy Adelman and Stephen Aron, 'From Borderlands to Borders: Empires, Nation-States, and the Peoples in Between in North American History,' *American Historical Review* 104 (1999): 814–41. The phrase is from Samuel Truett and Elliott Young, 'Making Transnational History: Nations, Regions, and Borderlands,' in Samuel Truett and Elliott Young, eds, *Continental Crossroads: Remapping U.S.–Mexico Borderlands History* (Durham and London, 2004), 23.

23 Baud and Van Schendel, 'Toward a Comparative History,' 227; J.I. Little, 'American Sinner / Canadian Saint? The Further Adventures of the Notorious Stephen Burroughs, 1799–1840,' *Journal of the Early Republic* 27 (Summer 2007): 203-31; and Little, *State and Society,* 50, 52, 55–7, 67, 70, 76.

24 Peter Sahlins, *Boundaries: The Making of France and Spain in the Pyrenees* (Berkeley, 1989), 8.

25 Benjamin Johnson, 'Problems and Prospects in North American Borderlands History,' *History Compass* 4, no. 1 (2006): 189. On this theme, see also Elizabeth Jameson, 'Dancing on the Rim, Tiptoeing through Minefields: Challenges and Promises of Borderlands,' *Pacific Historical Review* 75, no. 1 (2006): 5, 21–2.

26 See Little, *State and Society,* 101–17.

27 Errington, *The Lion,* 15. While Errington (18–19) still stresses the Upper Canadian pioneers' links with the outside world, early Eastern Townships settlers were more cut off from the colonial centres and therefore the press and postal system.

28 Jane Errington makes a somewhat similar point about the impact of the war on the Kingston area. See her 'Friends and Foes: The Kingston Elite and the War of 1812 – A Case Study in Ambivalence,' *Journal of Canadian Studies* 20, no. 1 (1985): 76–7.

29 Baud and Van Schendel, 'Toward a Comparative History,' 241.

30 Elizabeth Jameson and Jeremy Mouat, 'Telling Differences: The Forty-Ninth Parallel and Historiographies of the West and Nation,' *Pacific Historical Review* 75 (2006): 189.

31 Nancy Christie, 'Introduction: Theorizing a Colonial Past: Canada as a Society of British Settlement,' in Nancy Christie, ed., *Transatlantic Subjects: Ideas, Institutions, and Social Experience in Post-Revolutionary British North America* (Montreal and Kingston, 2008). For a similar perspective, see P.A. Buckner, 'The Borderlands Concept: A Critical Appraisal,' in Stephen Hornsby, Victor Konrad, and James J. Herlan, eds, *The Northeastern Borderlands: Four Centuries of Interaction* (Orono and Fredericton, 1989). For an example of how localism could subvert reform legislation, see J.I. Little, 'School Reform and Community Control in the 1840s: A Case Study from the Eastern Townships,' *Historical Studies in Education* 9 (1997): 153–64.

32 Randy William Widdis, 'Borders, Borderlands and Canadian Identity: A Canadian Perspective,' *International Journal of Canadian Studies* 15 (Spring 1997): 61.

33 See Benedict Anderson, *Imagined Communities: Reflections on the Origin and Spread of Nationalism* (London, 1983).

The War of 1812

1 See H.N. Muller III, 'A "Traitorous and Diabolical Traffic": The Commerce of the Champlain–Richelieu Corridor during the War of 1812,' *Vermont History* 44 (1976): 78–96. (The smuggling corridor was wider than Muller's title suggests.)

2 Allan S. Everest, *The War of 1812 in the Champlain Valley* ([Syracuse], 1981) does not even include 'Eastern Townships' in its index. Two brief accounts of war in the region are the unpublished and undated paper by J.A.H. Richardson, 'The War of 1812,' located in the archives of the Brome County Historical Society [hereafter BCHS], but with most of the footnotes missing; and George H. Montgomery, *Missisquoi Bay (Philipsburg, Que.)* (Granby, QC, 1950), chap. 12. Useful bits of information can also be found in the unfinished and undated manuscript by Walter N. Beattie, 'Stanstead's Historical Traditions, Their Ancestors, Their Firsts, Their Struggles and Their Politics,' located in the BCHS archives.

3 S.F. Wise, 'The War of 1812 in Popular History,' in *God's Peculiar Peoples: Essays on Political Culture in Nineteenth-Century Canada* (Ottawa, 1993), 153.

4 S.F. Wise, 'Upper Canada and the Conservative Tradition,' in *Profiles of a Province: Studies in the History of Ontario* (Toronto, 1967). This interpretation is questioned in George Sheppard, *Plunder, Profit, and Paroles: A Social History of the War of 1812 in Upper Canada* (Montreal and Kingston, 1994), 8–9.

5 See Jane Errington, *The Lion, the Eagle, and Upper Canada: A Developing Colonial Ideology* (Montreal and Kingston, 1987), 22–3.

6 See J.I. Little, *Ethno-Cultural Transition and Regional Identity in the Eastern Townships of Quebec* (Ottawa, 1989), 3–8.

7 Fernand Ouellet, 'Officiers de milice et structure sociale au Québec (1660–1815),' *Histoire sociale / Social History* 12 (1979): 51–2; Christian Dessureault and Roch Legault, 'Évolution organisationelle et sociale de la milice sédentaire canadienne: le cas du bataillon de Saint-Hyacinthe, 1808–1830,' *Journal of the Canadian Historical Association*, n.s., no. 8 (1997): 41–2; Sean Mills, 'French Canadians and the Beginning of the War of 1812: Revisiting the Lachine Riot,' *Histoire sociale / Social History* 38 (2005): 44.

8 National Archives of Canada [hereafter NA], MG23, G3, 13, pp. 178–81, Henry Cull's Militia Record Book, Organization in 1805 of Three Battalions of Militia. Township boundaries were not always convenient for militia purposes. As of 1813, the thinly settled eastern part of Farnham Township was separated from the local militia company and the Sixth Battalion so that its men could drill with Dunham if they lived south of Beaver Meadow Brook and with Shefford if they lived north of it. NA, MG8, F13, IX, Township Papers, Farnham, Order, 28 Jan. 1813.

9 According to the local historian B.F. Hubbard, the three Stanstead Township companies were organized in 1803, one Barnston company in 1805, and one Hatley company in 1807. He claims that by 1812 there were seven companies in Stanstead, four in Hatley, and three in Barnston. B.F Hubbard, *Forests and Clearings; the History of Stanstead County, Province of Quebec* (Montreal, 1874), 12.

10 NA, MG23, G3, 13, p. 261, Henry Cull to Adjutant-General, Hatley, 6 July 1813; p. 262, Henry Cull to Sir John Johnson, Hatley [July 1813].

11 Dessureault and Legault, 'Évolution organisationelle,' 48. Reflecting the urban character of much of the province's English-speaking population, however, 65 per cent of Lower Canada's English-speaking militia officers during the War of 1812 were merchants and 16 per cent were professionals. Ouellet, 'Officiers de milice,' 58. On the failure of the government to establish a more professional militia commanded by British officers, see Roch Legault, 'L'Organisation militaire sous le régime Britannique et le rôle assigné à la gentilhommerie canadienne (1760–1815),' *Revue d'histoire de l'Amérique française* 45 (1991): 245–7.

12 Marie-Paule LaBrèque, 'Pennoyer, Jesse,' *Dictionary of Canadian Biography* [hereafter *DCB*], vol. 6, 574–6; NA, RG9, 1A1, vol. 5, p. 1321, J. Pennoyer to F. Vassal de Monviel, Compton, 30 June 1812.

13 Andrée Désilets, 'Cull, Henry,' *DCB*, vol. 6, 174; Hubbard, *Forests and Clearings*, 77–8; Jean-Pierre Kesteman, Peter Southam, and Diane Saint-Pierre, *Histoire des Cantons de l'Est* (Sainte-Foy, QC, 1998), 91; NA, RG4 A1, Civil Secretary's Correspondence (Incoming), vol. 134, 42813–15, Petition of Henry Cull to Sir George Prevost, Hatley, 29 Jan. 1814.

14 NA, MG23, G3, 13, p. 276, H.C., Lt Col., to Mr Secretary Brenton, Hatley, 5 April 1814.

15 NA, RG4, A1, vol. 126, 40251, H.W. Ryland to E.B. Brenton, Quebec, 14 Nov. 1812.

16 NA, Pennoyer Papers, MG24, I11, p. 148, J. Pennoyer to James Woolrich, Compton, 5 July 1813.

17 NA, MG24, I11, p. 149, J. Pennoyer to Ezekiel Hart, Compton, 27 Nov. 1813.

18 NA, MG23, G3, 13, p. 165, Henry Cull to Captain Thomas Chaddock, Hatley, 8 Sept. 1807; p. 168, Cull to Captain Bishop, Hatley, 8 Sept. 1807; p. 187, Circular, General Order, Adjutant-General's Office, Quebec, 5 Dec. 1808; NA, RG4, A1, vol. 117, 37392, Captain Jacob Glen to Sir George Prevost, Chambly, 22 Jan. 1812.

19 NA, MG23, G3, 13, pp. 171–2, Henry Cull to Sir John Johnson, Hatley, 28 Sept. 1807.

20 NA, MG23, G3, 13, pp. 172–3, Henry Cull to Captain Glen, Hatley, 13 Feb. 1808. On the relationship between authority and uniform, see Brian Young, 'The Volunteer Militia in Lower Canada, 1837–50,' in Tamara Myers et al., eds, *Power, Place and Identity: Historical Studies of Social and Legal Regulation in Quebec* (Montreal, 1998), 49–50.

21 NA, MG23, G3, 13, p. 185, Henry Cull to Sir John Johnson, Stanstead, 15 Aug. 1808.

22 NA, MG23, G3, 13, p. 217, Report of Henry Cull, Hatley, 10 June 1812.

23 NA, MG23, G3, 13, p. 186, Field Return of the the 3rd Battalion, Stanstead, 15 Aug. 1808. Cull later deducted the names of several young men under the age of eighteen 'who had acknowledged themselves man enough to appear at the *General Review* (which you probably noticed).' NA, MG23, G3, 13, p. 196, Henry Cull to Captain Jacob Glen, Hatley, 30 Dec. 1809.

24 NA, MG23, G3, 13, p. 184, Henry Cull to Sir John Johnson, Stanstead, 15 Aug. 1808; p. 189, Circular from Henry Cull, Hatley, 6 Jan. 1809.

25 Hovey moved from Vermont to Hatley in 1793, and the land grant was made in 1803. Hubbard claims, however, that an amicable division of the 23,000 acres was made, 'and all parties were satisfied.' Hubbard, *Forests and Clearings*, 67–8, 77. See also Mrs C.M. Day, *History of the Eastern Townships* (Montreal, 1869), 447–8.

26 NA, MG23, G3, 13. p. 196, Henry Cull to Captain Jacob Glen, Hatley, 30 Dec. 1809.
27 NA, MG23, G3, 13, p. 204, Henry Cull to Captain Glen, Hatley, 27 Sept. 1810.
28 NA, MG23, G3, 13, p. 205, Henry Cull to Major Kilborn, Hatley, 28 Sept. 1810.
29 NA, MG23, G3, 13, p. 209, Henry Cull to Colonel John Johnson, Hatley, 14 Oct. 1811.
30 NA, MG23, G3, 13, p. 210, Henry Cull to Colonel John Johnston, Hatley, 7 Jan. 1812.
31 NA, MG23, G3, 13, p. 211, Henry Cull to Sir, Hatley, 1 June 1812.
32 Sheppard, *Plunder, Profit, and Paroles*, 42–4.
33 NA, MG23, G3, 13, pp. 212, 217, Henry Cull's report, Hatley, 10 June 1812.
34 NA, RG9, 1A1, Adjutant-General, Lower Canada, Correspondence, vol. 5, Henry Cull to Vassal de Monviel, Hatley, 10 June 1812; NA, MG 23, G3, 13, p. 219, Henry Cull to Sir, Hatley, 12 June 1812; p. 220, Henry Cull to Captain James Bangs, Hatley, 17 June 1812.
35 NA, MG23, G3, 13, p. 221, Henry Cull to Adjutant-General, Hatley, 17 June 1812. See also Cull's inquiry to the Executive Council in NA, RG4, A1, vol. 122, pp. 39064–5, Quebec, 10 July 1812.
36 NA, MG 24, I11, Pennoyer Papers, J. Pennoyer to Capt. Thomas Chaddock or Lieut. Abel Bennet, Compton, 10 June 1812.
37 NA, RG9, 1A1, vol. 5, J. Pennoyer to F. Vassal de Monviel, Compton, 30 June 1812.
38 NA, MG23, I11, p. 9, J. Pennoyer to Capt. Joseph Perkins, Compton, 30 July 1812.
39 *The Loyalists of the Eastern Townships of Quebec* (Belleville, ON, 1992), 118.
40 NA, RG9, 1A1, vol. 5, Henry Cull to Vassal de Monviel, Hatley, 10 June 1812; MG 23, G3, 13, p. 219, Henry Cull to Sir, Hatley, 12 June 1812; p. 220, Henry Cull to Captain James Bangs, Hatley, 17 June 1812; RG4, A1, vol. 122, pp. 38973–6, F. de Monviel to Government House, Quebec, 7 July 1812.
41 Quoted in Walter Hill Crockett, *Vermont: The Green Mountain State* (New York, 1921), vol. 3: 41.
42 NA, RG4, A1, vol. 122, 38925–32, Petition to governor-general dated at Compton, 6 July 1812.
43 Everest, *War of 1812*, 36.
44 J.I. Little, *State and Society in Transition: The Politics of Institutional Reform in the Eastern Townships, 1838–1852* (Montreal and Kingston, 1997), 63.

45 NA, RG4, A1, vol. 124, 39680–4, O. Barker to Lieut.-Col. James Cuthbert, Compton, 30 Aug. 1812.
46 NA, RG9, 1A1, vol. 5, Henry Cull to Adjutant-General, Hatley, 8 Nov. 1812; RG4, A1, vol. 126, 40319–21, Petition to Governor-General Prevost, Compton, 28 Nov. 1812.
47 NA, RG4 A1, vol. 134, 42813–14, Petition of Henry Cull to Sir George Prevost, Hatley, 29 Jan. 1814.
48 NA, RG4, A1, vol. 127, 40673–4, O. Barker to Col. James Cuthbert, Montreal, 21 Jan. 1813. Cuthbert vouched for Barker's character and loyalty. NA, RG8, I, C688c, p. 8, James Cuthbert to E.B. Brenton, Quebec, 28 Jan. 1813.
49 NA, MG23, G3, 13, p. 167, Henry Cull to Captain Elmer Cushing, [Jan. 1808]; pp. 169–70, Henry Cull to Captain Elmer Cushing, [Jan. 1808].
50 NA, RG4, A1, vol. 123, 39353–62, Petition from inhabitants of Shipton, 27 July 1812.
51 NA, RG4, A1, vol. 123, 39417–20, Petition from inhabitants of Eaton, 1 Aug. 1812.
52 NA, mf M-5904, Bishop's University, Special Collections, John Savage Papers, 1770–1859, Shefford Township, George Prevost to S. Willard, Montreal, 9 Oct. 1812 (copy). The petition itself has not been located.
53 NA, RG9, 1A1, vol. 5, John Johnson to Adjutant-General, Montreal, 10 Nov. 1812.
54 NA, MG23, G3, 13, p. 223, Henry Cull to Capt. Norton, Hatley, 12 Aug. 1812. Pennoyer would register the same complaint nearly two years later. NA, MG24, I11, p. 64, J. Pennoyer to F. Vassal de Monviel, Compton, 9 March 1814.
55 NA, RG9, 1A1, vol. 5, Henry Cull to Lt. Col. Vassal, Hatley, 22 Aug. 1812.
56 NA, MG24, I11, p. 11, J. Pennoyer to James Cuthbert, Compton, 30 Aug. 1812; RG9, 1A1, vol. 5, Philip Luke to Adjutant-General, 6 Sept. 1812.
57 See Mills, 'French Canadians.'
58 NA, MG23, G3, 13, p. 228, Henry Cull to Captain Kezar, Hatley, 3 Dec. 1812; p. 230, Henry Cull to Vassal de Monviel, Hatley, 14 Dec. 1812.
59 NA, MG24, I11, p. 20, J. Pennoyer to Captain, Compton, 28 Nov. 1812; p. 21, J. Pennoyer to Capt., Compton, 4 Dec. 1812; NA, RG9, 1A1, vol. 5, pp. 2646–7, Jesse Pennoyer to F. Vassal de Monviel, Compton, 16 Dec. 1812; pp. 2652–4, Jesse Pennoyer to E.B. Brenton, Compton, 16 Dec. 1812.
60 NA, RG9, 1A1, vol. 5, Henry Ruiter to Sir, Potton, 27 Oct. 1812.

61 NA, RG9, 1A1, vol. 15, J. Pennoyer to F. Vassal de Monville, Compton, 13 Feb. 1814; 17 Feb. 1814; J. Pennoyer's recommendations, Compton, 8 March 1814.

62 NA, RG9, 1A1, vol. 11, letter from Henry Ruiter, Potton, 4 Oct. 1813; letter from Henry Ruiter, Potton, 8 Oct. 1813; vol. 15, Henry Ruiter to Sir, Potton, 17 Jan. 1814.

63 NA, RG9, 1A1, vol. 15, Henry Ruiter to Sir, Potton, 21 Feb. 1814; Henry Ruiter to Sir, Potton, 30 April 1814. Captain Jacob Glen, adjutant for the Royal Eastern Regiment, also served as adjutant for the Third Battalion. NA, MG23, G3, 13, p. 304, Organization of the 3rd Battalion, 21 Aug. 1817; p. 305, H.Cull to Adjutant-General, Hatley, 18 April 1818

64 NA, RG4, C1, vol. 131, 41946, Roll of the Officers and Men of the Fourth Battalion, St Armand, 10 Oct. 1813.

65 NA, RG9, 1A1, vol. 5, Joseph Powell to F. Vassal de Monviel, Saint Armand, 22 July 1812.

66 NA, RG9, 1A1, vol. 15, Henry Ruiter to Sir, Potton, 19 July 1814.

67 NA, RG9, 1A1, vol. 5, E. Cushing to Sir John Johnson, Shipton, 25 June 1812.

68 NA, RG4, A1, vol. 123, 39300–3, Petition of Elmer Cushing to Governor-General, Shipton, 23 July 1812. On Cushing and the McLane case, see Bernard Epps, *The Eastern Townships Adventure*, vol. 1: *A History to 1837* (Ayer's Cliff, QC, 1992), 108–15, 118–21; and F. Murray Greenwood, *Legacies of Fear: Law and Politics in Quebec in the Era of the French Revolution* (Toronto, 1993), chap. 7.

69 NA, RG9, vol. 11, Elmer Cushing to Jesse Pennoyer, Shipton, 27 March 1813. Cushing complained eight months later that there had been no response to his resignation, which 'places us in a state of awkward suspence.' NA, RG4, A1, vol. 132, 42162, E. Cushing to Major Jesse Pennoyer, Shipton, 7 Nov. 1813.

70 Epps, *Eastern Townships Adventure*, 149–52.

71 NA, RG9, 1A1, vol. 15, J. Pennoyer to F. Vassal de Monviel, Compton, 9 March 1814; RG4, A1, vol. 135, 42967–8, Gordon Lawrence to Col. Brenton, Shipton, 7 March, 1814; 42981, J. Pennoyer to Col. E.B. Brenton, Compton, 9 March 1814.

72 J.I. Little, 'Gale, Samuel,' *DCB*, vol. 6, 270.

73 See Marie-Paule LaBrèque, 'Savage, John,' *DCB*, vol. 6, 688–9; and Marie-Paule LaBrèque, 'Willard, Samuel,' *DCB*, vol. 6, 816–17; and Jimmy W. Manson, *The Loyal Americans of New England and New York: Founders of the Townships of Lower Canada* ([Knowlton, QC], 2001), 41–3.

74 NA, RG4, A1, vol. 126, 40329–33, Memorial of the undersigned

Inhabitants of the New Townships in the Eastern District, Farnham,
Dec. 1812.

75 NA, RG4, A1, vol. 126, 40334, Observations relative to the Memorial,
S. Gale. See also NA, MG8, F13, I, Samuel Willard Papers, p. 861, S.
Gale to S. Willard, Farnham, 29 Dec. 1812; p. 863, S. Gale to S.
Willard, Farnham, 3 Feb. 1813; NA, MG8, F13, II, Samuel Gale
Papers, Correspondence: 1787–1840, p. 44, S. Gale to Samuel Willard,
Esq., Farnham, 15 Jan. 1813.

76 NA, RG9, vol. 11, abstract from Colonel Murray's letter to General de
Rottenburg, St John, 30 Jan. 1813.

77 The provincial quota was to be 2,000 men. NA, RG4, A1, vol. 118,
37888-90; NA, MG24, I11, p. 31; John Johnson to Sir, Montreal, 10
Jan. 1813; NA, MG8, F13, I, p. 863, S. Gale to S. Willard, Farnham, 3
Feb. 1813.

78 A dozen Canadian infantry battalions contributed about half the
strength of the regular units in Canada. Everest, *War of 1812*, 36.

79 NA, RG4, A1, vol. 118, 37890–1, E.B. Brenton to O. Barker, Quebec,
2 Feb. 1813 (copy).

80 NA, British Military and Naval Records, RG8, I, C1203 1/2H, p. 23;
G.F.G. Stanley, *The War of 1812: Land Operations* ([Ottawa], 1983),
249. In June Pennoyer wrote that Barker was unlikely to succeed in
raising his company of volunteers because the man who was to be his
lieutenant would probably join Kilborn's company as lieutenant. NA,
MG24, I11, p. 53, J. Pennoyer to Louis Ritter, Compton, 1 June 1813.

81 NA, RG8, I, C91, pp. 151-3, 157-8, Petition of Oliver Barker to Sir
Gordon Drummond, Quebec, 18 March 1816; pp. 183–5, Petition of O.
Barker to Sir Gordon Drummond, Drummondville, 22 April 1816.

82 NA, MG23, 13, p. 231, H. Cull to Capt. Kezar, Hatley, 1 Feb. 1813.

83 NA, RG9, vol. 11, J. Jones to Capt. Joseph Richardson, 28 Jan. 1813.

84 NA, RG9, vol. 11, abstract from Colonel Murray's letter to General
deRottenburg, St John, 30 Jan. 1813; *Loyalists of the Eastern Townships*, 127–8.

85 NA, MG23, G3, 13, p. 231, H. Cull to Capt Kezar, Hatley, 1 Feb. 1813.

86 NA, MG23, G3, 13, p. 232, Record of Journal, Hatley, 8 Feb. 1813.

87 NA, MG23, G3, 13, pp. 235–6, Henry Cull to Sir John Johnson,
Stanstead, 16 Feb. 1813.

88 NA, MG24, I11, p. 26, J. Pennoyer to Captain __, Compton, 3 Feb.
1813; pp. 27–30, Journal concerning the subject of a circular letter.

89 NA, MG23, G3, 13, pp. 235–6, Henry Cull to Sir John Johnson,
Stanstead, 16 Feb. 1813.

90 NA, MG23, G3, 13, p. 237, Henry Cull to Captain Kezar, Stanstead,
17 Feb. 1813 (circular); *Sherbrooke Daily Record*, 30 April 1910;

Hubbard, *Forests and Clearings*, 153–4; Kesteman et al., *Histoire des Cantons de l'Est*, 133–4.

91 NA, MG24, I11, p. 30, Compton, 23 February 1813. The Pennoyer Papers (p. 32) also include an undated and unsigned copy of a petition to the governor-general committing its signatories to serve for one year under their own militia officers.

92 NA, RG4, A1, vol. 127, 40909–10, George Prevost to Sir John Johnson, Montreal, 19 Feb. 1813.

93 NA, MG23, G3, 13, p. 238, John Johnson to Gentlemen, Montreal, 20 Feb. 1813 (circular).

94 NA, MG23, G3, 13, p. 240, Henry Cull to Sir John Johnson, Hatley, 17 March 1813.

95 The salary was presumably the same as in Upper Canada, where it was just over £9 per year. George Sheppard, '"Wants and Privations": Women and the War of 1812 in Upper Canada,' *Histoire sociale / Social History* 28 (1995): 166. In contrast, Vermont's detached militia in service received $10 per month from a state tax. Crockett, *Vermont*, 53–4.

96 NA, MG23, G3, 13, p. 240, Henry Cull to Sir John Johnson, Hatley, 17 March 1813.

97 NA, MG23, G3, 13, p. 241, Henry Cull to Sir, Stanstead, 23 March 1813.

98 NA, MG23, G3, 13, p. 244, Henry Cull to Captain Ruiter, Hatley, 20 April 1813. On payment of substitutes in Upper Canada, see Sheppard, *Plunder, Profits, and Paroles*, 60.

99 NA, MG8, F13, IX, Township Papers, Stukely, D. Militia, Resolutions formed at a meeting of the Inhabitants. While this document is not dated, an adjoining one states that while one of the men in question returned home the other was thought to have been killed at Queenston Heights.

100 The Newport Township minutes for 1799–1814 appear to be the only ones to have survived. There would be no official system of local government in Lower Canada until 1840. See Little, *State and Society*, 119–20.

101 NA, MG23, G3, 13, p. 243, H. Cull to Capt. Kezar, Hatley, 27 March 1813.

102 NA, MG23, G3, 13, p. 247, Henry Cull to Capt, Norton, Hatley, 14 May 1813 (circular).

103 NA, MG23, G3, 13, p. 267, Henry Cull to Captain Ritter, Hatley, 3 Sept. 1813.

104 NA, MG23, G3, 13, p. 249, Henry Cull to Adjutant-General, Hatley, 25 May 1813.

105 NA, MG23, G3, 13, p. 259, Henry Cull to Sir John Johnson, Hatley, 22 June 1813.

106 NA, MG23, G3, 13, pp. 256–7, Henry Cull to Captain Ritter, Hatley, 21 June 1813. Edmund Davis, who had fled to the United States after being drafted in April 1813, returned a year later with the support of his company's officers and two local justices of the peace. NA, RG4, A1, vol. 135, 43193, Petition of Edmund David to Sir George Prevost, Barnston, 31 March 1814.

107 NA, MG23, G3, 13, pp. 245–6, Henry Cull to S. Levesque, Hatley, 28 April 1813; pp. 258–9, 4 captains, 3 lieut.'s, and 2 ensigns to Major Kilborn, 7 June 1813 (copy); A Gentleman in Stanstead to Sir (copy).

108 NA, MG23, G3, 13, p. 259, Henry Cull to Sir John Johnson, Hatley, 22 June 1813.

109 NA, MG23, G3, 13, p. 260, Henry Cull to Sir John Johnson, Hatley, 24 June 1813.

110 *Sherbrooke Daily Record*, 30 April 1910.

111 NA, MG23, G3, 13, pp. 262–5, Henry Cull to Sir John Johnson, Hatley [July 1813].

112 Ibid.

113 Little, *State and Society*, 171–4; Kathleen H. Brown, *Schooling in the Clearings: Stanstead 1800–1850* (Stanstead, 2001), chaps 3 and 4.

114 NA, MG24, I11, p. 36, J. Pennoyer to Sir John Johnson, Compton, 17 March 1813; p. 37, J.P. to commanding officer at St Johns, Compton, 17 March 1813; p. 38, J. Pennoyer to Colonel Johnson, Compton, 23 March 1813; p. 39, J. Pennoyer to Major Charles Kilborn, Compton, 4 April 1813.

115 NA, MG24, I11, p. 40, J. Pennoyer to Captain David Steel, Compton, 7 April 1813.

116 NA, MG24, I11, p. 45, J.P., Major, to Sir, Compton, 27 April 1813; pp. 46–7, J.P., Major, to Louis Ritter, Compton, 27 April 1813.

117 NA, MG24, I11, p. 49, J. Pennoyer to Captain Napthali Bishop et al., Compton, 12 May 1813.

118 NA, MG24, I11, pp. 50–1, J. Pennoyer to Louis Ritter, Compton, 24 May 1813.

119 NA, MG24, I11, p. 53, J. Pennoyer to Louis Ritter, Compton, 1 June 1813.

120 NA, RG8, I, C797, p. 100, Philip Luke to Sir, Saint Armand, 15 April 1813.

121 NA, RG8, I, C797, pp. 133–6, Louis Ritter to Sir, St John's, 20 July 1813.

122 NA, RG8, I, C797, pp. 140–2, Louis Ritter to Sir, St John's, 8 August 1813.

123 NA, RG8, I, C797, pp. 145–7, Louis Ritter to Sir, St John's, 12 Aug. 1813. An officer was supposed to be supplied by each battalion. Pennoyer's belief was that Major Kilborn represented the Third as captain, a lieutenant was to come from the Second or Fourth, and Ensign Harvel represented the Fifth. NA, MG24, I11, pp. 50–1, J. Pennoyer to Captain Louis Ritter, Compton, 24 May 1813.

124 NA, RG8, I, C797, pp. 149–50, Louis Ritter to Major Kilborn, St John's, 21 Aug. 1813; pp. 151–2, Charles Kilborn to Major Ritter, Dorchester near Fort St John's, 20 Aug, 1813; pp. 154–8, Charles Kilborn's petition to Sir George Prevost, Dorchester near Fort St John's, 23 Aug. 1813.

125 NA, RG8, I, C1221, p. 58, Noah Freer to Capt. Ritter, Head Quarters, Kingston, 11 Sept. 1813. Local historians claim that the John Savage in question was the Shefford Township leader, who was then seventy-three years old, but he did have a son of the same name who would presumably have been more suitable for active service. LaBrèque, 'Savage, John,' 688–9; Winona Lawrence Matthews, *The Story of West Shefford (Bromont), Quebec* (n.p., n.d.), 13; C. Thomas, *The History of Shefford* (Montreal, 1877), 15.

126 The other members were from the First Battalion, which covered the St Jean area, and the Sixth Battalion from west of Lake Champlain. Four men from the First Battalion had deserted by 7 December, and three were prisoners of war, while the contingent from the largely French-speaking Sixth Battalion was complete except for one man killed in action.

127 NA, RG4, A1, vol. 132, 42381–2, Nominal list of men drafted from the Six Battalions, 7 Dec. 1813.

128 See Sheppard, *Plunder, Profit, and Paroles*, 96–7.

129 NA, RG4, A1, vol. 132, 42383, Louis Ritter's humble proposition to the Governor in Chief [7 Dec. 1813].

130 NA, RG9, 1A1, vol. 12, Louis Ritter to Col. Vassal de Monviel, Lacolle, 24 March 1814.

131 NA, MG23, G3, 13, p. 269, H. Cull to Captain Simon Kezar et al., 11 Jan. 1814.

132 NA, RG9, 1A1, vol. 12, Louis Ritter to Lt Col. Taschereau, Lacolle, 27 Jan. 1814.

133 NA, RG9, 1A1, vol. 15, Henry Ruiter to Vassal de Monviel, Potton, 12 June 1814.

134 NA, RG9, 1A1, vol. 15, Philip Luke to Sir, St Armand, 9 Feb. 1814.

135 NA, RG9, 1A1, vol. 15, Jacob Ruiter to Col. Luke, Dunham, 24 Feb. 1814; Philip Luke to Adjutant General, St Armand, 8 July 1814; *The Loyalists*, 121.

136 NA, RG9, 1A1, vol. 15, Philip Luke to Sir, St Armand, 29 April 1814; Philip Luke to F. Vassal de Monviel, St Armand, 10 May 1814.
137 NA, RG9, 1A1, vol. 15, Philip Luke to Adjutant General, St Armand, 8 July 1814 (copy).
138 NA, MG24, I11, p. 61, J.P., Major, to F. Vassal de Monviel, Compton, 17 Feb. 1814; p. 62, J. Pennoyer to Col. Williams, Compton, 22 Feb. 1814; p. 63, J.P. Major, to Col. Williams, Compton, 2 March 1814.
139 NA, MG24, I11, p. 69, J.P., Major, to Captain __, Compton, 1 April 1814 (circular); p. 71a, J.P., Major, to Captain __, Compton, 13 July 1814; p. 72, J. Pennoyer to Commanding Officer of Frontier Light Infantry, Compton, 11 Aug. 1814.
140 NA, MG23, G3, 13, p. 275, H.C., Lt Col., to Col. Heman Bangs, Hatley, 5 April 1814; p. 277, H.C., Lt Col., to Mr Secretary Brenton, Hatley, 5 April 1814; p. 278, H.C., Lt Col., to Capt. Enoch Bailey, Hatley, 20 May 1814; p. 279, [Henry Cull] to Col. Bangs, Hatley, 20 May 1814; p. 281, H.C., Lt Col., to Adjutant-General, Hatley, 15 June 1814.
141 NA, MG23, G3, 13, p. 285, names of militiamen, 13 July 1814.
142 NA, RG9, 1A1, vol. 12, Louis Ritter to Col. Vassal de Monviel, Montreal, 23 April 1814.
143 NA, RG9, 1A1, vol. 12, Louis Ritter to Lt Col. Taschereau, Lacolle, 27Jan. 1814.
144 NA, MG23, G3, 13, p. 286, H.C., Lt. Col. to E.B. Brenton, Hatley, 18 Aug. 1814.
145 NA, MG23, G3, 13, pp. 289–91, H.C., Lt Col., to Captain John Ruiter, n.d.; RG9, 1A1, vol. 17, Lt. Col. P. Luke to Sir, [?] Jan. 1815.
146 NA, RG9, 1A1, vol. 17, Philip Luke to F. Vassal de Monviel, St Armand, 28 Feb. 1815.
147 NA, RG8, I, C1172, p. 128A, General Orders, Quebec, 1 March 1815.
148 Everest, *War of 1812*, 107.
149 Muller, 'A "Traitorous and Diabolical Traffic,"' 80–1; Hubbard, *Forests and Clearings*, 28, 30.
150 Pierre Berton, *Flames across the Border, 1813–1814* (Toronto, 1981), 209.
151 Quoted in Everest, *War of 1812*, 128.
152 Quoted in Colonel E.A. Cruickshank, 'From Isle aux Noix to Chateauguay. A Study of the Military Operations on the Frontier of Lower Canada in 1812 and 1813,' part 2, *Transactions of the Royal Society of Canada*, Section II, Series III, vol. 8 (1914): 75.
153 Cruickshank, 'Isle aux Noix,' part 2, 75. A local historian attributed Powell's decision not to arm the men 'either to cowardice or treachery.' Cyrus Thomas, *Contributions to the History of the Eastern Townships* (Montreal, 1866), 27.

154 Quoted in J. Russel, Jr, comp., *The History of the War between the United States and Great Britain* (Hartford, 1815), 232–3.

155 NA, RG9, vol. 11, Philip Luke to Sir Roger Sheaffe, St Armand, Philipsburg, Missisquoi Bay, 16 Oct. 1813; Bishop's University, Quebec Diocesan Archives [hereafter QDA], D8, Sewell Papers, p. 1, C. Stewart to Rev. Dr. Morice, 1 Nov. 1813.

156 NA, RG4, A1, vol. 131, 41945, Roll of the Officers and Men of the Fourth Battalion, St Armand, 10 Oct. 1813. According to Sheppard ('"Wants and Privations,"' 168) the practice of plundering private property began only in late 1813.

157 Philip Ruiter to Hon. Thomas Dunn, 10 Dec. 1813. Quoted in Montgomery, *Missisquoi Bay*, 97–8. Philip Ruiter was Lieutenant-Colonel Henry Ruiter's nephew. Rick J. Ashton, *The Life of Henry Ruiter, 1742–1819* (n.p., 1974), 32–3.

158 QDA, D8, p. 2, C. Stewart to Rev. Dr Morice, 1 Nov. 1813 (typescript); NA, MG23, G3, 3, p. 253, Philip Ruiter to Hon. Thomas Dunn, 10 Dec. 1813. The *Vermont Republican* reported the higher number of ninety cattle, adding that 'in this excursion the Colonel is said to have behaved very honourably.' Quoted in Beattie, 'Stanstead's Historical Traditions,' 71.

159 NA, RG4, A1, vol. 131, 41995–6, Philip Ruiter to the Hon. and Rev. C. Stewart, St Armand, 19 Oct. 1813.

160 NA, RG4, A1, vol. 131, 42067–70, C. Stewart to Lt. Col. Brenton, St Armand, 25 Oct. 1813.

161 NA, RG4, A1, vol. 131, 42071–2, C. Stewart to Lt. Col. Brenton, St Armand, 25 Oct. 1813; vol. 132, 42145–7, C. Stewart Col. Brenton, St Armand, 5 Nov. 1813. On this theme, see Everest, *War of 1812*, 82–4.

162 QDA, D8, pp. 1–2, C. Stewart to Rev. Dr Morice, 1 Nov. 1813 (typescript).

163 NA, RG4, A1, vol. 132, 42143, C. Stewart to Colonel Bedel [document fragment]; p. 42197, Meedy Bedel to Respected Sir, Burlington, 12 Nov. 1813. On the management of prisoners of war, see Everest, *War of 1812*, 79–86.

164 Quoted in Stanley, *War of 1812*, 249.

165 NA, RG4, A1, vol. 132, 42283–4, C. Stewart to Lt. Col. Brenton, St Armand, 1 Dec. 1813.

166 NA, RG4, A1, vol. 132, 42293, Petition and Memorial of Amos Davis, Montreal, 2 Dec. 1813 (submitted by agent); 42294, affidavit by Capt. George Sax, Montreal, 30 Nov. 1813.

167 NA, RG4, A1, vol. 133, 42500–1, C. Stewart to Lt Col. Brenton, St Armand, 20 Dec. 1813. Stewart stated that his community had donated £100 to the Patriotic Society in Upper Canada in July 1813.

QDA, Unbound Manuscripts, Case I, Folder 5, 1807–15, C. Stewart to Rev. Sir, 1 Nov. 1813.

168 NA, MG23, G3, 3, Ruiter Papers, vol. 2, p. 762, order of Col. Cobb, Burlington, 6 Dec. 1813.

169 NA, MG23, G3, 3, p. 252, Christian Snyder et al. to Phillip Ruiter, Burlington, 8 Dec. 1813.

170 NA, RG8, I, C1203 1/2, p. 208. Adjutant-General Edward Baynes, Montreal, 27 Jan. 1814; QDA, D8, C.S. to Rev. Dr Morice, St Armand, 2 May 1814 (typescript).

171 NA, RG8, I, C692, pp. 44-5; Everest, *War of 1812*, 83.

172 NA, RG9, 1A1, vol. 17, Philip Luke to A.W. Cochran, St Armand, 7 July 1815; RG8, I, C692, p. 267.

173 NA, RG4, A1, vol. 134, 42915–16, C. Stewart to Lt Colonel Brenton, St Armand, 19 Feb. 1814; RG8, I, C86, p. 69, Philip Ruiter to Lieut, Fermell, St Armand, 26 [?] June 1814; pp. 109–10, petition of Samuel Gelston to Sir George Prevost, St Armand, 16 June 1814; pp. 111–12, petition of Ephraim Hungerford and James Taylor to Sir George Prevost, St Armand, 16 June 1814.

174 NA, RG4, A1, vol. 134, 42814, Petition of Henry Cull to Sir George Prevost, Hatley, 29 Jan. 1814.

175 NA, RG8, I, C688E, p. 144, General Orders, Adjutant-General's Office, Quebec, 9 Jan. 1814; C91, p. 153, Petition of O. Barker to Sir Gordon Drummond, Quebec, 18 March 1816.

176 Crockett, *Vermont*, 86; NA, MG23, G3, 13, p. 272, Heman Bangs et al. to Lt. Col. Henry Cull, Stanstead, 19 March 1814. Crockett (*Vermont*, 85–6) states that in March 1814 several parties of American troops were sent to various places along the border 'to break up an irregular intercourse that had been carried on with the British troops during the winter.' He adds that orders had been issued to respect private property.

177 NA, MG23, G3, 13, p. 273, Lt. Col. H.C. to Major Pennoyer, Hatley, 19 March 1814. In response, Pennoyer ordered that the government arms be distributed within his battalion, which should be prepared to march at the shortest notice, and that every man who had 'any sort of fire arms' should 'bring them forward in order that they may be received.' NA, MG23, I11, p. 67, J. Pennoyer to Lieut. Thomas Fuller, Compton, 24 March 1814.

178 The rendezvous locations were to be determined by Colonel Heman Bangs as acting adjutant. NA, MG23, G3, 13, pp. 273–4, orders issued by Lt. Col. Henry Cull, Stanstead, 24 March 1814.

179 NA, MG23, G3, 13, p. 260, Henry Cull to Sir John Johnson, Hatley, 24 June 1813.

180 NA, MG23, G3, 13, p. 266, Henry Cull to Capt. Joseph Ives, Hatley, 18 July 1813 (circular).

181 NA, RG9, 1A1, vol. 11, Simon Kezar to Lt. Col. Henry Cull, Hatley, 23 July 1813.

182 Quoted in Richardson, 'War of 1812,' 6.

183 NA, RG9, 1A1, vol. 11, Gordon Lawrence to F. V. de Monviel, Township of Shipton, 27 May 1813; vol. 15, J. Pennoyer to F. Vassal de Monviel, Compton, 9 March 1814; RG4, A1, vol. 135, pp. 42967–8, Gordon Lawrence to Col. Brenton, Shipton, 7 March, 1814; p. 42981, J. Pennoyer to Col. E.B. Brenton, Compton, 9 March 1814. In November, Pennoyer requested that the 'appointment for Twenty horsemen' delivered to Josiah Sawyer not be given to the Shipton cavalry because of its distance from the border and because of the untrustworthy character of its commanding officer, Gordon Lawrence. NA, MG24, I11, p. 75, J. Pennoyer to F. Vassal de Monviel, Compton, 28 Nov. 1814.

184 NA, RG9, 1A1, vol. 5, Joseph Powell to F. Vassal de Monviel, Saint Armand, 22 July 1812; NA, RG4, A1, vol. 132, pp. 42218–19, Retour Générale pour l'Année 1813.

185 NA, MG23, G3, 13, p. 270, H. Cull to J.F. Taschereau, Hatley, 26 Jan. 1814; RG4, A1, vol. 134, 42835, Oliver Barker E.B. Brenton, Compton, 2 Feb. 1814. The loan included twenty cartridges for each musket, but Pennoyer complained that while two flints were provided for each Ascot musket, those from Compton came with only one or none at all. He also queried the charge of one dollar per musket. NA, RG9, 1A1, vol. 15, J. Pennoyer to F. Vassal deMonville [sic], Compton, 13 Feb. 1814; NA, RG4, A1, vol. 134, 42930–1, E.B. Brenton to Major Pennoyer, Quebec, 24 Feb. 1814; NA, MG24, I11, p. 68, J.P., Major, to Josiah Sawyer, Compton, 1 April 1814; NA, RG9, 1A1, vol. 17, J. Pennoyer to Adjutant-General, Compton, 10 Sept. 1815.

186 In 1819 a Royal Engineer officer stated that the Lake Memphremagog–St Francis River water route 'would never afford an Enemy that facility of transport requisite for him to possess in any extensive military Operations against Lower Canada.' Quoted in Richardson, 'War of 1812,' 7.

187 Later the state assumed these costs. Crockett, Vermont, 41, 55.

188 Richardson, 'War of 1812,' 5–6; Montgomery, Missisquoi Bay, 99.

189 See the correspondence in NA, RG8, C86, pp. 216–24.

190 NA, RG8, I, C1224, pp. 43–5, Noah Freer, Mil. Sec., to General de Rottenburg, Quebec, 25 March 1814; C1222, pp. 71–2, George Prevost to Lt.-Gen. Drummond, Quebec, 26 March 1814; C1219, pp. 200–1, Sir George Prevost's report to Earl of Bathurst, Lacadie, 31

March 1814; D.C.L. Gosling, 'The Battle at Lacolle Mill, 1814,' *Journal of the Society for Army Historical Research* 47 (1969): 169–74; Everest, *War of 1812*, 142–3.

191 See Harvey Scrum, 'Smuggling in the War of 1812,' *History Today* 29 (1979): 532–7; and H.N. Muller, 'Smuggling into Canada: How the Champlain Valley Defied Jefferson's Embargo,' *Vermont History* 38 (1970): 5–21.

192 Scrum, 'Smuggling,' 537.

193 Muller, 'A "Traitorous and Diabolical Traffic,"' 80.

194 Ibid., 79. The legislation was repealed after the Federalist Martin Chittenden was elected governor in the fall of 1812. Crockett, *Vermont*, 71–4.

195 Muller, 'A "Traitorous and Diabolical Traffic,"' 90; Everest, *War of 1812*, 151.

196 Cruickshank, 'From Isle aux Noix,' part 2, 26.

197 Quoted in Everest, *War of 1812*, 108.

198 Quoted in ibid., 151.

199 Quoted in Muller, 'A "Traitorous and Diabolical Traffic,"' 91. See also the incidents described in Crockett, *Vermont*, 78–80.

200 QDA, D8, C.S. to Rev. Sir, St Armand, 1 Nov. 1814 (typescript).

201 Quoted in Montgomery, *Missisquoi Bay*, 95–6.

202 NA, MG23, G3, 13, p. 193, Henry Cull to Captain Glen [January 1809].

203 NA, RG4, A1, vol. 125, 40225–8, Petition of Levi Bigelow to Governor-General Prevost, Quebec, 9 Nov. 1812. Muller ('A "Traitorous and Diabolical Traffic,"' 83) mistakenly identifies the town as Montreal and specifies 400 barrels of potash rather than 4,000 barrels of ashes, as the document states.

204 NA, RG4, A1, vol. 125, 40225–8, Petition of Levi Bigelow, 7 Nov. 1812; J.I. Little, ed., *The Child Letters: Public and Private Life in a Canadian Merchant-Politician's Family, 1841–1845* (Montreal and Kingston, 1995), 6–7.

205 Cruickshank, 'From Isle aux Noix,' part 1, 148.

206 NA, RG4, A1, vol. 129, 40859–60, Thomas Coffin to E.B. Brenton, 12 Feb. 1813; vol. 130, 41546, T. Coffin to Civil Secretary, 29 July 1813.

207 NA, RG9, 1A1, vol. 15, Jacob Ruiter to Col. Luke, Dunham, 24 Feb. 1814.

208 NA, RG4, A1, vol. 132, 42265–6, Petition of John Jones, Montreal, 30 Nov. 1813.

209 NA, RG4, A1, vol. 132, 42301–5, Committee of Executive Council petition to George Prevost [3 Dec. 1813].

210 'Smuggling in 1813–1814: A Personal Reminiscence,' *Vermont History* 38 (1970): 22–6. This unsigned handwritten account is dated January 1868. See also the reminiscence in Thomas, *Contributions*, 124–6.

211 NA, MG23, G3, 13, p. 283, Regimental Order, Henry Cull, Lt. Col., Hatley, 30 June 1814; p. 284, H.C., Lt Col., to Mr Secretary Brenton, Hatley, 30 June 1814.

212 Muller, 'A "Traitorous and Diabolical Traffic,"' 90–1.

213 NA, RG9, vol. 11, Henry Cull to S. Levesque, Hatley, 28 April 1813; Richardson, 'War of 1812,' 8.

214 Thomas, *Contributions*, 101–3; Beattie, 'Stanstead's Historical Traditions,' 72.

215 Epps, *Eastern Townships Adventure*, 151.

216 NA, MG24, I11, pp. 86–8, Compton, to Thomas Coffin, 24 April 1813 (not forwarded).

217 Beattie, 'Stanstead's Historical Traditions,' 64–5; Richardson, 'War of 1812,' 9; *Sherbooke Daily Record*, 18 June 1910; NA, RG4 A1, vol. 139, 44567–71, Henry Cull to Civil Secretary, Stanstead, 21 Dec. 1814; 44572–4, affidavit of Nathan Morrill, Stanstead, 20 Dec. 1814; NA, RG8, I, C1225, pp. 63–4, George Prevost to Major-General Macomb, Que., 13 Feb. 1815. According to an American account, Hugh was found innocent of homicide but convicted of a minor offence and sentenced to be branded and imprisoned for three months but was released soon after peace was declared. *Vermont Historical Magazine*, vol. 1: 1015, 1033–5.

218 Kenneth Scott, 'Counterfeiting in Early Vermont,' *Vermont History* 32 (1965): 303; Stephen Burroughs, *A View of Practical Justice as Administered in Lower Canada Displayed in a Memorial to His Excellency the Earl of Gosford* (Three Rivers, 1836), 6–7.

219 Scott, 'Counterfeiting,' 304–6; NA, RG4 A1, vol. 118, 37921–5. S. Sewell to E.B. Brenton, 8 April 1812. Cull apparently sided with Burroughs in his conflict with Barker. Burroughs, *A View of Practical Justice*, 8–13; NA, RG4, A1, vol. 134, 42813-14, Petition of Henry Cull to Sir George Prevost, Hatley, 29 Jan. 1814.

220 NA, MG23, G3, 3, Ruiter Family Papers, vol. 2, pp. 47–9, Petition of the undersigned Magistrates & Militia officers and others, [incomplete].

221 In addition to petitioning for a half-pay pension for this and other services – such as infiltrating General Izard's position prior to his attack at Châteauguay – Barker later requested £500 to compensate for his efforts and to keep him from debtors' prison. NA, RG4, A1, vol. 133, 42584–6, O. Barker to E.B. Brenton, Stanstead, 31 Dec.

1813; 42676–9, affidavit of Charles Burnham of the Township of Stanstead, Montreal, 6 Jan. 1814; vol. 134, 42834–6, Oliver Barker to Col. E.B. Brenton, Compton, 2 Feb. 1814; RG8, I, C91, 154, Petition of O. Barker to Sir Gordon Drummond, Quebec, 18 March 1816. Counterfeiting remained a significant feature of the border townships' economy until the 1840s. See Little, *State and Society*, 55–7.

222 NA, RG4, A1, vol. 122, 39006, Proclamation signed by H.W. Ryland, Quebec, 8 July 1812.

223 NA, RG4, A1, vol. 129, 41266–7, J.M. Mondelet to Jesse Pennoyer, Montreal, 19 May 1813.

224 NA, MG24, I11, p. 143, signed by J. Pennoyer, Compton, 5 Feb. 1813.

225 NA, MG8, F13, IX, Township Papers, Hatley, Petition signed Hatley, 2 April 1814.

226 Georgeville Historical Society, Abraham Channel, Jr, to Robert Channel, 17 June 1813 (document kindly transcribed and forwarded by John Scott).

227 NA, MG24, I11, p. 90, declaration by J. Pennoyer, Compton, 24 Aug. 1813; p. 92, Compton, 29 Aug. 1813; p. 93, testimony, 30 Aug. 1813.

228 NA, MG23, G3, 13, p. 254, Henry Cull to Thomas McCord and J.M. Mondelet, Hatley, 7 June 1813.

229 NA, RG4, A1, vol. 133, 42537, M. Nichols, j.p. to Thos. Coffin, Ascott, 23 Dec. 1813.

230 NA, RG4, A1, vol. 133, 42570–1, T. Coffin to E.B. Brenton, Three Rivers, 29 Dec. 1813; pp. 42572–3, declaration of Jesse Moor, Three Rivers, 29 Dec. 1813. Coffin did support the case of Jacob Burnham, who was in the process of moving from the United States to his newly purchased property in Newport Township when the war broke out. NA, RG4, A1, vol. 128, 41144–6, Jacob Burnham to Thomas Coffin, Three Rivers, 20 April 1813; 41152–3, Samuel Heard to Thomas Coffin, Three Rivers, 22 April 1813; 41163–5, Thomas Coffin to E.B. Brenton, Three Rivers, 24 April 1813.

231 NA, RG4, A1, vol. 136, 43519, C.D. Shekleton to Thos McCord, Montreal, 31 May 1814; vol. 138, 44053, T. Coffin to E.B. Brenton, Three Rivers, 25 Aug. 1814.

232 NA, RG4, A1, vol. 134, 42889–91, Oliver Barker to Col. E.B. Brenton, Compton, 16 Feb. 1814.

233 J.I. Little, 'American Sinner / Canadian Saint? The Further Adventures of the Notorious Stephen Burroughs, 1799–1840,' *Journal of the Early Republic* 27 (Summer 2007), 216–17.

234 NA, RG4 A1, vol. 138, 43971, T. Coffin to E.B. Brenton, Three Rivers, 10 Aug. 1814; 43994, T. Coffin to E.B. Brenton, Three Rivers, 15 Aug. 1814.

235 NA, RG4, A1, vol. 133, 42687–9, C. Stewart to McCord, St Armand, Jan. 1814.
236 NA, RG4, A1, vol. 136, 43450, Petition of Ephraim Knight, Montreal, 20 May 1814.
237 NA, Collections of BCHS, VIII, Miscellaneous Papers, John Savage (reel M-136), pass assigned to John Savage by Jonathan James Judge, n.d.
238 NA, RG4, A1, vol. 134, 42889–91, Oliver Barker to Col. E.B. Brenton, Compton, 16 Feb. 1814.
239 NA, MG23, G3, 13, p. 239, Henry Cull to Solicitor-General, Hatley, March 1813; Sheppard, *Plunder, Profit, and Paroles*, 79–84, 88–9, 92, 98, 221.
240 NA, MG23, G3, 13, p. 264, Henry Cull to Sir John Johnson, Hatley [July 1813].
241 Crockett (*Vermont*, 56) claims that Orleans County was slow to recover because many settlers never returned.
242 QDA, D8, Rev. C.J. Stewart to Rev. Dr Morice, 1 May 1813; NA, MG23, G3, 13, p. 249, Henry Cull to Adjutant-General, Hatley, 25 May 1813.
243 NA, MG23, G3, 13, p. 264, Henry Cull to Sir John Johnson, Hatley [July 1813]. Pennoyer issued a warrant for an Eaton resident's arrest in August 1813 simply on the grounds that a bailiff had reported that he planned to move to the United States. NA, MG24, I11, p. 91, arrest warrant, Compton, 25 Aug. 1813.
244 NA, G24 J47, C.C. Cotton Letters (typescript), 163, C.C. Cotton to Anna, Dunham, 20 July 1814.
245 NA, RG8, I, C693, pp. 53–4, petition of Elmer Cushing to George Prevost, Montreal, 12 July 1814.
246 NA, RG8, I, C688D, pp. 66–7, E.B.B. to Elmer Cushing, Montreal, 17 July 1814.
247 See J.I. Little, *Borderland Religion: The Emergence of an English-Canadian Identity, 1792–1852* (Toronto, 2004), 31–2, 38–9.
248 Joseph's father was Peaslee Badger, and the man charged was Peaslee Badger, Jr. Joseph Badger was served a subpoena to testify in this case. NA, MG23, G3, 13, 215, Henry Cull's bill for services to the government; MG24 I11, p. 95, Affidavit of Benjamin Sleeper, 7 Oct. 1813; p. 96, J. Pennoyer to Ensign Page Bull, 7 Oct. 1813.
249 See Little, *Borderland Religion*, 29–30.
250 NA, MG23, G3, 13, p. 213. On Moulton, see Little, *Borderland Religion*, 27, 29, 35, 96.
251 NA, RG9, 1A1, vol. 17, Philip Luke to F. Vassal de Monviel, St Armand, 7 July 1815.

252 NA, RG9, 1A1, vol. 17, Philip Luke to F. Vassal de Monviel, St Armand, 3 Oct. 1815; 30 Oct. 1815.

253 Peter Sahlins, *Boundaries: The Making of France and Spain in the Pyrenees* (Berkeley, 1989), 3.

254 Alan Taylor, '"The Late Loyalists": Northern Reflections on the Early American Republic,' *Journal of the Early Republic* 27, no. 1 (2007): 30.

255 While Mills ('French Canadians,' 54–6) argues that there was a sense of loyalty to the monarch in the French-Canadian parishes, the settlers of the Eastern Townships had a more democratic tradition.

256 Charles Stewart, *A Short View of the Present State of the Eastern Townships in the Province of Lower Canada* (London, 1817; reprint from Montreal, 1815), 9.

257 Eli Whitcomb, who had recently moved to Hereford from Maine, was accused in September 1813 by a neighbour of having frequent interviews with the American guard, several members of which reportedly helped to dig his potatoes, and of having claimed that he would be given the accuser's land after the American army had invaded. Whitcomb admitted that he had been interviewed by the Vermont state attorney but denied providing any information about smuggled cattle. He also pointed out that the only grist mill available to Hereford residents was in Stewartston, New Hampshire, close to the American blockhouse. Pennoyer and Cull, serving as magistrates, acquitted Whitcomb of all charges upon his promise to take the oath of allegiance (NA, MG24, I11, p. 94, affidavit of Thomas McCoy, Compton, 30 Sept. 1813; *Sherbrooke Daily Record*, 16 July 1910; Epps, *Eastern Townships Adventure*, 151). In October of the same year, Philip Ruiter issued a warrant for the arrest of Dr Jonathan W. Phillips of St Armand in response to the oath of a surgeon who had deserted the American army to the effect that Phillips had informed him 'that he had a regular correspondence with several officers in the United States army. That they had promised him the appointment of Surgeon if he would leave this Government and join them, and had been making his arrangements accordingly.' NA, MG23, G3, 3, pp. 758–61, Philip Ruiter to John Pier, Sergeant of Militia, this to execute, 20 Oct. 1813.

The Rebellions of 1837–8

1 Jean-Paul Bernard, *Les rébellions de 1837–1838* (Montreal, 1983), 339. Allan Greer clearly supports the first position, despite what Marcel Bellavance claims in a recent critique, but he also argues that the habitant participants were drawing on traditions of popular culture,

which Bellavance assumes is a contradiction. See Allan Greer, *The Patriots and the People: The Rebellions of 1837 in Lower Canada* (Toronto, 1993), esp. 4–9, 132–6, 154–6; and Marcel Bellavance, *Le Québec au siècle des nationalités (1791–1918)* (Montreal, 2004), chap. 4. For a critique of the bourgeois revolution concept propounded by Bellavance, among others, see Colin M. Coates, 'The Rebellions of 1837–38, and Other Bourgeois Revolutions in Quebec Historiography,' *International Journal of Canadian Studies* 20 (Fall 1999): 19–34.

2   One notable exception is Gérald Bernier and Daniel Salée, 'Les Patriotes, la question nationale et les rébellions de 1837–1838 au Bas-Canada,' in Michel Sarra-Bournet, ed., *Les nationalismes au Québec du XIXe au XXIe siècle* ([Sainte-Foy], 2001), 25–36.

3   In his recent survey of the ideas propagated by the Lower Canadian press during this era, for example, Yvan Lamonde makes no reference whatsoever to the newspapers of the Eastern Townships. *Histoire sociale des idées au Québec, 1760–1896* (Montreal, 2000), chaps 6–8. The only exceptions are Denyse Beaugrand-Champagne, 'Les mouvements patriote et loyal dans les comtés de Missisquoi, Shefford, et Stanstead' (MA thesis, Université du Québec à Montréal, 1990); and Gilles Laporte, *Patriotes et loyaux: Leadership régional et mobilisation politique en 1837 et 1838* (Sillery, QC, 2004). Excellent as it is, the first study relies largely on the press and ends with the outbreak of the Rebellion; the second study is more comprehensive but somewhat marred by errors, such as the assumption that most of the American settlers were Loyalists when only a small minority were.

4   See Louis-Georges Harvey, 'La Révolution américaine et les Patriotes, 1830–1837,' in Sarra-Bournet, ed., *Les nationalismes*, 15–24; and *Le printemps de l'Amérique française. Américanité, anticolonialisme et républicanisme dans le discours politique québécois, 1805–1837* (Montreal, 2004).

5   On this point, see Greer, *The Patriots*, 164–8, though his emphasis on 'the militant Constitutionalism of the English minority' underestimates the political divisions within the Eastern Townships.

6   J.I. Little, *Ethno-Cultural Transition and Regional Identity in the Eastern Townships of Quebec* (Ottawa, 1989), 8–9; Jean-Pierre Kesteman, Peter Southam, and Diane Saint-Pierre, *Histoire des Cantons de l'Est* (Sainte-Foy, 1998), 112–15, 119–24.

7   Kesteman et al., *Histoire des Cantons de l'Est*, 131, 142–5, 152, 158–62; Mario Gendron et al., *Histoire du Piémont-des-Appalaches: La Montérégie* (Sainte-Foy, 1999), 82–8.

8   Kesteman et al., *Histoire des Cantons de l'Est*, 101–6, 121–4; Gendron

et al., *Histoire de Piémont*, 64–5, 75–80; Jules Martel, *Histoire du système routier des Cantons de l'Est avant 1855* (Victoriaville, QC, 1960). According to the census for 1844, 60 per cent of the English-speaking population of 47,700 was Canadian-born. There were also 14,600 French Canadians, most of whom had settled in the outlying townships after the Rebellions. Little, *Ethno-Cultural Transition*, 9, 13–14, 16, 21.

 9 Jeffrey McNairn, *The Capacity to Judge: Public Opinion and Deliberative Democracy in Upper Canada, 1791–1854* (Toronto, 2000), 70.

10 These lodges were established in Philipsburg (1795), Stanstead (1803), Ascot (1805), and Eaton (1813). John H. Graham, *Outlines of the History of Freemasonry in the Province of Quebec* (Montreal, 1892), 103, 112–13, 132, 140.

11 Arthur Henry Moore, *History of Golden Rule Lodge* (Toronto, 1905), 14–21, 66.

12 Two exceptions were Marcus Child and Elias Lee. Moore, *History of Golden Rule*, 23–6, 160–1, 167–8, 181–6, 188, Appendix D. McNairn (*Capacity to Judge*, 82–3) concedes that Freemasonry 'upheld the status quo by valuing loyalty to existing authorities and prohibiting partisan discussions,' but concludes that it 'offered a glimpse at another world: a world where men could be equal, rational, and benevolent, transcend social divisions, and cooperate in the governing of their order.'

13 John J. Duffy and H. Nicholas Muller, III, *Anxious Democracy: Aspects of the 1830s* (Westport, CT, 1982), 13; Moore, *History of Golden Rule*, 32–42; Graham, *Outlines*, 114, 132–3, 140.

14 J.I. Little, '"A Moral Engine of Such Incalculable Power": The Temperance Movement in the Eastern Townships, 1830–52,' in *The Other Quebec: Microhistorical Essays on Nineteenth-Century Religion and Society* (Toronto, 2006), 137–9.

15 See McNairn, *Capacity to Judge*, 103–7. The Rechabite order, which emerged in the Eastern Townships during the mid-1840s, conformed more closely to a ritualistic, lay-controlled, voluntary society. See Little, '"A Moral Engine,"' 145–7.

16 See Cecil J. Houston and William J. Smyth, *The Sash Canada Wore: A Historical Geography of the Orange Order in Canada* (Toronto, 1980), 52, 54.

17 Sherbrooke also hosted two agricultural exhibitions a year, beginning in September 1823 when 500 people attended. Jean-Pierre Kesteman, *Histoire de Sherbrooke*, tome 1: *De l'âge de l'eau à l'ère de la vapeur* (Sherbrooke, 2000), 68. On the role of agricultural societies in creating a civic consciousness, see McNairn, *Capacity to Judge*, 96.

18 See J.I. Little, *Borderland Religion: The Emergence of an English-Canadian Identity, 1792–1852* (Toronto, 2004).

19 These demands were articulated as early as 1815 in the Reverend Charles Stewart, *A Short View of the Present State of the Eastern Townships* (London, 1817; reprint Montreal 1815). For a brief overview, see Matthew F. Farfan, *The Stanstead Region 1792–1844: Isolation, Reform, and Class on the Eastern Townships Frontier* (Hull, QC, 1992), 34–46.

20 *Missiskoui Standard*, 26 May 1835; Beaugrand-Champagne, 'Les mouvements,' 30; Kesteman et al., *Histoire des Cantons de l'Est*, 198–200, 205.

21 The Townships also benefited substantially from the school subsidies that followed from the Assembly Schools' Act of 1829. Beaugrand-Champagne, 'Les mouvements,' 50–1, 145–8; Gendron et al., *Histoire du Piémont*, 116, 121–2; Kesteman et al., *Histoire des Cantons de l'Est*, 179–82, 206–8; and J.I. Little, *State and Society in Transition: The Politics of Institutional Reform in the Eastern Townships, 1838–1852* (Montreal and Kingston, 1997), 17–22, 171–5.

22 See D.G. Creighton, 'The Economic Background of the Rebellion of Eighteen Thirty-Seven,' *Canadian Journal of Economics and Political Science* 3, no. 3 (1937): 322–34; and Fernand Ouellet, *Lower Canada, 1791–1840: Social Change and Nationalism* (Toronto, 1980), chaps 8–10.

23 Kesteman et al., *Histoire des Cantons de l'Est*, 162–5; Gendron et al., *Histoire du Piémont*, 53–4, 98–9.

24 Jane Errington, *The Lion, the Eagle and Upper Canada: Developing a Colonial Ideology* (Montreal and Kingston, 1987), 102.

25 See ibid., chap. 9.

26 Quoted in Little, *State and Society*, 23.

27 See T.H. Breen, 'Ideology and Nationalism on the Eve of the American Revolution: Revisions Once More in Need of Revising,' *Journal of American History*, 84, no. 1 (1997): 13–39.

28 Quoted in J.I. Little, 'British Toryism amidst "a horde of disaffected and disloyal squatters": The Rise and Fall of William Bowman Felton and Family in the Eastern Townships,' *Journal of Eastern Townships Studies* 1 (1992): 18. See also the many disparaging comments by the English newcomer Lucy Peel in J.I. Little, ed., *Love Strong as Death: Lucy Peel's Canadian Journal, 1833–1836* (Waterloo, ON, 2001).

29 Quoted in Little, 'British Toryism,' 25.

30 Elmer Cushing, *An Appeal, Addressed to a Candid Public* (Stanstead, 1826), 75–8.

31 See Little, 'British Toryism'; Kesteman et al., *Histoire des Cantons de l'Est*, 128; and J.I. Little, 'Contested Land: Squatters and Agents in the Eastern Townships of Lower Canada,' *Canadian Historical Review* 80 (1999): 381–412.

32 See *Missiskoui Standard*, 23 Feb. 1836; Little, *State and Society*, 22–5; Beaugrand-Champagne, 'Les mouvements,' 115–22, 128–30; and Kesteman et al., *Histoire des Cantons de l'Est*, 208–9.

33 On the New England exodus, see Harold Fisher Wilson, *The Hill-Country of Northern New England: Its Social and Economic History, 1790–1930* (New York, 1936); and Steven Stoll, *Larding the Lean Earth: Soil and Society in Nineteenth-Century America* (New York, 2002). On the Lower Canadian crop failures, see R.L. Jones, 'French-Canadian Agriculture in the St. Lawrence Valley, 1815–1850,' in W.T. Easterbrook and M.H. Watkins, eds, *Approaches to Canadian Economic History* (Toronto, 1967), 116–17; and Allan Greer and Léon Robichaud, 'La Rébellion de 1837–1838 au Bas-Canada: une approche géographique,' *Cahiers de Géographie du Québec*, 33, no. 90 (1989): 36, 372.

34 See *Missiskoui Standard*, 7 June, 14 June, 12 July, 18 Oct. 1836, 23 May 1837; and J.I. Little, 'Canadian Pastoral: Promotional Images of British Colonization in Lower Canada's Eastern Townships during the 1830s,' *Journal of Historical Geography* 20, no. 2 (2003): 189–211. On the region's early woollen mills, the first in Lower Canada, see Kesteman et al., *Histoire des Cantons de l'Est*, 153–5.

35 Laporte (*Patriotes et loyaux*, 27–8) claims that the term 'Parti patriote' is somewhat anachronistic, having originally been applied by historians after the Rebellions took place.

36 Jean-Pierre Kesteman, 'Une bourgeoisie et son espace: industrialization et développement du capitalisme dans le District de Saint-François (Québec), 1823–1879' (PhD dissertation, Université du Québec à Montréal, 1985), v, 693.

37 For a social analysis of the 1834 election in Stanstead, see Farfan, *Stanstead Region*, 48–51.

38 See the detailed analysis in Beaugrand-Champagne, 'Les mouvements,' 165–7.

39 McNairn, *Capacity to Judge*, 174. For McNairn's discussion of the press, see his chap. 3.

40 See Jean-Pierre Kesteman, 'Les premiers journaux du District de Saint-François (1823–1845),' *Revue d'histoire de l'Amérique française* 31 (1977): 241–3.

41 The new name was the *St. Francis Courier and Stanstead Gazette*.

Kesteman, 'Les premiers journaux,' 244; Beaugrand-Champagne, 'Les mouvements,' 34–5; Matthew F. Farfan, 'Stanstead's Other Journals,' *Journal of the Stanstead Historical Society* 13 (1989): 29.

42 Beaugrand-Champagne, 'Les mouvements,' 35–6; Daughter of H.J. Thomas, 'Incidents of the Canadian Rebellion of 1837–38,' *Second Report of the Missisquoi County Historical Society*, 1907, 44–5; Stephen Kenny, 'The Canadian Rebellions and the Limits of Historical Perspective,' *Vermont History* 58, no. 3 (1988): 188–9; Laporte, *Patriotes et loyaux*, 354.

43 *Township Reformer*, 8 Aug. 1837, 21 Nov. 1837; Beaugrand-Champagne, 'Les mouvements,' 36–7; Laporte, *Patriotes et loyaux*, 352.

44 National Archives of Canada [hereafter NA], Civil Secretary's Correspondence (Incoming), RG4 A1, vol. 541, 101, P. Hubbard to C.R. Ogden, Stanstead, 12 July 1838; vol. 542, T.A. Stayner to Charles Buller, Quebec, 25 July 1838; Laporte, *Patriotes et loyaux*, 361; Farfan, 'Stanstead's Other Journals,' 30–1. Only two copies of the *Patriot* and apparently none of the *Democrat* have survived.

45 *Missiskoui Standard*, 8 Aug., 3 Oct. 1837; Beaugrand-Champagne, 'Les mouvements,' 38–9, 40–1; Kesteman, 'Les premiers journaux,' 247–8, 250–1.

46 The surviving issues of the *Standard* become very scattered after 10 April 1838, and it ceased publication in 1839. *Missiskoui Standard*, 6 Dec. 1836, 10 April 1838; Beaugrand-Champagne, 'Les mouvements,' 39–40; Laporte, *Patriotes et loyaux*, 347–8; Lorne Ste Croix, 'Ferres, James Moir,' *Dictionary of Canadian Biography* [hereafter *DCB*], vol. 9, 257–8.

47 See McNairn, *Capacity to Judge*, 187–8. Due largely to the location of the constituency's polling station, the voters of Dunham, Stanbridge, and St Armand did manage until 1821 to elect their candidate in Bedford, which included the seigneuries of Rouville, Monnoir, Bleury, and Sabrevois. Kesteman et al., *Histoire des Cantons de l'Est*, 199, 201–4.

48 See J.I. Little, ed., *The Child Letters: Public and Private Life in a Merchant-Politician's Family* (Montreal and Kingston, 1995), 12–14.

49 Beaugrand-Champagne, 'Les mouvements,' 43–6, 60–1; Laporte, *Patriotes et loyaux*, 356.

50 S.D. Clark, *Movements of Political Protest in Canada, 1640–1840* (Toronto, 1959), 277–8.

51 Beaugrand-Champagne, 'Les mouvements,' 49; Laporte, *Patriotes et loyaux*, 356.

52 Quoted in Beaugrand-Champagne, 'Les mouvements,' 49.

53 Ibid., 50; Laporte, *Patriotes et loyaux*, 360.

54 Laporte, *Patriotes et loyaux*, 345–6.

55 Beaugrand-Champagne, 'Les mouvements,' 47–8; Laporte, *Patriotes et loyaux*, 347.

56 For details, see Kesteman, *Histoire de Sherbrooke*, vol. 1: 129–31.

57 Laporte, *Patriotes et loyaux*, 361–2.

58 Quoted in ibid., 374.

59 See McNairn, *Capacity to Judge*, chap. 4.

60 Beaugrand-Champagne, 'Les mouvements,' 53; Laporte, *Patriotes et loyaux*, 372.

61 Little, *Child Letters*, 14–15.

62 Beaugrand-Champagne, 'Les mouvements,' 57–9, 65n66; Laporte (*Patriotes et loyaux*, 351) states that the conversion took place *before* the election.

63 Laporte, *Patriotes et loyaux*, 357.

64 Kesteman, 'Une bourgeoisie,' 695; Clark, *Movements*, 329.

65 Beaugrand-Champagne, 'Les mouvements,' 65–6.

66 Ibid., 62–3.

67 Ibid., 66.

68 Quoted in ibid., 70.

69 A southern division of the Sherbrooke Constitutional Association was established in Lennoxville in January 1836 when ten township sub-committees were also formed. *Missiskoui Standard*, 2 Feb. 1835; Laporte, *Patriotes et loyaux*, 367–8, 372, 374.

70 Layfield claimed that the founding meeting had actually voted thirty-three to seventeen against forming a branch of the association, but forty-two joined the association at that meeting. *Quebec Mercury*, 6 Jan., 15 Jan., 21 Jan. 1835, 12 Jan. 1836.

71 *Missiskoui Standard*, 28 April 1835; Beaugrand-Champagne, 'Les mouvements,' 70–1; Laporte, *Patriotes et loyaux*, 347, 360, 363.

72 Beaugrand-Champagne, 'Les mouvements,' 78–9; Laporte, *Patriotes et loyaux*, 358.

73 Beaugrand-Champagne, 'Les mouvements,' 69; Laporte, *Patriotes et loyaux*, 29, 350.

74 *Missiskoui Post and Canada Record*, 5 Aug. 1835.

75 Laporte, *Patriotes et loyaux*, 350–1; Beaugrand-Champagne, 'Les mouvements,' 72–7, 79, 80–1, 86–7 (quoted on 77).

76 *Missiskoui Standard*, 30 June 1835; Beaugrand-Champagne, 'Les mouvements,' 133–4.

77 *Missiskoui Standard*, 22 Dec. 1835.

78 *Missiskoui Standard*, 16 Feb. 1836; Beaugrand-Champagne, 'Les mouvements,' 87–9; Laporte, *Patriotes et loyaux*, 347.

79 *Missiskoui Standard*, 15 March 1836; Beaugrand-Champagne, 'Les mouvements,' 90–1; Laporte, *Patriotes et loyaux*, 363.

80 NA, RG4 A1, vol. 508, 26, petition of William Colclough, Leeds, 17 April 1837.

81 NA, RG4 A1, vol. 502, file 7–10, printed minutes, Leeds, 25 March 1836; Laporte, *Patriotes et loyaux*, 374–5.

82 The *Missiskoui Standard* also objected to the Montreal Association's opposition to Catholic Church tithes and the clergy reserves. *Missiskoui Standard*, 8 March, 22 March 1836, 14 June, 21 June 1836, 3 Jan. 1837; Beaugrand-Champagne, 'Les mouvements,' 92–3, 148–50; Laporte, *Patriotes et loyaux*, 348.

83 *Missiskoui Standard*, 29 March 1836. The Montreal Association voted in early April to proceed with the provincial convention, which finally took place in July. *Missiskoui Standard*, 3 May, 19 July 1836.

84 In reply, the commissioners suggested that they might be willing to consider municipal government for the region. *Missiskoui Standard*, 31 May 1836.

85 Quoted in Beaugrand-Champagne, 'Les mouvements,' 94.

86 Laporte, *Patriotes et loyaux*, 43–4; Little, 'British Toryism,' 27–31; Little, *State and Society*, 22–31.

87 Beaugrand-Champagne, 'Les mouvements,' 89–90; Laporte, *Patriotes et loyaux*, 358.

88 *Missiskoui Standard*, 21 July, 28 July, 4 Aug. 1835; Laporte, *Patriotes et loyaux*, 351; Little, *Child Letters*, 15.

89 *Missiskoui Standard*, 10 Jan. 1837. Grannis died soon afterward. Laporte, *Patriotes et loyaux*, 357–8.

90 B.F. Hubbard, *Forests and Clearings: The History of Stanstead County, Province of Quebec* (Montreal, 1874), 156, 158–9. On Elias Lee's religious fervour, see Little, *Borderland Religion*, 186.

91 Charles Carroll Colby was named in honour of Charles Carroll. Marguerite Van Die, *Religion, Family, and Community in Victorian Canada: The Colbys of Carrollcroft* (Montreal and Kingston, 2005), 11.

92 Stanstead Historical Society, M.F. Colby Papers, Political Tracts, 1836–51, 'Electors of the County of Stanstead,' 26 Dec. 1836.

93 Quoted in Beaugrand-Champagne, 'Les mouvements,' 97.

94 See, for example, Charles Sellar, *The Market Revolution: Jacksonian America, 1815–1846* (New York, 1991).

95 *Vindicator and Canadian Advertiser* (Montreal), 7–20 Jan. 1837; Beaugrand-Champagne, 'Les mouvements,' 95–7; Laporte, *Patriotes et loyaux*, 358; Little, *Child Letters*, 16–17.

96 NA, RG4 A1, vol. 500, 34–34A, Number of Persons in arrear of 2 or more years for Quit Rents, 1 Jan. 1837.

97 *Missiskoui Standard*, 8 Aug. 1837. See also 17 Jan., 7 March, 16 May, 29 Aug. 1837.

98 NA, RG4 A1, vol. 502, 80–1, John Clapham to Earl of Gosford, Que-
    bec, 8 Feb. 1837; vol. 503, 194, Petition of quit rent inhabitants of the
    Township of Inverness to Earl of Gosford; 195–7, Resolutions passed
    by quit-rent settlers of Inverness, 15 Feb. 1837; vol. 506, 52, Charles
    Drury to S. Walcott, Quebec, 5 April 1837; 53, petition of quit renters
    of Leeds, County of Megantic. Seventy-four of those leasing crown
    reserves were in arrears four to five years, while thirty of those leas-
    ing clergy reserves (by far the largest number in the region) owed for
    five years. NA, RG4 A1, vol. 500, 34–34A, Number of Persons in
    arrear of 2 or more years for Quit Rents due on Crown & Clergy
    Lands, 1 Jan. 1837.

99 Quoted in Beaugrand-Champagne, 'Les mouvements,' 129–30.

100 Laporte, *Patriotes et loyaux*, 352.

101 *Missiskoui Standard*, 11 July 1837; Beaugrand-Champagne, 'Les
    mouvements,' 100–3, 139.

102 Beaugrand-Champagne, 'Les mouvements,' 103–4.

103 See Carol Wilton, *Popular Politics and Political Culture in Upper
    Canada, 1800–1850* (Montreal and Kingston, 2000), chap. 6.

104 See the petitions in NA, RG4 A1, vol. 505, pp. 262–65A; and
    Missiskoui Standard, 19 April, 26 April, 13 Sept., 8 Nov. 1836, 14
    March, 23 May, 11 July, 18 July, 8 Aug., 15 Aug., 12 Sept. 1837, 2
    Jan. 1838.

105 Quoted in *Missiskoui Standard*, 9 May 1837.

106 On this project, see *Missiskoui Standard*, 8 Sept., 13 Oct., 20 Oct., 1
    Dec. 1835, 26 July 1836; and Little, *Child Letters*, 15.

107 *Missiskoui Standard*, 18 May, 11 Aug., 24 Nov., 1 Dec. 1835, 31 May
    1836; Beaugrand-Champagne, 'Les mouvements,' 120, 142–3.

108 *Sherbrooke Gazette*, 23 Sept. 1837.

109 See, for example, Beaugrand-Champagne, 'Les mouvements,' 176.

110 *Missiskoui Standard*, 5 Dec. 1837.

111 Ibid., 26 Dec. 1837, 2 Jan. 1838.

112 Archives Nationales du Québec à Québec [hereafter ANQQ], E17,
    Fonds Ministère de la Justice, Événements de 1837–1838 [hereafter
    Événements], no. 71, voluntary examination of Dr Leonard Brown,
    Montreal, 15 Feb. 1838.

113 Laporte, *Patriotes et loyaux*, 351–2, 354; ANQQ, Événements, no.
    1172, testimony of Ephraim Knight, 16 Nov. 1838.

114 M. Child to Franklin Mack, Stanstead, 4 Dec. 1837, cited in *Stanstead
    Journal*, 6 April 1916.

115 Amédée Papineau, *Journal d'un Fils de la Liberté, réfugié aux États-
    Unis, par suite de l'insurrection canadienne, en 1837* (Montreal,
    1972), vol. 1: 106–8.

116 NA, MG24 B2, Papiers Papineau, no. 2583, J.B. Ryan to Louis Perreault, 22 Jan. 1838.

117 Prominent local anti-Patriots had protested that as 'the head of that party in this vicinity who are endeavouring to overthrow the present form of Government and establish a French republic,' Child could not be trusted with the mail. They recommended the former Eaton postmaster, Phineas Hubbard, in his stead. NA, RG4 A1, vol. 525, 212, Memorial of loyal inhabitants of Stanstead, 29 Nov. 1837; 213, affidavit of Jas. C. Peasley, j.p., Stanstead, 29 Nov. 1837.

118 Little, *Child Letters*, 12, 17–18.

119 NA, RG4 A1, vol. 526, 27, W. Ritchie to S. Walcott, Stanstead, 2 Dec. 1837.

120 NA, RG4, A1, vol. 530, 251, Wm Ritchie to S. Walcott, Stanstead, 27 Jan. 1838.

121 Quoted in Little, *Borderland Religion*, 191.

122 On Chamberlin, see Reisner, *Diary of a Country Clergyman*, 190–2.

123 See Little, *Borderland Religion*, 114.

124 Little, *State and Society*, 53.

125 Stanstead Historical Society, 'A Memoir of Ralph Merry IV, 1786–1863' (typescript), 3 Feb. 1838.

126 NA, RG4 A1, vol. 531, 133, John R. Lambly to Sir, Halifax, 24 Feb. 1838; vol. 557, 234, Lt Col. Head to Goldie, Frost Village, 7 Dec. 1838.

127 NA, RG4 A1, vol. 532, 30, Wm Ritchie to W.P. Christie, Stanstead, 8 March 1838.

128 NA, RG9, 1A1, Adjutant-General, Lower Canada, Correspondence, vol. 48, Sherbrooke, Major Charles Whitcher to Deputy Adjutant-General, Sherbrooke, 12 Aug. 1837; Edward Hale et al. to Civil Secretary, Sherbrooke, 27 Nov. 1837. The same request came from Melbourne. See D. Thomas and Edward Tourneaux to Sir, Melbourne Township, 27 Nov. 1837.

129 NA, RG9, 1A1, vol. 49, Sherbrooke, Charles Whitcher to Colonel Antrobus, Sherbrooke, 24 Nov. 1838; vol. 52, Sherbrooke, Lt Col. C. Whitcher to Major Goldie, Sherbrooke, 10 June 1839.

130 Dominique Dion and Roch Legault, 'L'organisation de la milice de la région montréalaise de 1792 à 1837: de la paroisse au comté,' *Bulletin d'histoire politique* 8, nos 2–3 (2000): 116; Brian Young, 'The Volunteer Militia in Lower Canada, 1837–50,' in Tamara Myers et al., eds, *Power, Place and Identity: Historical Studies of Social and Legal Regulation in Quebec* (Montreal, 1998), 40.

131 ANQQ, Événments, no. 3786, C.R. Ogden to Earl of Gosford, Montreal, 18 July 1837. See also NA, RG4 A1, vol. 524, 53, memorial of inhabitants of Sherbrooke and vicinity to Stephen Walcott, [n.d.].

132 NA, RG4 A1, vol. 11, 2984, Gosford to Colborne, Castle of St Lewis, 21 Nov. 1837; Laporte, *Patriotes et loyaux*, 369–71; Marie-Paule LaBrèque, 'Heriot, Frederick George,' *DCB*, vol. 7, 397–8.

133 NA, RG4 A1, vol. 527, 121, F.G. Heriot to Sir John Colborne, Melbourne, 11 Dec. 1837.

134 ANQQ, Événements, no. 3793, Jno. Moore to S. Walcot, Sherbrooke, 3 Jan. 1838; no. 3794, Jno. Moore to S. Walcot, Sherbrooke, 22 Jan. 1837 [*sic*].

135 Moore was employed by the British American Land Company, lending some support to Laporte's claim (*Patriotes et loyaux*, 343) that this and other volunteer companies were funded by the company.

136 McCord Museum, Hale Papers, Edward Hale to F.H. [*sic*] Heriot (copy), Jan. 1838; Heriot to Hale, Melbourne, 29 Jan. 1838; John Eden to Edward Hale, Montreal, 5 Feb. 1838; Edward Hale to Col. Eden (copy), [n.d.]; Little, *State and Society*, 26–7.

137 NA, RG 4 A1, vol. 528, 145–8, minutes of a meeting held at Lodge's Hotel, 18 Dec. 1837.

138 NA, RG4 A1, vol. 556, 297, J.S. Jones to Sir John Colborne, Compton, Nov. 1838; ANQQ, Événements, no. 3810, J.S. Jones to Sir, Montreal, 8 March 1838.

139 NA, RG4 A1, vol. 526, 27, W. Ritchie to S. Walcott, Stanstead, 2 Dec. 1837; 28, resolutions of Loyal meeting at Stanstead, 30 Nov. 1837.

140 ANQQ, Événements, no. 1200, William Ritchie to Col. Rowan, Stanstead, 12 Nov. 1838.

141 NA, RG4 A1, vol. 525, 111–11a, W.A. [?] Chaffus [?], j.p., to S. Walcott, Frost Village, 25 Nov. 1837; Laporte, *Patriotes et loyaux*, 363.

142 *Township Reformer*, 21 Nov. 1837.

143 NA, RG9, 1A1, vol. 47, Missisquoi, Captains Peleg Thomas, Oren J. Kemp, and Henry Baker to Col. Robert Jones, Frelighsburg, 21 Nov. 1837; R. Jones to L. Juchereau Duchenay, Bedford, 23 Nov. 1837; *Missiskoui Standard*, 21 Nov., 28 Nov., 5 Dec., 12 Dec. 1837, 10 April 1838; Beaugrand-Champagne, 'Les mouvements,'105–8; Laporte, *Patriotes et loyaux*, 349.

144 ANQQ, Événements, 559, Thomas Stark to Attorney-General Ogden, Frelighsburg, 20 Nov. 1837.

145 Clapham was also concerned about the loyalty of the Irish Catholics in the neigbouring parishes of St Gilles and St Patrick. NA, RG4 A1, vol. 525, 173, Jno. G. Clapham to S. Walcott, St Giles, 28 Nov. 1837, Ireland, 2 Dec. 1837. See also Laporte, *Patriotes et loyaux*, 376–7.

146 NA, RG4 A1, vol. 525, 126–26a, Jno. G. Clapham to S. Walcott, Quebec, 25 Nov. 1837. When completed in 1843, the Gosford Road would run parallel to the effectively abandoned Craig Road from Saint-Gilles-de-Lotbinière to Inverness Township, then to Sherbrooke.

147   *Quebec Mercury*, 16 Dec. 1837. See also NA, RG4 A1, vol. 525, 153, Thos. W. Lloyd to Sir, Quebec, 27 Nov. 1837.

148   NA, RG4 A1, vol. 525, 173–4, Jno. G. Clapham to S. Walcott, Ireland, 2 Dec. 1837.

149   NA, RG4 A1, vol. 525, 114, Jno. G. Clapham to S. Walcott, Quebec, 25 Nov. 1837; vol. 526, 46, minutes of a meeting held in Upper Ireland, 4 Dec. 1837; minutes of a meeting held in Lower Inverness, 6 Dec. 1837; minutes of a meeting of the inhabitants of Hamilton, Inverness, 8 Dec. 1837; ANQQ, Événements, nos. 3847–9, enrolment pledges, Inverness, 1 Dec. 1837; no. 3850, Ireland, 4 Dec. 1837; no. 3851, Inverness, 8 Dec. 1837; *Quebec Mercury*, 16 Dec. 1837, 11 Jan. 1838, 21 April 1838. Presumably because the Megantic company was considered to be part of the Royal Quebec Volunteers, it was not included as a distinct unit in the list of volunteer corps printed on 29 December 1837 (see Appendix A). When it was disbanded in April 1838, McKillop was allowed to take thirty stand of arms home with him. *Quebec Mercury*, 21 April 1838. On McKillop's role in the Arran settlement, see J.I. Little, 'From the Isle of Arran to Inverness Township: A Case Study of Highland Emigration and North American Settlement, 1829–34,' *Scottish Economic and Social History* 20, part 1 (2000): 3–30.

150   ANQQ, Événements, no. 3852, S.W. to J.G. Clapham, 26 Jan. 1838; no. 3853, Colonel Baird to S. Walcot, Quebec, 27 Jan. 1838; no. 3854, Jno. G. Clapham to S. Walcot, Quebec, 29 Jan. 1838; no. 3855, affidavit of Jno. G. Clapham, jr., Quebec, 2 Feb. 1838; no. 3856, affidavit of Capt. Archibald McKillop, 3 Feb. 1838; no. 3857, affidavit of J. Greaves, Quebec, 2 Feb. 1838; no. 3859, Jno. Clapham to Col. Rowan, Quebec, 5 March 1838; no. 3860, R. to J.G. Clapham, Quebec, 16 March 1838; no. 3867, Jno. Clapham to Col. Baird, Quebec, 1 May 1838; no. 3868, James Baird to Colonel Rowan, Quebec, 4 May 1838; no. 3869, R. to J.G. Clapham, Quebec, 8 May 1838.

151   NA, MG8, F13, Collections of the Brome County Historical Society, XIV, Rebellion of 1838, D. Wood to A. Willard, Shefford, 29 Jan. 1838; A.W. to Lieut. Col. John Eden, Stukeley, 1 Feb. 1838.

152   NA, RG4 A1, vol. 527, 121, F.G. Heriot to Sir John Colborne, Melbourne, 11 Dec. 1837; vol. 530, 250, Thos. Taine to H. Jessop, Quebec, 27 Jan. 1838. Several men from Philipsburg reported in later November that they had seen approximately twenty armed Canadians and as many Americans gathered in Swanton who were preparing to join a force of approximately 300 in invading Canada. NA, RG4 A1, vol. 525, 210, affidavit of Abraham B. Merrill, 29 Nov. 1837; 211, affidavit of James Taylor and Paschal P. Russell, 29 Nov. 1837. See

also ANQQ, Événements, 866, testimony of P. Russell, Philipsburg, 26 May 1838; 868, testimony of Ralph Taylor, Philipsburg, 26 May 1838.

153 Quoted in Little, *Borderland Religion*, 189.

154 *Missiskoui Standard*, 12 Dec., 19 Dec. 1837, 2 Jan. 1838; Duffy and Muller, *Anxious Democracy*, 92; Charles O. Jones, 'The Moore's Corner Battle in 1837,' *Fourth Annual Report of the Missisquoi Historical Society for 1908–9*, 67–73; ANQQ, Événements, nos. 547–58. The quote is from Elinor Kyte Senior, *Redcoats and Patriotes: The Rebellions in Lower Canada, 1837–38* (Stittsville, ON, 1985), 108.

155 *Missiskoui Standard*, 12 Dec. 1837.

156 Laporte, *Patriotes et loyaux*, 370.

157 Quoted in Duffy and Muller, *Anxious Democracy*, 65–6, 144; see also 91–2, 145.

158 *Missiskoui Standard*, 26 Dec. 1837.

159 *Canadian Patriot*, 2 Feb. 1838.

160 *Missiskoui Standard*, 13 March 1838.

161 Senior, *Redcoats and Patriotes*, 152.

162 NA, MG8, F13, XIV, A.W. to Lieut. Col. John Eden, Stukeley, 1 Feb. 1838; IX, Township Papers, Shefford, [Abijah Willard] to Sir, Stukely, 9 July 1838 (incomplete draft); Brome, Soldiers' Oath signed by George Pettes and ten others.

163 The paymaster, Abijah Willard, was in turn accused of changing Colborne's mind. NA, MG8, F13, XIV, A.W. to Lieut. Col. John Eden, Stukeley, 1 Feb. 1838; Abijah Willard to Lieut. Col. John Eden, Stukeley, 15 Feb. 1838; W.P. Christie to Abijah Willard, Montreal, 21 Feb. 1838; Capt. Sheppard Parker to Major W.P. Christie, Stukely, 9 July 1838 (copy); IX, Township Papers, Shefford, Abijah Willard to Major Head, Stukeley, 19 Nov. 1838. For the units that were to paid, and those that were not, see Appendix A.

164 *Sherbrooke Gazette*, 28 Dec. 1837.

165 When McMahon again asked for an *exeat* in late January, however, he was refused once more. Mgr Albert Gravel, *Messire Jean-Baptiste McMahon, premier curé-missionnaire de Sherbrooke, 1834–1840* (Sherbrooke, 1960), 19, 25; Jules Martel, 'Les troubles de 1837–38 dans la région de Sherbrooke,' *La Revue de l'Université de Sherbrooke* 5, no. 1 (1964): 40–1; Little, *State and Society*, 95–6.

166 ANQQ, Événements, no. 1198, 'Extract of a letter from L. Spalding, Esq. a Merchant of Stanstead, L.C. to his partner, dated Montpelier, Vt. Dec 30, 1837,' no. 3788, Alex Kilborn to Col. Heriot, Stanstead, 1 Jan. 1838; no. 3789, Jas. Thompson to Col. Heriot, Melbourne, 2 Jan. [1838].

167 The letter is printed in *Montreal Herald*, 22 March 1838. The New-
foundland-born John B. Ryan had established the 'People's Line' in
competition with the Molson steamboat line on the St Lawrence. His
biographer states that in January 1838 he offered to purchase guns,
powder, and shot in Chelsea, Vermont, 'to further the Sacred Cause ...
of opposing British misrule in our native Country,' but she makes no
mention of his involvement in Nelson's planned attack. Marianna
O'Gallagher, 'Ryan, John B.,'*DCB*, vol. 9, 695.

168 The other names given by the informants (some of whom may have
been coerced into naming family members) as having been in Derby
Line or involved in the plot are Harvey Merriman, John Tuck, George
Islip, Julius Ives, David Jewitt 2d, Uriah Jewett, Abraham Channell
2d, Samuel Mann, Joseph P. Allen, Asa L. Harvey, William Harvey,
Amos Morgan, Hazen Lawrence, Daniel Miller, Asaph (presumably
Asa) Hollister, Harrison Wheeler, John Ewings, Thomas Ewings,
James Ewings, Ira Daniels, Welcome Daniels, Daniel Sprague, Erastus
Sprague, Hiram Aldrich, George Sanborn, Carlisle Sanborn, James
McDuffee, Heman Durkee, Sheldon Durkee, and Charles Hoeg. NA,
RG4 A1, vol. 532, 167, affidavit of Asa Lillie, 3 March 1838; affi-
davit of C.S. Channell, 3 March 1838; 168, affidavit of Joseph Ward,
3 March 1838; 6 March 1838, affidavit of Wm Lewis; 169, affidavit
of Moses McDuffee, 7 March 1838.

169 Ryan was, admittedly, an outsider, and O'Gallagher claims that his
first attempt to enter Lower Canada in the spring of 1838 was
blocked, but, aside from the fact that Nelson's letter was addressed to
him in Stanstead, he is identified as a Stanstead resident (albeit as J.
Ruan) in the *Canadian Patriot*'s report of the Newport pro-Patriot
meeting of 1 February. Martel, 'Les troubles,' 45; O'Gallagher,
'Ryan,' 695. My thanks to John Scott for this observation.

170 NA, RG4 A1, vol. 542, 102, P. Hubbard to T.A. Stayner, Stanstead, 11
July 1838; Aegidius Fauteux, *Patriotes de 1837–1838* (Montreal,
1950), 116–17. Hubbard, based on the memory of J.S. Walton, who
served as ensign, mistakenly claims that the plot was to unfold in January 1837. Hubbard, *Forests and Clearings*, 12–13. Several Stanstead
justices of the peace complained to the governor-general in April that
men identified as being part of the plot were returning to their homes
'without any notice being taken.' NA, RG4 A1, 1838, vol. 533, Selah
Pomroy, j.p., Ichabod Smith, j.p., Jas. C. Peasley, j.p., and Wilder
Pierce, j.p. to William Rowan, Civil Secretary, Stanstead, 9 April
1838.

171 McCord Museum, Hale Papers, undated correspondence from Edward
Hale to Eliza Hale.

172 NA, RG4 A1, vol. 532, 104, Memorial of Harvey Elkins to Colborne, Montreal, 20 March 1838; Duffy and Muller, *Anxious Democracy*, 62; Hubbard, *Forests and Clearings*, 13–14; Rev. Ernest M. Taylor, *History of Brome County, Quebec* (Montreal, 1937), vol. 2: 6–11.

173 H.N. Muller III, 'Trouble on the Border, 1838: A Neglected Incident from Vermont's Neglected History,' *Vermont History* 44 (1976): 100–2. Muller identifies the correspondent as N.R. Woods, but internal evidence suggests that he mistook the H. for an N. The Ritchie notarial index lists a deed in 1840 from Henry B. Woods (Muller's R. would therefore be a B.) to Warren S. Howland, the husband of Henry's sister, Sarah. The Woods letter mentions Howland, stating that some of his letters to him had been intercepted. Henry Woods also had a brother, Charles, who was obviously the individual referred to in the letter as a rebel. Charles Woods was in charge of issuing oaths for the Potton branch of the Hunters' Lodge. My thanks to John Scott for this information.

174 McCord Museum, Hale Papers, undated correspondence from Edward Hale to Eliza Hale. Martel ('Les troubles,' 47) claims that they conducted raids into the nearby Vermont villages searching for arms and ammunition.

175 NA, RG4 A1, vol. 532, 104, Memorial of Harvey F. Elkins, S. Potton, to Colborne, Montreal, 20 March 1838.

176 Quoted in Little, *Borderland Religion*, 189.

177 Senior, *Redcoats and Patriotes*, 153–4; Duffy and Muller, *Anxious Democracy*, 62–3; *Missiskoui Standard*, 6 March, 13 March 1838.

178 See Senior, *Redcoats and Patriotes*, 155–7; Laporte, *Patriotes et loyaux*, 40–2; Greer, *The Patriots*, 338–44; Richard Chabot, Jacques Monet, and Yves Roby, 'Nelson, Robert,' *DCB*, vol. 10, 544–7.

179 Duffy and Muller attribute this phenomenon to the search for 'an identity with the rest of their countrymen.' Elsewhere, and more convincingly, Muller states that Vermonters were seeking an identification with their own revolutionary past in order to gain 'a needed sense of security.' Duffy and Muller, *Anxious Democracy*, 52, 65–72, 127–37; Muller, 'Trouble on the Border,' 98. Focusing on Ohio, a recent article links American support for the Patriots with resistance to the rise of the 'commercial market economy based on a banking oligarchy, credit, and paper money,' an analysis that does not appear to apply to Vermont given the prominent social status of many of the Hunters' Lodge members. Andrew Bonthius, 'The Patriot War of 1837–1838: Locofocoism with a Gun?' *Labour / Le Travail* 52 (Fall 2003): 12. See also Albert B. Corey, *The Crisis of 1830–1842 in Canadian–American Relations* (New York, 1941; reissued 1970); and

Oscar A. Kinchen, *The Rise and Fall of the Patriot Hunters* (New York, 1956).

180 Allan Greer, '1837–38: Rebellion Reconsidered,' *Canadian Historical Review* 76 (1995): 15. The entire United States force had, however, consisted of less than 400 soldiers from Maine to Michigan. NA, RG4 A1, vol. 14, 4106–7, H.S. Fox to Sir John Colborne, Washington, 11 March 1838.

181 See, for example, NA, RG4 A1, vol. 18, 5329–30, Lt Col. W. Williams to Sir John Colborne, Bedford, 25 Oct. 1838.

182 Louis Perrault, *Lettres d'un Patriote réfugié au Vermont, 1837–1839* (Montreal, 1999), 81; Jean-Paul Bernard, 'Vermonters and the Lower Canadian Rebellions of 1837–1838,' *Vermont History* 58 (Fall 1990): 260–1, 263n35.

183 NA, RG4 A1, vol. 563, 122, Major Head, j.p., to Captain Goldie, Frost Village, 29 Dec. 1838; ANQQ, Événements, no. 1173, testimony of Samuel Stocker of Potton, 15 Feb. 1839; no. 1174, testimony of Samuel Stocker, 15 Dec. 1838; no. 1175, testimony of Artemus Newton of Shefford, 24 Dec. 1838; no. 1177, testimony of Moses Elkins of Potton, 25 Dec. 1838; Farfan, *Stanstead Region*, 51.

184 *Missiskoui Standard*, 3 April 1838. Jacquay is mistakenly identified as Enoch Jacquies, a farmer, in Alain Messier, *Dictionnaire encyclopédique et historique des patriotes, 1837–1838* (Montreal, 2002), 246, and as Enoch Jakes in Bernard, *Les rébellions*, 306.

185 ANQQ, Événements, no. 1180, testimony of Calvin Harvey, Shefford, 26 Dec. 1838; testimony of Daniel Miltmore of Potton, 27 Dec. 1838.

186 ANQQ, Événements, no. 1178, deposition of William Lebaron of Potton Township, 26 Dec. 1838; no. 1180, testimony of Daniel Miltmore of Potton, 27 Dec. 1838.

187 See Senior, *Redcoats and Patriotes*, 159, and chaps 13 and 14.

188 NA, RG4 A, vol. 526, 52, John Ployart to Stephen Walcott, Township of Durham, 5 Dec. 1837.

189 ANQQ, Événements, no. 1202, affidavit of L.B. David, Drummondville, 5 Nov. 1838; no. 1203, John Ployart to Captain Goldie, Durham Township, 9 Nov. 1838; no. 1204, John Ployart to Captain Goldie, Durham Township, 28 Nov. 1838; no. 3523, affidavit of Simon Dell, Durham Township, 11 Dec. 1838; NA, RG4 A1, vol. 557, 129, petition to Colborne by H. Robson, Drummondville, missionary; 130, Col. F.G. Heriot to Charles Montizambert, Melbourne, 6 Dec. 1838; Martel, 'Les troubles,' 49–50; Fauteux, *Patriotes*, 165–6; Messier, *Dictionnaire encyclopédique*, 103–4.

190 Hubbard, *Forests and Clearings*, 14.

191 Hubbard, *Forests and Clearings*, 154–5; NA, RG4 A1, vol. 554,

381–2, Wm Ritchie to Col. Rowan, Stanstead, 15 Nov. 1838; 383, affidavit of Jos. Martin of Stanstead, 14 Nov. 1838.
192 Quoted in Little, *Borderland Religion*, 192.
193 Hubbard, *Forests and Clearings*, 14–15. The *Montreal Gazette* (20 Nov. 1838) reported that 'strong detachments' of the Queen's Mounted Rangers, the Sherbrooke Rifles, and the Sherbrooke Dragoons were sent to Stanstead.
194 A local historian claims that all the boats on Lake Memphremagog were sunk to interfere with the military's movements, but the *Montreal Gazette* (17 Nov. 1838) mentioned only the sinking of a single horse boat. William Bryant Bullock, *Beautiful Waters: Devoted to the Memphremagog Region and Adjacent Counties* (Newport, VT, 1938), vol. 2: 40.
195 NA, RG4 A1, vol. 532, 170, affidavit of Taylor L. Parsons, 10 April 1838. On Channell and Tuck, see Messier, *Dictionnaire encyclopédique*, 99–100, 467.
196 Laporte, *Patriotes et loyaux*, 360.
197 John M. Scott, 'Stanstead Cavalry Occupies Georgeville; Three Jailed; Bullock, Ives Flee for Border,' *Georgeville Enterprise* 3, no. 1 (Spring/Summer 1994): 3–5.
198 NA, RG4 A1, vol. 554, 388, W. Ritchie to Col. Rowan, Stanstead, 15 Nov. 1838; vol. 539, 30, petition of Increase Bullock to Lord Durham, Georgeville, 19 June 1838. Ritchie's suggestion was supported by the local military authorities and a number of local magistrates who stressed the vulnerability of Georgeville to American attack. Ritchie himself became the registrar. NA, RG4 A1, vol. 556, 208, Lt Col. Wright Chamberlin et al., to Civil Secretary, Stanstead Plain, 24 Nov. 1838.
199 Little, *Borderland Religion*, 192. The *Montreal Gazette* (20 Nov. 1838) reported that Elias Lee was 'a leader of the discontented in Barnston' and that he had been identified by Captain Kilborn as the person who fired on him, but there is no other documentation of this claim.
200 NA, RG4 A1, vol. 554, 381–2, Wm Ritchie to Col. Rowan, Stanstead, 15 Nov. 1838.
201 *Montreal Gazette*, 20 Nov. 1838.
202 Ibid., 6 Dec. 1838.
203 Jared Blanchard would not be released until 15 April 1839, and an arson charge in 1844 would result in his imprisonment in the Kingston Penitentiary, where he would die in 1851. Little, *State and Society*, 64–5, 89–90. On the list of political prisoners he compiled in December 1838 (see Appendix B), Sheriff Whitcher crossed out the

name Jared and replaced it with Gerard, which presumably explains why Fauteux (followed by Bernard and Messier) identifies him mistakenly as Gérard Blanchard. Fauteux, *Patriotes de 1837–38*, 116.

204 Hubbard, *Forests and Clearings*, 326; Bernard, *Les rébellions*, 306; Messier, *Dictionnaire encyclopédique*, 59. Bernard mistakenly spells Hoeg as Horf. I am grateful to John Scott for information on the Sanborn-Blanchard family.

205 Hubbard, *Forests and Clearings*, 210. On Burpee, see Messier, *Dictionnaire encyclopédique*, 89. Whitcher wrote 'Blandel' rather than 'Blaisdell Kent,' but Blaisdell was the brother of Jonas and Jacob, and Blaisdell was their mother's maiden name. My thanks to John Scott for this information. As critics of Read's study of the revolt in western Upper Canada have pointed out, a meaningful socioeconomic comparison would require analysis of all the families in the township. See Colin Read, *The Rising in Western Upper Canada, 1837–8: The Duncombe Revolt and After* (Toronto, 1982).

206 ANQQ, Événements, no. 1181, Petition of Taylor Wadleigh to Sir John Colborne, Montreal Gaol, 14 Jan. 1839; no. 1182, Petition of undersigned inhabitants of Stanstead and Sherbrooke Counties to Sir John Colborne, Stanstead, 7 Jan. 1839; *Journals of the Legislative Assembly*, 23 April 1839; Laporte, *Patriotes et loyaux*, 359.

207 It is also not clear why Whitcher did not include Brooks in his list of political prisoners, but he was certainly in the Sherbrooke jail in October 1839 when he was granted bail. ANQQ, Événements, no. 3747, J. Fletcher to Major Goldie, Sherbrooke, 16 Oct. 1839; 19 Oct. 1839. Laporte (*Patriotes et loyaux*, 366) is therefore mistaken when he states that Brooks was released several days after his arrest.

208 ANQQ, Événements, 3259, T.A. Young to W.L. Coffin, Quebec, 25 Jan. 1839.

209 None of their names appeared in my search through the trial records. See also Kesteman et al., *Histoire des Cantons de l'Est*, 216.

210 Quoted in Little, *Borderland Religion*, 61.

211 Quoted in ibid.

212 Quoted in ibid., 193.

213 Quoted in ibid., 83.

214 ANQQ, Événements, no. 1194, Rotus Parmelee to Charles Buller, Waterloo, 7 Sept. 1838; no. 1195, Rotus Parmelee to Charles Buller, Waterloo, 28 Sept. 1838; no. 1196, D. Wood et al. to Charles Buller, Waterloo, 1 Oct. 1838. For the affidavits, see nos. 1183–93.

215 Quoted in Little, *Borderland Religion*, 84–5.

216 Quoted in ibid., 193.

217 Senior, *Redcoats and Patriotes*, 200–1; Duffy and Muller, *Anxious Democracy*, 72. On the destruction of Patriot properties after the 1838 Rebellion, see Beverley Boissery and Carla Paterson, '"Women's Work": Women and Rebellion in Lower Canada, 1837–9,' in F. Murray Greenwood and Barry Wright, eds, *Canadian State Trials*, vol. 2: *Rebellion and Invasion in the Canadas, 1837–1839* (Toronto, 2002), 372–5.
218 Gerald M. Craig, *Upper Canada: The Formative Years, 1784–1841* (Toronto, 1963), 249.
219 Elinor Kyte Senior, 'The Presence of French Canadians in American Towns Bordering Lower Canada, 1837–1840: Disaffection, Terror or Economic Pulls?' *Lifelines* 4 (Fall 1987): 23–4.
220 NA, RG4 A1, vol. 563, 30, Lt Col. Williams to Col. Charles Gore, Philipsburg, 30 Dec. 1838; vol. 565, 42–3, S.H. Jenison to Colborne, Middlebury, Vt, 10 Jan. 1839.
221 NA, RG4 A1, vol. 565, 48, J. Colborne to Lord Glenelg, Montreal, 15 Jan. 1839; 153, Report of Committee of Executive Council, Montreal, 7 Jan. 1839; RG9, 1A1, vol. 51, Missisquoi, C.S. Reynolds to Lt. Col. Williams, St Armand, 16 Feb. 1839.
222 For example, William Miller, whose apocalyptic prophecies would soon result in a major religious upheaval in New England and New York, as well as the border townships, wrote to his son from Hatley in 1840 that the American government should arrest the 'villains' or 'they will soon commit crimes on either side of the line.' Quoted in Little, *Borderland Religion*, 130–1. See also Senior, 'Presence of French Canadians,' 24, 26.
223 Montreal Diocesan Archives, James Reid Papers, MG 2045, James Reid to Bishop of Montreal, St Armand, 18 Feb. 1839.
224 Quoted in Little, *Borderland Religion*, 190.
225 *Missiskoui Standard*, 12 Dec. 1837, 2 April 1839.
226 NA, RG4 B24, Stipendiary Magistrates, vol. 4, Col. Nickle to Capt. Griffin, Stanstead, 26 June 1839; affidavit of Wm Burroughs, Capt, sworn 26 June 1839.
227 ANQQ, Événements, no. 3588, W.L. Coffin to C.N. Montizambert, Lennoxville, 7 Dec. 1839; no. 3589, names of prisoners; Little, *State and Society*, 56–7.
228 Senior, 'Presence of French Canadians,' 27.
229 NA, MG24 A40, Colborne Papers, vol. 25, 7538–9, Thos. Austin et al. to Lieutenant-General Lord Somerset, Hatley, 5 March 1840; 7541–2, Address of the Clergy, Magistrates, Militia and Volunteer Officers, and Loyal Inhabitants of the Counties of Stanstead, Sherbrooke and Shefford to Colonel Robert Nickle, K.H., commanding these Districts.

230 NA, RG4, A1, vol. 567, 201, Williams to Capt. Goldie, Bedford, 24 Jan. 1839.
231 NA, RG4, A1, vol. 563, 79, Lt Col. Williams to Capt. Goldie, Philipsburg, 27 Dec. 1838.
232 *Missiskoui Standard*, 2 April 1839.
233 NA, RG1E1, Minute Books (State Matters), 1764–1867, State Book K, 233, revocation of martial law in District of St Francis, 13 April 1839; NA, MG8, F13, X, County Papers, Missisquoi, Circular to Officers Commanding Districts; District order by Lt Col. Williams, Bedford, 11 April 1839.
234 NA, RG9, 1A1, vol. 51, Missisquoi, Henry Baker to Lt Col. Jones, Cooksville, 19 June 1839; Oren Kemp to Lt Col. R. Jones, Frelighsburg, 21 June 1839; Lt Col. Jones to Lt Col. P. Young, Bedford, 14 June 1839, 22 June 1839. On militia discontent in the fall of 1838, see Senior, *Redcoats and Patriotes*, 159–60.
235 NA, RG8, I, British Military and Naval Records, Rebellion Correspondence, vol. 615, 149, General Order signed by John Eden, HQ, Montreal, 14 October 1839.
236 ANQQ, Événements, no. 1201, Jas. C. Peasley et al. to Major Goldie, Stanstead Plain, 13 May 1839.
237 The three men were Luther Bullard, Ichiel Cross, and Joshua Fisher. McCord Museum, Hale Papers, Edward Hale to Attorney General (copy), 2 Aug. 1839; E. Hale to Civil Secretary (copy), Sherbrooke, 30 Aug. 1829.
238 McCord Museum, Hale Papers, C.M. Montizambert to E. Hale, Montreal, 3 Sept. 1839.
239 NA, RG9, 1A1, vol. 52, Shefford, P.H. Knowlton to D.A.G.M., Brome, 20 June 1839; Little, *State and Society*, 41. As an MLA, Knowlton had himself initially supported Papineau. Laporte, *Patriotes et loyaux*, 362.
240 J.I. Little, 'The Short Life of a Local Protest Movement: The Annexation Crisis of 1849–50 in the Eastern Townships,' *Journal of the Canadian Historical Association*, n.s., no. 2 (1992): 73; Gendron et al., *Histoire du Piémont*, 127.
241 See Gordon T. Stewart, *The Origins of Canadian Politics: A Comparative Approach* (Vancouver, 1986), 29–31; S.F. Wise, 'Tory Factionalism: Kingston Elections and Upper Canadian Politics, 1820–1836,' *Ontario History* 57 (1965): 205–25; H.V. Nelles, 'Loyalism and Local Power. The District of Niagara, 1792–1837,' *Ontario History* 58 (1966): 99–116; F.H. Armstrong, 'The Oligarchy of the Western District of Upper Canada, 1788–1841,' Canadian Historical Association, *Historical Papers*, 1977, 87–102; and Colin Read, 'The London Dis-

trict Oligarchy in the Rebellion Era,' *Ontario History* 72 (1980): 195–209.

242 Quoted in Bonthius, 'Patriot War,' 27.

243 Duffy and Muller attribute Vermont's turmoil to economic crisis as well as the legacy of 'the Age of Jackson's claims for the sovereignty of the individual.' (*Anxious Democracy*, 4–6, 21–4, 36–7). For a more detailed and somewhat more sympathetic analysis, though one that emphasizes the conspiratorial frame of mind, see Randolph A. Roth, *The Democratic Dilemma: Religion, Reform, and the Social Order in the Connecticut River Valley of Vermont, 1791–1850* (Cambridge, MA, 1987), esp. chaps 5 and 6.

244 See Little, *Borderland Religion*, esp. 6–11.

245 See ibid., chaps 3–5.

246 See J.I. Little, 'The Fireside Kingdom: A Mid-Nineteenth-Century Anglican Perspective on Marriage and Parenthood,' in Nancy Christie, ed., *Households of Faith: Family, Gender, and Community in Canada, 1760–1969* (Montreal and Kingston, 2002), 77–102.

247 *Missiskoui Standard*, 28 Nov. 1837.

248 *Missiskoui Standard*, 16 Jan. 1838 – mistakenly self-identified as 9 Jan. 1838.

249 See Kesteman et al., *Histoire des Cantons de l'Est*, chap. 4; and Gendron et al., *Histoire du Piémont*, chap. 3.

250 On Côté's radical agrarianism, see Greer, *The Patriots*, 276–83.

251 Quoted in Little, *Borderland Religion*, 119.

252 See ibid., chap. 6.

253 For a brief discussion, see Kenny, 'Canadian Rebellions,' 191–3.

254 Greer, 'Rebellion Reconsidered,' 17; Michael S. Cross, '1837: The Necessary Failure,' in Michael S. Cross and Gregory S. Kealey, eds, *Readings in Canadian Social History*, vol. 2: *Pre-Industrial Canada, 1760–1849* (Toronto, 1982). See also Brian Young, 'Positive Law, Positive State: Class Realignment and the Transformation of Lower Canada, 1815–1866,' in Allan Greer and Ian Radforth, eds, *Colonial Leviathan: State Formation in Mid-Nineteenth-Century Canada* (Toronto, 1992), 51.

255 See, for example, Marcel Bellavance, 'La rébellion de 1837 et les modèles théoriques de l'émergence de la nation et du nationalisme,' *Revue d'histoire de l'Amérique française* 53 (2000), esp. 389–92. Anxious as he is to emphasize the modernizing impulse of the Rebellion of 1837, Bellavance focuses on what he sees as European parallels while ignoring the American literature that stresses the radical agrarian resistance to capitalist expansion during this era.

256 The Rouges were not enthusiastic about the establishment of a munic-

ipal system in the 1840s. Little, *State and Society*, 120–1; J.I. Little, 'Colonization and Municipal Reform in Canada East,' *Histoire sociale / Social History* 14, no. 27 (1981): 118. Carol Wilton-Siegel has noted that much of the pressure for administrative reform in Upper Canada came from local elites whose ties were with the Tory party. Carol Wilton-Siegel, 'Administrative Reform: A Conservative Alternative to Responsible Government,' *Ontario History* 78 (June 1986): 105–25.

257 Laporte, *Patriotes et loyaux*, 368.
258 Ibid., 44.
259 The quotes are from Little, *State and Society*, 121–2; on the demands for judicial and other reforms, see 53–4.
260 See ibid., chap. 1.
261 Laporte, *Patriotes et loyaux*, 10.
262 While outlining other factors, Jean-Paul Bernard is clearly sympathetic to this interpretation, as is Gilles Laporte. See Bernard, *Les rébellions*, 59–60; Jean-Paul Bernard, *The Rebellions of 1837 and 1838 in Lower Canada* (Ottawa, 1996), 23; and Laporte, *Patriotes et loyaux*, 38–40. While Bellavance (*Le Québec*, 144–5) accuses Greer of arguing that the Rebellions were essentially a tribal conflict, Greer actually emphasizes class conflict. See Greer, *The Patriots*, chap. 9. The population estimate for the Eastern Townships is a conservative one, for it was 37,040 in 1831, when it was almost entirely English-speaking, and 62,068 in 1842, of whom 47,707 were of British origin. Little, *Ethno-Cultural Transition*, 9, 13.
263 According to Laporte's analysis (*Patriotes et loyaux*, 53), 15.5 per cent of the Patriot leaders were not French Canadian, which is not far below the English-speaking ratio of the province's population.
264 Bernier and Salée, 'Les Patriotes.' This is not to deny that French-Canadian nationalism was the main driving force behind this anti-imperialist movement, but, in his attempt to prove that it was a nationalist bourgeois revolution on the mid-nineteenth-century model, Bellavance assumes an exaggerated degree of industrialization in Lower Canada which had not yet entered the railway era. See his 'La rébellion,' 367–400.
265 Gérard Bouchard, *Entre l'Ancien et le Nouveau Monde. Le Québec comme population neuve et culture fondatrice* (Ottawa, 1996), 9. For a critique of Bouchard's attempt to create an inclusive nationalist vision of history, see Jocelyn Létourneau, 'Going from Heirs to Founders: The Great Collective Narrative of Quebecers as Revisited by Gérard Bouchard,' in *A History for the Future: Rewriting Memory and Identity in Quebec* (Montreal and Kingston, 2004).

Afterword

1 Rev. Ernest M. Taylor, *History of Brome County, Quebec* (Montreal, 1937), vol. 2: 102–5.
2 C.M. Day, *History of the Eastern Townships* (Montreal, 1869), 282–5; J.I. Little, *Borderland Religion: The Emergence of an English-Canadian Identity, 1792–1852* (Toronto, 2004), 94, 123–5.
3 J.I. Little, *State and Society in Transition: The Politics of Institutional Reform in the Eastern Townships, 1838–1852* (Montreal and Kingston, 1997), 58–9.
4 See, for example, Mario Gendron et al., *Histoire du Piémont-des-Appalaches: La Montérégie* (Sainte-Foy, 1999), 120, 124.
5 See J.I. Little, 'The Short Life of a Local Protest Movement: The Annexation Crisis of 1849–50 in the Eastern Townships,' *Journal of the Canadian Historical Association*, n.s., no. 2 (1992): 45–67.

Bibliography

Manuscript Sources

Archives Nationales du Québec à Québec
Fonds Ministère de la Justice, Événements de 1837–1838 (E17).

Georgeville (QC) Historical Society
Abraham Channel, Jr, to Robert Channel, 17 June 1813.

McCord Museum
Hale Papers

National Archives of Canada
Adjutant-General, Lower Canada, Correspondence (RG9, 1A1).
British Military and Naval Records (RG8, I, C Series).
C.C. Cotton Letters (typescript) (G24 J47).
Civil Secretary's Correspondence (Incoming) (RG4 A1).
Colborne Papers (MG24 A40).
Collections of Brome County Historical Society (MG8, F13, reels M133–8). I, Samuel Willard Papers; II, Samuel Gale Papers, Correspondence: 1787–1840; VIII, Miscellaneous Papers, John Savage; IX, Township Papers; X, County Papers; XIV, Rebellion of 1838.
Henry Cull's Militia Record Book (MG23, G3, 13).
John Savage Papers, 1770–1859 (reel M-5904, from Bishop's University, Special Collections).
Minute Books (State Matters), 1764–1867 (RG1E1).
Papiers Papineau (MG24 B2).
Pennoyer Papers (MG24, I11).

Ruiter Family Papers (MG23, G3, 3).
Stipendiary Magistrates (RG4 B24).

Quebec Diocesan Archives (Bishop's University)
Sewell Papers (D8).

Stanstead Historical Society
'A Memoir of Ralph Merry IV, 1786–1863' (typescript).
M.F. Colby Papers.

Printed Primary Sources

Burroughs, Stephen. *A View of Practical Justice as Administered in Lower Canada Displayed in a Memorial to His Excellency the Earl of Gosford.* Three Rivers: G. Stobbs, 1836.
Cushing, Elmer. *An Appeal, Addressed to a Candid Public.* Stanstead: S.H. Dickerson, 1826.
Daughter of H.J. Thomas. 'Incidents of the Canadian Rebellion of 1837–38.' *Second Report of the Missisquoi County Historical Society,* 1907, 44–5.
Journals of the Legislative Assembly, 23 April 1839.
Papineau, Amédée. *Journal d'un Fils de la Liberté, réfugié aux États-Unis, par suite de l'insurrection canadienne, en 1837,* vol. 1. Montreal, 1972.
Perrault, Louis. *Lettres d'un Patriote réfugié au Vermont, 1837–1839.* Montreal: Méridien, 1999.
Russel, J., Jr, comp. *The History of the War between the United States and Great Britain.* Hartford: B. and J. Russell, 1815.
'Smuggling in 1813–1814: A Personal Reminiscence.' *Vermont History* 38 (1970): 22–6.
Stewart, Charles. *A Short View of the Present State of the Eastern Townships in the Province of Lower Canada.* London: J. Hatchard, 1817; reprint from Montreal, 1815.
Vermont Historical Magazine, vol. 1, 1015, 1033–5.

Newspapers

Canadian Patriot.
Missiskoui Post and Canada Record.
Missiskoui Standard.
Montreal Gazette.
Montreal Herald.
Quebec Mercury.

St Francis Courier and Stanstead Gazette.
Sherbrooke Gazette.
Sherbrooke Record, 1910.
Stanstead Journal, 6 April 1916.
Township Reformer.
Vindicator and Canadian Advertiser.

Published Secondary Sources

Abbott, Louise. 'Marion Phelps: A Guardian of Townships History.' *Journal of Eastern Townships Studies* 16 (2000): 5–16.

Adelman, Jeremy, and Stephen Aron. 'From Borderlands to Borders: Empires, Nation-States, and the Peoples in between in North American History.' *American Historical Review* 104 (1999): 814–41.

Anderson, Benedict. *Imagined Communities: Reflections on the Origin and Spread of Nationalism.* London: Verso, 1983.

Armstrong, F.H. 'The Oligarchy of the Western District of Upper Canada, 1788–1841.' Canadian Historical Association, *Historical Papers*, 1977, 87–102.

Ashton, Rick J. *The Life of Henry Ruiter, 1742–1819.* Self-published, 1974.

Baud, Michiel, and Willem Van Schendel. 'Toward a Comparative History of Borderlands.' *Journal of World History* 8, no. 2 (1997): 211–42.

Bellavance, Marcel. *Le Québec au siècle des nationalités (1791–1918).* Montreal: VLB Éditeur, 2004.

– 'La rébellion de 1837 et les modèles théoriques de l'émergence de la nation et du nationalisme.' *Revue d'histoire de l'Amérique française* 53 (2000): 367–400.

Bernard, Jean-Paul. *Les rébellions de 1837–1838.* Montreal: Boréal Express, 1983.

– *The Rebellions of 1837 and 1838 in Lower Canada.* Ottawa: Canadian Historical Association, Historical Booklet no. 55, 1996.

– 'Vermonters and the Lower Canadian Rebellions of 1837–1838.' *Vermont History* 58 (Fall 1990): 250–63.

Bernier, Gérald, and Daniel Salée. 'Les Patriotes, la question nationale et les rébellions de 1837–1838 au Bas-Canada.' In *Les nationalismes au Québec du XIXe au XXIe siècle*, edited by Michel Sarra-Bournet. [Sainte-Foy]: Les Presses de l'Université Laval, 2001.

Berton, Pierre. *Flames across the Border, 1813–1814.* Toronto: McClelland and Stewart, 1981.

Bliss, Michael. 'Privatizing the Mind: The Sundering of Canadian History, the Sundering of Canada.' *Journal of Canadian Studies* 26, no. 4 (1991–2): 5–17.

Boissery, Beverley, and Carla Paterson. '"Women's Work": Women and Rebellion in Lower Canada, 1837–9.' In *Canadian State Trials*, vol. 2: *Rebellion ad Invasion in the Canadas, 1837–1839*, edited by F. Murray Greenwood and Barry Wright. Toronto: University of Toronto Press, 2002.

Bonthius, Andrew. 'The Patriot War of 1837–1838: Locofocoism with a Gun?' *Labour / Le Travail* 52 (Fall 2003): 9–43.

Bouchard, Gérard. *Entre l'Ancien et le Nouveau Monde. Le Québec comme population neuve et culture fondatrice*. Ottawa: Les Presses de l'Université d'Ottawa, 1996.

Breen, T.H. 'Ideology and Nationalism on the Eve of the American Revolution: Revisions Once More in Need of Revising.' *Journal of American History* 84, no. 1 (1997): 13–39.

Brown, Kathleen H. *Schooling in the Clearings: Stanstead 1800–1850*. Stanstead: Stanstead Historical Society, 2001.

Buckner, P.A. 'The Borderlands Concept: A Critical Appraisal.' In *The Northeastern Borderlands: Four Centuries of Interaction*, edited by Stephen Hornsby, Victor Konrad, and James J. Herlan. Orono and Fredericton: Canadian-American Center, University of Maine, and Acadiensis Press, 1989.

Bullock, William Bryant. *Beautiful Waters: Devoted to the Memphremagog Region and Adjacent Counties*, vol. 2. Newport, VT: Bullock, 1938.

Calloway, Colin G. *The Western Abenakis of Vermont, 1600–1800: War, Migration, and the Survival of an Indian People*. Norman and London: University of Oklahoma Press, 1990.

Careless, J.M.S. '"Limited Identities" in Canada.' *Canadian Historical Review* 50 (1969): 1–10.

Chabot, Richard, Jacques Monet, and Yves Roby. 'Nelson, Robert.' *Dictionary of Canadian Biography*, vol. 10, 544–7.

Christie, Nancy. 'Introduction: Theorizing a Colonial Past: Canada as a Society of British Settlement.' In *Transatlantic Subjects: Ideas, Institutions, and Social Experience in Post-Revolutionary British North America*, edited by Nancy Christie. Montreal and Kingston: McGill-Queen's University Press, 2008.

Clark, S.D. *Movements of Political Protest in Canada, 1640–1840*. Toronto: University of Toronto Press, 1959.

Coates, Colin M. 'The Rebellions of 1837–38, and Other Bourgeois Revolutions in Quebec Historiography.' *International Journal of Canadian Studies* 20 (Fall 1999): 19–34.

Corey, Albert B. *The Crisis of 1830–1842 in Canadian-American Relations*. New York: Russell and Russell, 1941; reissued 1970.

Craig, Gerald M. *Upper Canada: The Formative Years, 1784–1841*. Toronto: McClelland and Stewart, 1963.

Creighton, D.G. 'The Economic Background of the Rebellion of Eighteen Thirty-Seven.' *Canadian Journal of Economics and Political Science* 3, no. 3 (1937): 322–34.

Crockett, Walter Hill. *Vermont: The Green Mountain State*, vol. 3. New York: The Century History Company, 1921.

Cross, Michael S. '1837: The Necessary Failure.' In *Readings in Canadian Social History*, vol. 2: *Pre-Industrial Canada, 1760–1849*, edited by Michael S. Cross and Gregory S. Kealey. Toronto: McClelland and Stewart, 1982.

Cruickshank, Colonel E.A. 'From Isle aux Noix to Chateauguay. A Study of the Military Operations on the Frontier of Lower Canada in 1812 and 1813.' *Transactions of the Royal Society of Canada*, Series IIII, vol. 7, Section II (1913): 129–73; vol. 8, Section I (1914–15): 25–102.

Daniell, Jere R. *Experiment in Republicanism: New Hampshire Politics and the American Revolution, 1741–1794*. Cambridge, MA: Harvard University Press, 1970.

Day, C.M. *History of the Eastern Townships*. Montreal: John Lovell, 1869.

Day, Gordon M. *The Identity of the St Francis Indians*. Ottawa: National Museums of Canada, 1981.

Désilets, Andrée. 'Cull, Henry.' *Dictionary of Canadian Biography*, vol. 6, 174.

Dessureault, Christian, and Roch Legault. 'Évolution organisationelle et sociale de la milice sédentaire canadienne: le cas du bataillon de Saint-Hyacinthe, 1808–1830.' *Journal of the Canadian Historical Association*, n.s., no. 8 (1997): 36–61.

Dion, Dominique, and Roch Legault. 'L'organisation de la milice de la région montréalaise de 1792 à 1837: de la paroisse au comté.' *Bulletin d'histoire politique* 8, nos 2–3 (2000): 108–18.

Duffy, John J., and H. Nicholas Muller, III. *Anxious Democracy: Aspects of the 1830s*. Westport, CT: Greenwood Press, 1982.

Epps, Bernard. *The Eastern Townships Adventure*, vol. 1: *A History to 1837*. Ayer's Cliff, QC: Pigwidgeon Press, 1992.

Errington, Jane. 'Friends and Foes: The Kingston Elite and the War of 1812 – A Case Study in Ambivalence.' *Journal of Canadian Studies* 20, no. 1 (1985): 58–79.

– *The Lion, the Eagle, and Upper Canada: A Developing Canadian Ideology*. Montreal and Kingston: McGill-Queen's University Press, 1987.

Everest, Allan S. *The War of 1812 in the Champlain Valley*. [Syracuse]: Syracuse University Press, 1981.

Farfan, Matthew F. 'Hunters' Lodges, in Potton and Bolton, and the Rebellions of 1837–38.' *Yesterdays of Brome County* 8 (1991): 40–3.

– *The Stanstead Region 1792–1844: Isolation, Reform, and Class on the Eastern Townships Frontier.* Hull, QC: Townships Publications, 1992.

– 'Stanstead's Other Journals.' *Journal of the Stanstead Historical Society* 13 (1989): 27–35.

Fauteux, Aegidius. *Patriotes de 1837–1838.* Montreal: Les Éditions des Dix, 1950.

Fyson, Donald. *Magistrates, Police and People: Everyday Criminal Justice in Quebec and Lower Canada, 1764–1837.* Toronto: University of Toronto Press, 2006.

Gendron, Mario et al. *Histoire du Piémont-des-Appalaches: La Montérégie.* [Sainte-Foy]: Les Presses de l'Université Laval, 1999.

Gosling, D.C.L. 'The Battle at Lacolle Mill, 1814.' *Journal of the Society for Army Historical Research* 47 (1969): 169–74.

Graham, John H. *Outlines of the History of Freemasonry in the Province of Quebec.* Montreal: John Lovell and Son, 1892.

Gravel, Mgr Albert. *Messire Jean-Baptiste McMahon, premier curé-missionnaire de Sherbrooke, 1834–1840.* Sherbrooke: Pages d'histoire Régionale, Cahier no. 3, 1960.

Greenwood, F. Murray. *Legacies of Fear: Law and Politics in Quebec in the Era of the French Revolution.* Toronto: University of Toronto Press, 1993.

Greer, Allan. '1837–38: Rebellion Reconsidered.' *Canadian Historical Review* 76 (1995): 1–18.

– *The Patriots and the People: The Rebellion of 1837 in Rural Lower Canada.* Toronto: University of Toronto Press, 1993.

Greer, Allan, and Léon Robichaud. 'La Rébellion de 1837–1838 au Bas-Canada: une approche géographique.' *Cahiers de Géographie du Québec* 33, no. 90 (1989): 345–77.

Harris, R.C. 'The Canadian Archipelago and the Border Thesis.' *Association of American Geographers Annual Meeting and Abstracts.* Washington: Association of American Geographers, 1990.

– 'The Historical Geography of North American Regions.' *American Behavioral Scientist* 22, no. 1 (1978): 115–30.

Harvey, Louis-Georges. *Le printemps de l'Amérique française: Américanité, anticolonialisme et républicanisme dans le discours politique québécois, 1805–1837.* Montreal: Boréal, 2004.

– 'La Révolution américaine et les Patriotes, 1830–1837.' In *Les nationalismes au Québec du XIXe au XXIe siècle*, edited by Michel Sarra-Bournet. [Sainte-Foy]: Les Presses de l'Université Laval, 2001.

Houston, Cecil J., and William J. Smyth. *The Sash Canada Wore: A Historical Geography of the Orange Order in Canada.* Toronto: University of Toronto Press, 1980.

Hubbard, B.F. *Forests and Clearings; the History of Stanstead County, Province of Quebec.* Edited by John Lawrence. Montreal: Lovell Printing and Publishing, 1874.

Jameson, Elizabeth. 'Dancing on the Rim, Tiptoeing through Minefields: Challenges and Promises of Borderlands.' *Pacific Historical Review* 75, no. 1 (2006): 1–24.

Jameson, Elizabeth, and Jeremy Mouat. 'Telling Differences: The Forty-Ninth Parallel and Historiographies of the West and Nation.' *Pacific Historical Review* 75 (2006): 183–230.

Johnson, Benjamin. 'Problems and Prospects in North American Borderlands History.' *History Compass* 4, no. 1 (2006): 186–92.

Jones, Charles O. 'The Moore's Corner Battle in 1837.' *Fourth Annual Report of the Missisquoi Historical Society for 1908–9,* 67–73.

Jones, R.L. 'French-Canadian Agriculture in the St. Lawrence Valley, 1815–1850.' In *Approaches to Canadian Economic History,* edited by W.T. Easterbrook and M.H. Watkins. Toronto: McClelland and Stewart, 1967.

Kenny, Stephen. 'The Canadian Rebellions and the Limits of Historical Perspective.' *Vermont History* 58, no. 3 (1988): 179–98.

Kesteman, Jean-Pierre. *Histoire de Sherbrooke,* tome 1: *De l'âge de l'eau à l'ère de la vapeur.* Sherbrooke: Éditions GGC, 2000.

– 'Les premiers journaux du District de Saint-François (1823–1845).' *Revue d'histoire de l'Amérique française* 31 (1977): 239–53.

Kesteman, Jean-Pierre, Peter Southam, and Diane Saint-Pierre. *Histoire des Cantons de l'Est.* Sainte-Foy: Les Presses de l'Université Laval, 1998.

Kinchen, Oscar A. *The Rise and Fall of the Patriot Hunters.* New York: Bookman Associates, 1956.

LaBrèque, Marie-Paule. 'Heriot, Frederick George.' *Dictionary of Canadian Biography,* vol. 7, 397–8.

– 'Pennoyer, Jesse.' *Dictionary of Canadian Biography,* vol. 6, 574–6.

– 'Savage, John.' *Dictionary of Canadian Biography,* vol. 6, 688–9.

– 'Willard, Samuel.' *Dictionary of Canadian Biography,* vol. 6, 816–17.

LaDow, Beth. *The Medicine Line: Life and Death on North American Borderland.* New York and London: Routledge, 2001.

Lamonde, Yvan. *Histoire sociale des idées au Québec, 1760–1896.* Montreal: Fides, 2000.

Laporte, Gilles. *Patriotes et loyaux: leadership régional et mobilisation politique en 1837 et 1838.* Sillery, QC: Septentrion, 2004.

Laxer, James. *The Border: Canada, the U.S. and Dispatches from the 49th Parallel.* [Toronto]: Doubleday Canada, 2001.

Legault, Roch. 'L'organisation militaire sous le régime Britannique et le role assigné à la gentilhommerie canadienne (1760–1815).' *Revue d'histoire de l'Amérique française* 45 (1991): 229–49.

Létourneau, Jocelyn. 'Going from Heirs to Founders: The Great Collective Narrative of Quebecers as Revisited by Gérard Bouchard.' In *A History for the Future: Rewriting Memory and Identity in Quebec,* edited by Jocelyn Létourneau, translated by Phyllis Aronoff and Howard Scott. Montreal and Kingston: McGill-Queen's University Press, 2004.

Little, J.I. 'American Sinner / Canadian Saint? The Further Adventures of the Notorious Stephen Burroughs, 1799–1840.' *Journal of the Early Republic* 27 (Summer 2007): 203–31.

– *Borderland Religion: The Emergence of an English-Canadian Identity, 1792–1852.* Toronto: University of Toronto Press, 2004.

– 'British Toryism amidst "a horde of disaffected and disloyal squatters": The Rise and Fall of William Bowman Felton and Family in the Eastern Townships.' *Journal of Eastern Townships Studies* 1 (1992): 13–42.

– 'Canadian Pastoral: Promotional Images of British Colonization in Lower Canada's Eastern Townships during the 1830s.' *Journal of Historical Geography* 20, no. 2 (2003): 189–211.

– ed. *The Child Letters: Public and Private Life in a Canadian Merchant-Politician's Family, 1841–1845.* Montreal and Kingston: McGill-Queen's University Press, 1995.

– 'Colonization and Municipal Reform in Canada East.' *Histoire sociale / Social History* 14, no. 27 (1981): 93–121.

– 'Contested Land: Squatters and Agents in the Eastern Townships of Lower Canada.' *Canadian Historical Review* 80 (1999): 381–412.

– *Ethno-Cultural Transition and Regional Identity in the Eastern Townships of Quebec.* Ottawa: Canadian Historical Association, 1989.

– 'The Fireside Kingdom: A Mid-Nineteenth-Century Anglican Perspective on Marriage and Parenthood.' In *Households of Faith: Family, Gender, and Community in Canada, 1760–1969,* edited by Nancy Christie. Montreal and Kingston: McGill-Queen's University Press, 2002.

– 'From the Isle of Arran to Inverness Township: A Case Study of Highland Emigration and North American Settlement, 1829–34.' *Scottish Economic and Social History* 20, part 1 (2000): 3–30.

– 'Gale, Samuel.' *Dictionary of Canadian Biography,* vol. 6, 269–70.

– ed. *Love Strong as Death: Lucy Peel's Canadian Journal, 1833–1836.* Waterloo, ON: Wilfrid Laurier University Press, 2001.

– '"A Moral Engine of Such Incalculable Power": The Temperance Movement in the Eastern Townships, 1830–52.' In *The Other Quebec: Microhistorical Essays on Nineteenth-Century Religion and Society.* Toronto: University of Toronto Press, 2006.

– 'School Reform and Community Control in the 1840s: A Case Study from the Eastern Townships.' *Historical Studies in Education* 9 (1997): 153–64.

– 'The Short Life of a Local Protest Movement: The Annexation Crisis of 1849–50 in the Eastern Townships.' *Journal of the Canadian Historical Association*, n.s., no. 2 (1992): 45–67.

– *State and Society in Transition: The Politics of Institutional Reform in the Eastern Townships, 1838–1852.* Montreal and Kingston: McGill-Queen's University Press, 1997.

The Loyalists of the Eastern Townships of Quebec. Belleville, ON: Mika, 1992.

Ludlum, David M. *Social Ferment in Vermont.* New York: AMS Press, 1966; reprint 1939.

Mann, Bruce. *Neighbors and Strangers: Law and Community in Early Connecticut.* Chapel Hill, NC: University of North Carolina Press, 1987.

Manson, Jimmy W. *The Loyal Americans of New England and New York: Founders of the Townships of Lower Canada.* [Knowlton: QC]: Brome County Historical Society, 2001.

Marini, Stephen. *Radical Sects of Revolutionary New England.* Cambridge, MA: Harvard University Press, 1982.

Martel, Jules. *Histoire du système routier des Cantons de l'Est avant 1855.* Victoriaville, QC: s.n., 1960.

– 'Les troubles de 1837–38 dans la région de Sherbrooke.' *La Revue de l'Université de Sherbrooke* 5, no. 1 (Oct. 1964): 39–58.

Martinez, Oscar. *Border People: Life and Society in the U.S.–Mexico Borderlands.* Tucson: University of Arizona Press, 1994.

Matthews, Winona Lawrence. *The Story of West Shefford (Bromont), Quebec.* n.p., n.d.

McGuigan, Gerald F. 'Administration of Land Policy and the Growth of Corporate Economic Organization in Lower Canada, 1791–1809.' *Canadian Historical Association, Report*, 1963, 65–73.

McKinsey, L., and V. Konrad. *Borderlands Reflections: The United States and Canada.* Orono: Canadian-American Center, University of Maine, 1989.

McManus, Sheila. *The Line which Separates: Race, Gender, and the Making of the Alberta–Montana Borderlands.* Edmonton: University of Alberta Press, 2005.

McNairn, Jeffrey. *The Capacity to Judge: Public Opinion and Deliberative Democracy in Upper Canada, 1791–1854.* Toronto: University of Toronto Press, 2000.

Messier, Allain. *Dictionnaire encyclopédique et historique des patriotes, 1837–1838.* Montreal: Drolet, 2002.

Mills, Sean. 'French Canadians and the Beginning of the War of 1812:

Revisiting the Lachine Riot.' *Histoire sociale / Social History* 38 (2005): 37–58.

Montgomery, George H. *Missisquoi Bay (Philipsburg, Que.).* Granby: Granby Printing and Publishing, 1950.

Moore, Arthur Henry. *History of Golden Rule Lodge.* Toronto: William Briggs, 1905.

Muller, H.N., IIII. 'Smuggling into Canada: How the Champlain Valley Defied Jefferson's Embargo.' *Vermont History* 38 (1970): 5–21.

– 'A "Traitorous and Diabolical Traffic": The Commerce of the Champlain–Richelieu Corridor during the War of 1812.' *Vermont History* 44 (1976): 78–96.

– 'Trouble on the Border, 1838: A Neglected Incident from Vermont's Neglected History.' *Vermont History* 44 (1976): 97–102.

Nelles, H.V. 'Loyalism and Local Power. The District of Niagara, 1792–1837.' *Ontario History* 58 (1966): 99–116.

O'Gallagher, Marianna. 'Ryan, John B.' *Dictionary of Canadian Biography,* vol. 9, 695.

Ouellet, Fernand. *Lower Canada, 1791–1840: Social Change and Nationalism.* Toronto: McClelland Stewart, 1980.

– 'Officiers de milice et structure sociale au Québec (1660–1815).' *Histoire sociale / Social History* 12 (1979): 36–65.

Read, Colin. 'The London District Oligarchy in the Rebellion Era.' *Ontario History* 72 (1980): 195–209.

– *The Rising in Western Upper Canada, 1837–38: The Duncombe Revolt and After.* Toronto: University of Toronto Press, 1982.

Reisner, M.E., ed. *The Diary of a Country Clergyman, 1848–1851: James Reid.* Montreal and Kingston: McGill-Queen's University Press, 2000.

Richardson, A.J.H. 'Captain John Savage and the Settlement of Shefford: From 1740 to 1793.' *Journal of Eastern Townships Studies* 24 (2004): 5–30.

– 'Captain John Savage and the Settlement of Shefford: From 1792 to 1801.' *Journal of Eastern Townships Studies* 25 (2004): 45–78.

Roth, Randolph A. *The Democratic Dilemma: Religion, Reform, and the Social Order in the Connecticut River Valley of Vermont, 1791–1850.* Cambridge: Cambridge University Press, 1987.

Rotundo, E. Anthony. *American Manhood: Transformations in Masculinity from the Revolution to the Modern Era.* New York: Basic Books, 1993.

Sahlins, Peter. *Boundaries: The Making of France and Spain in the Pyrenees.* Berkeley: University of California Press, 1989.

Ste Croix, Lorne. 'Ferres, James Moir.' *Dictionary of Canadian Biography,* vol. 9, 257–8.

Scott, John M. 'Stanstead Cavalry Occupies Georgeville; Three Jailed;

Bullock, Ives Flee For Border.' *Georgeville Enterprise* 3, no. 1 (Spring/Summer 1994): 3–5.

Scott, Kenneth. 'Counterfeiting in Early Vermont.' *Vermont History* 32 (1965): 297–307.

Scrum, Harvey. 'Smuggling in the War of 1812.' *History Today* 29 (1979): 532–7.

Sellar, Charles. *The Market Revolution: Jacksonian America, 1815–1846.* New York: Oxford University Press, 1991.

Senior, Elinor Kyte. 'The Presence of French Canadians in American Towns Bordering Lower Canada, 1837–1840: Disaffection, Terror or Economic Pulls?' *Lifelines* 4 (Fall 1987): 17–30.

– *Redcoats and Patriotes: The Rebellions in Lower Canada, 1837–38.* Stittsville, ON: Canada's Wings, 1985.

Sheppard, George. *Plunder, Profit, and Paroles: A Social History of the War of 1812 in Upper Canada.* Montreal and Kingston: McGill-Queen's University Press, 1994.

– '"Wants and Privations": Women and the War of 1812 in Upper Canada.' *Histoire sociale / Social History* 28 (1995): 159–79.

Shirley, Glenn, ed. *Buckskin Joe, being the unique and vivid memoirs of Edward Jonathan Hoyt, hunter-trapper, scout, soldier, showman, frontiersman, and friend of the Indians, 1840–1918.* Lincoln: University of Nebraska Press, 1966.

Stanley, G.F.G. *The War of 1812: Land Operations.* Ottawa: National Museums of Canada, 1983.

Stewart, Gordon T. *The Origins of Canadian Politics: A Comparative Approach.* Vancouver: University of British Columbia Press, 1986.

Stoll, Steven. *Larding the Lean Earth: Soil and Society in Nineteenth-Century America.* New York: Hill and Wang, 2002.

Taylor, Alan. *The Divided Ground: Indians, Settlers, and the Northern Borderland of the American Revolution.* New York: Knopf, 2006.

– '"The Late Loyalists": Northern Reflections of the Early American Republic.' *Journal of the Early Republic* 27, no. 1 (2007): 1–34.

– *Liberty Men and Great Proprietors: The Revolutionary Settlement on the Maine Frontier, 1760–1820.* Chapel Hill: University of North Carolina Press, 1990.

Taylor, Rev. Ernest M. *History of Brome County, Quebec*, vol. 2. Montreal: John Lovell and Son, 1937.

Thomas, Cyrus. *Contributions to the History of the Eastern Townships.* Montreal: John Lovell, 1866.

– *The Frontier Schoolmaster.* Montreal: John Lovell, 1880.

– *The History of Shefford.* Montreal: Lovell, 1877.

Truett, Samuel, and Elliott Young. 'Making Transnational History: Nations,

Regions, and Borderlands.' In *Continental Crossroads: Remapping U.S.–Mexico Borderlands History*, edited by Samuel Truett and Elliott Young. Durham and London: Duke University Press, 2004.

Van Die, Marguerite. *Religion, Family, and Community in Victorian Canada: The Colbys of Carrollcroft*. Montreal and Kingston: McGill-Queen's University Press, 2005.

Widdis, Randy William. 'Borders, Borderlands and Canadian Identity: A Canadian Perspective.' *International Journal of Canadian Studies* 15 (Spring 1997): 49–66.

Williams, Daniel. 'In Defense of Self: Author and Authority in the *Memoirs of Stephen Burroughs*.' *Early American Literature* 25 (1990): 96–122.

Wilson, Harold Fisher. *The Hill-Country of Northern New England: Its Social and Economic History, 1790–1930*. New York: Columbia University Press, 1936.

Wilton, Carol. *Popular Politics and Political Culture in Upper Canada, 1800–1850*. Montreal and Kingston: McGill–Queen's University Press, 2000.

Wilton-Siegel, Carol. 'Administrative Reform: A Conservative Alternative to Responsible Government.' *Ontario History* 78 (June 1986): 105–25.

Wise, S.F. 'Tory Factionalism: Kingston Elections and Upper Canadian Politics, 1820–1836.' *Ontario History* 57 (1965): 205–25.

– 'Upper Canada and the Conservative Tradition.' In *Profiles of a Province: Studies in the History of Ontario*. Toronto: Ontario Historical Society, 1967.

– 'The War of 1812 in Popular History.' In *God's Peculiar Peoples: Essays on Political Culture in Nineteenth-Century Canada*. Ottawa: Carleton Univeristy Press, 1993.

Worster, Donald. 'Two Faces West: The Development Myth in Canada and the United States.' In *One West, Two Myths*, edited by Carol Higham and Robert Thacker. Calgary: University of Calgary Press, 2004.

Young, Brian. 'Positive Law, Positive State: Class Realignment and the Transformation of Lower Canada, 1815–1866.' In *Colonial Leviathan: State Formation in Mid-Nineteenth-Century Canada*, edited by Allan Greer and Ian Radforth. Toronto: University of Toronto Press, 1992.

– 'The Volunteer Militia in Lower Canada, 1837–50.' In *Power, Place and Identity: Historical Studies of Social and Legal Regulation in Quebec*, edited by Tamara Myers et al. Montreal: Montreal History Group, 1998.

Unpublished Secondary Sources

Beattie, Walter N. 'Stanstead's Historical Traditions, Their Ancestors, Their Firsts, Their Struggles and Their Politics.' Located in the archives of the Brome County Historical Society.

Beaugrand-Champagne, Denyse. 'Les mouvements patriote et loyal dans les comtés de Missisquoi, Shefford, et Stanstead.' MA thesis, Université du Québec à Montréal, 1990.

Holman, Andrew C. 'The Fourth of July in Eastern Canada: Negotiating the Identity of the Anglo-Canadian Borderlands, 1837–1870.' Paper presented to the annual meeting of the Canadian Historical Associaton, 2001.

Kesteman, Jean-Pierre. 'Une bourgeoisie et son espace: industrialisation et développement du capitalisme dans le District de Saint-François (Québec), 1823–1879.' PhD dissertation, Université du Québec à Montréal, 1985.

McGuigan, Gerald F. 'Land Policy and Land Disposal under Tenure of Free and Common Socage, Quebec and Lower Canada.' PhD dissertation, Laval University, 1962.

Richardson, J.A.H. 'The War of 1812.' Located in the archives of the Brome County Historical Society.

Index

Abenakis, vii, 3–4, 107
Adelman, Jeremy, 8
adjutant-general, 25
Albany, NY, 52
Alburg, VT, 43–4, 52, 96
Aldrich, Hiram, 92
Anglicans. *See* Church of England
annexation movement, 101, 108
Aron, Stephen, 8
arson. *See* border incidents
Ascot Township, 18, 27, 31, 41, 51, 53
Assembly of Six Counties, 75

Badger, Joseph, 53, 54
Bailey, Captain Ira A., 87, 89
Baker, Captain Henry, 99
Baker, Luther, 51
Bangor, ME, 93
Bangs, Lieutenant Lauren, 30
Baptists, 53, 65, 107
Barford Township, 98
Barker, Captain Oliver, 20, 25–6, 31, 40, 48, 49, 51, 52, 98
Barnston Township, 16, 27, 29–30, 31, 47, 50, 67, 86, 89, 90, 92, 93, 94, 98, 101
Bartlett, Captain Joseph, 27
Barton, VT, 41
Batchelder, Jacob, 92–3
Batchelders, 98

Bates, Roswell, 91
Battalions: First, 13, 35; Second, 13, 18, 22, 23, 26, 32, 34–6 *passim*; Third, 13, 14–17, 22, 24, 29–30, 33–6 *passim*, 41, 42; Fourth, 13, 18, 21, 22, 26, 32, 34, 37–8, 42; Fifth, 13, 14, 17, 21–3 *passim*, 27, 31–2, 34, 35, 41, 42, 62, 79; Sixth, 25
Baud, Michiel, 8, 9
Beaugrand-Champagne, Denyse, 65, 66
Bedel, Lieutenant-Colonel, 39
Bernier, Gérald, 105
Bigelow, Levi, 44–5
Bishop, Captain, 32
Blanchard, François-Benjamin, 85
Blanchard, Hiram Francis, 66, 86, 89, 92
Blanchard, Jared F., 92, 153n203
Bodwell, Captain James, 31
Bolton Township, 21, 50, 52, 68, 76, 89
border incidents, 20, 96–8, 103, 107
borderlands approach, 7–10, 12
Boston, 49
Bouchard, Gérard, 106
Bouchette, Robert Shore Milnes, 83
Bouchette, Surveyor-General Joseph, 57
boundary, Canadian–American, 4, 8, 55
British American Land Company, 63–4, 66, 71, 73, 74, 76, 102
British Colonist and St Francis Gazette, 61–2, 65, 66

British office holders, 61–2, 64
British settlers/settlement, 6, 54, 58, 60, 63–4, 76, 82, 85
Brock, William, 89
Brome Township, 21, 82, 87, 89
Brompton Township, 20
Brooks, George Washington, 93
Brooks, Samuel, 93, 104
Brown, Dr Leonard, 77
Brown, Thomas Storrow, 70–1, 75, 85
Bullock, Chauncey, 91
Bullock, Increase, 91
Burlington, VT, 37–9 passim
Burpee, Baruch, 92
Burroughs, Captain William, 98
Burroughs, Stephen, 48, 52, 98

Caldwell's Manor, 26, 37, 88, 96
Canaan, VT, 47
Canadian Patriot, 66, 78, 86
Canadien, Le, 71
cavalry, 15, 20, 21, 23–4, 41, 80, 82, 90, 98. See also militia
Chamberlin, Dr Joshua, 78–9
Chamberlin, Lieutenant-Colonel Wright, 68, 81
Chambly, 39
Champlain Canal, 58
Channell, Abraham, Jr, 50
Channell, Leon, 91
Chapin, Rev. H.B., 94, 95
Charpentier, Charles, 90, 92
Châteauguay, 42
Child, Marcus, 45, 67, 69, 73, 76, 77–8, 92, 95, 105
Christie, Nancy, 10
Church of England, 60, 65, 88, 96–7, 101–3 passim
churches. See religion
civic culture/consciousness, 58–61 passim, 67, 101
civil unrest, 62. See also political demands
Clapham, John Greaves, 70, 82
Clark, Colonel Isaac, 37–9 passim, 42, 43

Clark, S.D., 68, 69
Clifton Township, 47
Coffin, Police Inspector Thomas, 45, 51, 52
Coffin, Sheriff W.L., 98
Colborne, Sir John, 79, 80, 81, 83, 85, 96
Colby, Dr Moses, 73–4, 93
commissioners' court, 94, 95. See also justices of the peace
committees of safety, 21, 41; correspondence committees, 70; county committees, 68; township committees, 67–8, 71; vigilance committees, 73, 75. See also constitutional associations
Compton Township, 13, 18, 20, 27, 31, 41, 50, 57–8, 79, 80–1, 91, 98
Congregationalists, 94
Conroy, Lieutenant-Colonel Patrick, 13
conscription, 14–18, 21, 24–37
constitutional associations, 69–72 passim, 104
Constitutionalists' programme, 74, 76–7, 104
contact zone, Eastern Townships as, 3
Côté, Dr Cyrille, 89
Cotton, Rev. Charles, 24, 53, 103
counterfeiting, 8, 20, 48–9, 52, 77, 92, 98
Craig, G.M., 96
Cross, Michael, 103
cross-border migration, 49–54. See also desertion
crown and clergy reserves, tenants of, 74–5
Cull, Lieutenant-Colonel Henry, 13–14, 15–17, 18, 20–2 passim, 27–30 passim, 35, 36, 40, 41, 46, 50–4 passim
cultural identity, 7, 9, 54–6, 108. See also nationalism
Curtis, Captain David, 31
Cushing, Elmer, 20–1, 23–4, 51, 53, 63

Davis, Private Amos, 39
Democrat, 66

Derby (Line), VT, 40, 44, 49, 50, 52, 66, 73, 86, 87, 91, 92
de Rottenburg, General, 25, 26, 33
desertion, 18, 21, 23, 27, 29, 31–5, 51 *passim*, 54. *See also* conscription
Dickerson, Silas Horton, 65, 66, 89, 92
Dolbear, Dr Benjamin, 49
draft. *See* conscription
Drummond Constitutional Association, 70
Drummond County, 69, 80, 90
Drummondville, 80, 90
Dudswell Township, 32
Duffy, John J., 88
Dunham Flat, 70–1, 73
Dunham Township, 13, 21, 24, 26, 38, 46, 53, 65, 103
Durham Commission/Report, 103–5 *passim*
Durham Township, 76, 90

Eastern Townships Loyal Volunteers, 80
Eaton Township, 20, 21, 27, 98
economic development/conditions, 6, 57–64 *passim*, 74, 76, 102
election of 1834, 69, 78
Elkins, Captain Moses, 23, 107, 108
Elkins, Harvey, 87
Elkins, Josiah, 107
Elkins, Salmon, 107
Errington, Jane, 9
Eustis, Brigadier-General, 96

Farmer's Advocate and Townships Gazette, 66, 72–3, 74
Farnham Township, 21, 22, 24, 78
Felton, Charles, 73
Felton, Lieutenant-Colonel William Bowman, 62–3, 73, 79
Ferres, James Moir, 67, 71
firearms, 19, 21, 30, 31, 41–2, 46, 81, 82–3
flag, 75
Fletcher, Judge John, 65
Fowler, Lowell, 51–2
Freemasonry. *See* Masonic lodges

Free Will Baptists, 103
Frelighsburg, 68, 78, 81, 96, 99
French Canadians, 54, 55, 57, 61, 72, 75, 76, 82, 84, 85, 105
French Mills, VT, 44
Frères Chasseurs. *See* Hunters' Lodges
Frontier Light Infantry, 25, 28, 32–7 *passim*, 43
frontier thesis, 7, 62
Frost Village, 94
Frye, Northrop, 10

Gagnon, Lucien, 83
Gale, Samuel, 24–5, 26
Georgeville, 59, 65, 68, 77, 86, 91, 93, 101
Gibson, John, 96
Gilman, B.W., 89
Gilman, Joseph D., 67
Glen, Captain Jacob, 15, 20
Golden Rule Lodge, 59
Gosford, Governor-General Lord, 71, 75, 76, 79–80, 104
Gosford Commission, 72
Gosford Road, 82
Granby Township, 89, 94
Grannis, John, 69, 73
Grantham Township, 76
Greenbush, MA, 39
Greer, Allan, 103
Gugy, Lieutenant-Colonel B.C.A., 73, 98

Hadlock, Hazen, 87
Haldimand, General Frederick, 4
Hale, Edward, 80, 86, 87, 100
Hall, Rev. R.V., 94
Hampton, Major-General Wade, 37, 51
Hanson, Lewis, 86
Harris, Cole, 10
Harvel, Ensign James, 32, 33
Harvey, Calvin, 89
Hatley Township, 7, 13, 16, 27, 31, 41, 50, 67, 69, 70, 91, 93
Hayden, William, 89
Head, Lieutenant-Colonel, 79, 95

Head, Major, 89
Heard, Captain Samuel, 20
Hemmingford, 96
hemp, 14
Hereford Township, 17, 27, 31, 32, 35, 40, 47–8, 62
Heriot, Colonel Frederick G., 80, 90
Hervil. *See* Harvel
Highgate, VT, 97
Hoeg, Andrew, 92
Hollister, Asa, 90
Hovey, Ebenezer, 16, 121n25
Hubbard, B.F., 91, 93
Hudson, Sergeant, 32
Hugh, Samuel, 47–8
Hunters' Lodges, 8, 88–9

infantry, 82
Inverness Township, 74, 82
Ireland Township, 68, 82
Irish settlers. *See* British settlers
Isle aux Noix, 25
Ives, Captain Joseph, 31
Ives, Julius, 91
Izard, General George, 44

Jacquay, Dr Enoch, 89
Jameson, Elizabeth, 9
Jefferson's Embargo, 8, 11, 14, 43, 44, 54
Johnson, Benjamin, 8–9
Johnson, Colonel Sir John, 12–13, 14, 15, 21, 25, 28, 30, 31
Jones, Captain J., 26, 33
Jones, John, 45
Jones, Lieutenant-Colonel Robert, 81, 99, 101
Jones, Major J.S., 81
justices of the peace, 6, 16, 17, 21, 30, 35, 38, 48–53 *passim*, 62, 77–9 *passim*, 81, 87, 90, 91, 93–5 *passim*, 100

Kemp, Captain Oren, 83, 99
Kent, Blaisdell, 93
Kent, Jacob, 93
Kent, Jonas, 93

Kesteman, Jean-Pierre, 64, 69
Kezar, Captain Simon, 31, 41
Kilborn, Captain Alexander, 90–1, 93
Kilborn, Major Charles, 28, 29, 33, 34
Kilborn's Mills (Rock Island), 28
Kingsey Township, 17, 20, 76, 85
Knight, Ephraim, 52, 69, 75, 77, 105
Knowlton, Lieutenant-Colonel Paul Holland, 82, 85, 95, 100–1, 103, 104
Konrad, Victor, 8

L'Acadie, 82–3
Lachine Riot, 21
Lacolle, 34, 42, 89
Lake Champlain, 11, 25, 37, 43
Lake Memphremagog, 84, 91, 107
land grants, 4–5. *See also* squatters
Laporte, Gilles, 68, 73, 91, 104
Laprairie, 17, 86
Lawrence, Lieutenant Gordon, 23, 24
Lay, Dr Amos W., 89
Layfield, Robert, 70, 72, 105
leader and associates system / township leaders, 5, 13, 20, 24, 107
Lee, Elias, 73
Lee, Elias, Jr, 92
Leeds Township, 70, 93
Lennoxville, 83, 91
Létourneau, Jocelyn, vii
Lillie, Asa, 86
Lively Stone Lodge, 59
localism, 10, 19, 108
Lord Russell's Ten Resolutions, 75, 76
Loyal American Rifle Company, 80, 86
Loyalists, vii, 4, 5, 12, 13, 21, 24, 30, 61, 65
Loyal Megantic Volunteers, 82
loyalty petitions, 18–19, 20–1
Luke, Lieutenant, 35, 40
Luke, Lieutenant-Colonel Philip, 13, 21, 22–3, 24, 26, 32, 34–9 *passim*, 42, 54

Mackenzie, William Lyon, 85–6, 101
magistrates. *See* justices of the peace
Maidstone, VT, 47
Manson, Robert, 89

martial law, 83, 90, 94, 100
Martin, Lieutenant J.W., 90
Masonic lodges, 7, 59, 60, 101, 108
McComb, General, 42
McKeech, Dr Lovell, 86, 90, 92
McKillop, Archibald, 82
McKinsey, Lauren, 8
McLane, David, 23
McMahon, Rev. John Baptist, 85
McNairn, Jeffrey, 58–9, 60, 68–9
Megantic Constitutional Association,
    70, 71–2
Megantic County, 68, 79, 82, 90, 93
Melbourne Township, 20, 50
Merry, Ralph, 79
Methodists, 53, 60, 65, 78, 82, 91, 93–5
    passim, 97, 101; Protestant
    Methodists, 107
middle ground, 3
militia. See also Batallions and Frontier
    Light Infantry
Militia, Sedentary, 12
Militia, Select Embodied, 12, 21, 24,
    55; community payment of, 28–30
    passim
militia, Vermont, 15, 37, 42, 55–6, 75,
    83
militia, volunteer, 20, 25, 31, 79–82
    passim, 94–5, 98
Militia Act, 19
militia captains, 16, 30–2
militia officers, appointment of, 33
Miller, Captain Charles, 97
Millerites, 103, 108
Miltmore, Daniel, 89
Milton Township, 89
Missiskoui Post and Canada Record,
    66
Missiskoui Reform Association, 71
Missiskoui Standard and Farmer's
    Advocate, 66–7, 71, 72, 76, 77, 81,
    83, 84, 97, 99
Missisquoi Bay, 3, 13, 37, 43, 44, 65,
    75, 86, 88
Missisquoi Branch Constitutional Asso-
    ciation, 70, 71

Missisquoi County, 58, 65, 66, 68, 69,
    70, 81–2, 99
Missisquoi Volunteers, 82, 88
Montpelier, VT, 50, 85
Montreal, 46, 49, 50, 52, 58, 61, 66,
    68–70 passim, 73, 82, 85–7 passim,
    93, 105
Montreal Constitutional Association, 71,
    72
Montreal Express, 66
Montreal Gazette, 66, 92
Montreal Herald, 67
Montreal Temperance Convention, 60
Moore, John, 80
Moore's Corner, 82
Morgan, William, 59
Morin, Augustin-Norbert, 70
Morrill, Archibald, 47
Morrill, David, 47
Morris, Lieutenant-Colonel William,
    104
Mouat, Jeremy, 9
Moulton, Avery, 54
Muller, H.N., 46, 88
municipal system, 103–4
Murray, Colonel, 25, 26

Napierville, 88
nationalism, 54, 57, 61, 106. See also
    cultural identity
Nelson, Jonathan, 93
Nelson, Robert, 83–90 passim
New Hampshire, 8, 47, 48, 51
Newport, VT, 84
Newport Township, 20
newspapers, 65–7
Newton, Artemus, 89
Nickle, Colonel Robert, 90, 98
Ninety-Two Resolutions, 67, 68, 69,
    104
Noble, Levi, 50
North American, 66
North Hatley, 13
Norton, Captain Issachar, 31

oath of allegiance / oaths commission-

ers, 13, 16, 51, 78–9, 91, 93; Sol-
dier's Oath, 85
O'Callaghan, Edmund B., 57, 66, 69, 70
Odelltown, 40, 89, 96
officers, shortage of, 22, 100–1
Ogden, Attorney-General C.R., 79
Orange Lodge, 76
Orleans County, VT, 45, 52
Outlet, the (Magog), 79
out-migration, 30, 52–5 *passim*, 62, 78,
79, 92

Papineau, Amédée, 78
Papineau, André-Augustin, 85
Papineau, Louis-Joseph, 57, 68, 69, 73,
102, 105, 106
Parkhurst, Levi, 89
Parti patriote, 57, 61, 67–9 *passim*, 71,
76, 82–3, 85, 86, 89, 98, 102, 104,
105
Patriotic Society, Quebec, 39
Patriots. *See Parti patriote*
Peacham, VT, 107
Peck, Ebenezer, 103
Pennoyer, Major Jesse, 13, 14, 17, 18,
21–3 *passim*, 27, 28, 31–2, 35, 50,
53
Permanent Central Committee, 68
petitions, 67
Phelps, Elkanah, 66
Philadelphia, 40
Philipsburg, 35, 37, 42, 44, 55, 82, 83,
88, 96, 99
Plattsburg, 11, 42, 85, 96
Ployart, John, 90
police, 6, 45, 49, 50, 98, 99. *See also*
Coffin, Thomas
political demands/discontent, 61–3 *pas-
sim*, 67–75 *passim*, 105. *See also*
Constitutionalists' programme
population growth, 5, 58. *See also*
British settlers; out-migration
Potton Township, 21, 26, 46, 68, 70, 73,
76, 87, 89, 101, 107–8
Powell, Captain Bradford, 46–7
Powell, Major Joseph, 22–3, 37, 40

Prevost, Governor-General, 21, 25, 28,
35, 42, 44, 52
prisoners/imprisonment, 31, 38–40, 66

Quakers, 78
Quebec City, 39, 44, 48, 52, 58, 68, 73,
82, 86, 93
Quebec Constitutional Association, 69
Quebec Mercury, 82
Queen's Mounted Rangers, 80

Reid, Rev. James, 96–7, 99, 102
religion, 6–7, 60, 101–2
responsible government, 103
Revolution, American. *See* War of Inde-
pendence
Rhykert, Lieutenant, 40
Richards, Isaac W., 50
Richford, VT, 46
Richmond, 70
Ritchie, William, 78–9, 91, 92, 93
Ritter, Captain Louis, 32, 34, 35–6, 43
Robson, Rev. Hugh, 90
Roger's Rangers, 18
Royal Eastern Militia Regiment, 12, 19.
See also Battalions
Royal Institution of Learning, 60
Ruiter, Captain Jacob, 35
Ruiter, Captain James, 30
Ruiter, Captain John, 36
Ruiter, Lieutenant-Colonel Henry, 13,
18, 22, 23, 32, 34, 38
Ruiter, Philip, 38, 39–40
Ryan, J.B., 85–6, 150n169

Sahlins, Peter, viii, 8, 54
Saint-Césaire, 83
Saint-Hyacinthe, 86
Saint-Jean, 21, 25–7 *passim*, 29, 31–3
passim, 45, 83, 86
Salée, Daniel, 105
Sanborn, Carlisle, 92
Sanborn, George, 92
Sanborn, John, 92
Sanborn, Nancy, 92
Savage, Captain John, 24–5, 33, 52

schools. *See* Royal Institution of
  Learning
settlement, land, 6
Shefford County, 58, 68–71 *passim*,
  79–82 *passim*
Shefford Dragoons, 89
Shefford Loyal Volunteers, 81, 85
Shefford Township, 21, 22, 24, 74, 87,
  89, 94–5
Sherbrooke, 62, 64–5, 68, 73, 79, 85,
  86, 87, 90, 91, 92
Sherbrooke Constitutional Associations,
  72
Sherbrooke County, 93, 100, 103, 104
Sherbrooke Dragoons, 80
*Sherbrooke Gazette and Townships
  Advertiser*, 66, 77
Sheridan, Sergeant Thomas, 79
Shipton Township, 17, 20, 23, 32, 51–2,
  85, 89
Signay, Archbishop Joseph, 85
Smith, Ichabod, 92
smuggling, 8, 9, 11, 25, 37, 38, 43–8,
  59, 73, 76, 99
social development, 6–7
Spalding, Levi, 85
spying, 32, 49, 52
squatters, 5, 107–8
Squire, Rev. William, 82, 88, 97
St Albans, VT, 83–4
Stanbridge East, 66
Stanbridge Township, 26, 38, 39, 65
Stanbridge Upper Mills, 70, 75, 77
Stanstead by-election of 1837, 73–4
Stanstead County, 65, 67–70 *passim*, 78,
  90–4 *passim*, 98, 100
Stanstead Plain, 46, 50, 58, 61, 64–5,
  66, 78, 85, 86, 91, 93–5 *passim*
Stanstead Township, 15, 16, 27, 29,
  30–1, 40–1, 45, 47, 59, 60, 62, 64,
  67, 81, 85, 87, 89, 92, 98
St Armand, 13, 21, 24, 26, 34, 38, 45,
  48, 52–3, 65, 81
St Armand West, 84, 96–7
Stewart, Rev. Charles, 24, 38–9, 44,
  52–3, 55

Stewartson, N.H., 40, 47
St Francis Constitutional Association,
  70
*St Francis Courier and Sherbrooke
  Gazette*, 65–6, 86
St Francis District, 90, 100, 104
Stowe, VT, 83
Stukely Township, 20, 22, 24, 29, 89
Sutton Township, 21, 26, 89
Swanton, VT, 38, 66, 83, 85, 96

Taplin, Captain Johnson, 31
Taylor, Alan, 4, 5, 54–5
temperance movement, 58, 59–60,
  108
Thomas, Hiram J., 66
Tingwick Township, 85
Tolford, Calvin W., 66, 86
Tomkins, Rev. John, 94
Toomy, Edward, 69
town meeting system, 7, 29. *See also*
  municipal system
Township Reformer, 66, 81
Treaty of Ghent, 11
Trois-Rivières, 45, 47, 86
Troy, VT, 86, 87, 89, 107
Tuck, John Carty, 91
Turner, Rev. Thomas, 78

United States Congress/government, 48,
  88
Universalists, 102, 103
Upper Canada, 5, 9, 56, 58, 60, 61, 72,
  84, 85, 96, 101, 108

Van Schendel, Willem, 8, 9
Vermont, 4, 8, 18, 38, 43–54 *passim*,
  59, 66, 79, 81, 82, 84, 86–8 *passim*,
  91, 92, 96, 102, 108. *See also* militia,
  Vermont
Viger, Jacques, 69
vigilante societies, 7
Vindicator, 66, 67
Voltigeurs Canadiens, 80
voluntary societies, 58–9
Vosburgh, Abraham, 96

Wadleigh, Captain Taylor, 93, 105
Walton, Joseph, 66
War of Independence, American, 4, 6,
    16, 18, 26, 29, 75, 83
Waterloo, 68, 95
Whitcher, Sheriff and Major Charles,
    73, 79, 92
Wickham Township, 76
Widdis, Randy, 10

Wilkinson, Major-General, 42
Willard, Captain Samuel, 24–5
Williams, Lieutenant-Colonel,
    99–100
Windsor Township, 13
Wise, S.F., 11
Woods, Charles, 87
Woods, Henry, 87, 151n173
Wool, General John E., 85–6, 88

THE CANADIAN SOCIAL HISTORY SERIES

Terry Copp,
The Anatomy of Poverty:
The Condition of the Working Class
in Montreal, 1897–1929, 1974.
ISBN 0-7710-2252-2

Alison Prentice,
The School Promoters: Education
and Social Class in Mid-Nineteenth
Century Upper Canada, 1977.
ISBN 0-7710-7181-7

John Herd Thompson,
The Harvests of War:
The Prairie West, 1914–1918, 1978.
ISBN 0-7710-8560-5

Joy Parr, Editor,
Childhood and Family in
Canadian History, 1982.
ISBN 0-7710-6938-3

Alison Prentice and
Susan Mann-Trofimenkoff, Editors,
The Neglected Majority:
Essays in Canadian Women's History,
Volume 2, 1985.
ISBN 0-7710-8583-4

Ruth Roach Pierson,
'They're Still Women After All':
The Second World War and
Canadian Womanhood, 1986.
ISBN 0-7710-6958-8

Bryan D. Palmer,
The Character of Class Struggle:
Essays in Canadian Working Class
History, 1850–1985, 1986.
ISBN 0-7710-6946-4

Alan Metcalfe,
Canada Learns to Play:
The Emergence of Organized Sport,
1807–1914, 1987.
ISBN 0-7710-5870-5

Marta Danylewycz,
Taking the Veil: An Alternative to
Marriage, Motherhood, and Spinster-
hood in Quebec, 1840–1920, 1987.
ISBN 0-7710-2550-5

Craig Heron,
Working in Steel: The Early Years in
Canada, 1883–1935, 1988.
ISBN 0-7710-4086-5

Wendy Mitchinson and
Janice Dickin McGinnis, Editors,
Essays in the History of Canadian
Medicine, 1988.
ISBN 0-7710-6063-7

Joan Sangster,
Dreams of Equality: Women on the
Canadian Left, 1920–1950, 1989.
ISBN 0-7710-7946-X

Angus McLaren,
Our Own Master Race: Eugenics
in Canada, 1885–1945, 1990.
ISBN 0-7710-5544-7

Bruno Ramirez,
On the Move:
French-Canadian and Italian
Migrants in the North Atlantic Econ-
omy, 1860–1914, 1991.
ISBN 0-7710-7283-X

Mariana Valverde,
'The Age of Light, Soap and Water':
Moral Reform in English Canada,
1885–1925, 1991.
ISBN 978-0-8020-9595-4

Bettina Bradbury,
Working Families: Age, Gender, and
Daily Survival in Industrializing
Montreal, 1993.
ISBN 978-0-8020-8689-1

Andrée Lévesque,
Making and Breaking the Rules:
Women in Quebec, 1919–1939, 1994.
ISBN 0-7710-5283-9

Cecilia Danysk,
Hired Hands: Labour and the Devel-
opment of Prairie Agriculture,
1880–1930, 1995.
ISBN 0-7710-2552-1

Kathryn McPherson,
Bedside Matters: The Transformation of Canadian Nursing, 1900–1990, 1996.
ISBN 978-0-8020-8679-2

Edith Burley,
Servants of the Honourable Company: Work, Discipline, and Conflict in the Hudson's Bay Company, 1770–1870, 1997.
ISBN 0-19-541296-6

Mercedes Steedman,
Angels of the Workplace: Women and the Construction of Gender Relations in the Canadian Clothing Industry, 1890–1940, 1997.
ISBN 0-19-54308-3

Angus McLaren and Arlene Tigar McLaren, *The Bedroom and the State: The Changing Practices and Politics of Contraception and Abortion in Canada, 1880–1997,* 1997.
ISBN 0-19-541318-0

Kathryn McPherson, Cecilia Morgan, and Nancy M. Forestell, Editors, *Gendered Pasts: Historical Essays in Feminity and Masculinity in Canada,* 1999.
ISBN 978-0-8020-8690-7

Gillian Creese,
Contracting Masculinity: Gender, Class, and Race in a White-Collar Union, 1944–1994, 1999.
ISBN 0-19-541454-3

Geoffrey Reaume,
Remembrance of Patients Past: Patient Life at the Toronto Hospital for the Insane, 1870–1940, 2000.
ISBN 0-19-541538-8

Miriam Wright,
A Fishery for Modern Times: The State and the Industrialization of the Newfoundland Fishery, 1934–1968, 2001.
ISBN 0-19-541620-1

Judy Fudge and Eric Tucker,
Labour before the Law: The Regulation of Workers' Collective Action in Canada, 1900–1948, 2001.
ISBN 978-0-8020-3793-0

Mark Moss,
Manliness and Militarism: Educating Young Boys in Ontario for War, 2001.
ISBN 0-19-541594-9

Joan Sangster,
Regulating Girls and Women: Sexuality, Family, and the Law in Ontario, 1920–1960, 2001.
ISBN 0-19-541663-5

Reinhold Kramer and Tom Mitchell,
Walk Towards the Gallows: The Tragedy of Hilda Blake, Hanged 1899, 2002.
ISBN 978-0-8020-9542-8

Mark Kristmanson,
Plateaus of Freedom: Nationality, Culture, and State Security in Canada, 1940–1960, 2002.
ISBN 0-19-541866-2

Robin Jarvis Brownlie
A Fatherly Eye: Indian Agents, Government Power, and Aboriginal Resistance in Ontario, 1918–1939, 2003
ISBN 0-19-541891-3 (cloth)
ISBN 0-19-541784-4 (paper)

Steve Hewitt,
Riding to the Rescue: The Transformation of the RCMP in Alberta and Saskatchewan, 1914–1939, 2006.
ISBN 978-0-8020-9021-8 (cloth)
ISBN 978-0-8020-4895-0 (paper)

Robert B. Kristofferson,
Craft Capitalism: Craftsworkers and Early Industrialization in Hamilton, Ontario, 1840–1872, 2007.
ISBN 978-0-8020-9127-7 (cloth)
ISBN 978-0-8020-9408-7 (paper)

Andrew Parnaby,
*Citizen Docker: Making a New
Deal on the Vancouver Waterfront,
1919–1939,* 2007
ISBN 978-0-8020-9056-0 (cloth)
ISBN 978-0-8020-9384-4 (paper)

J.I. Little
*Loyalties in Conflict: A Canadian
Borderland in War and Rebellion,
1812–1840,* 2008
ISBN 978-0-8020-9773-6 (cloth)
ISBN 978-0-8020-9825-1 (paper)